ROYALLY OFF-LIMITS

A Sweet Royal Enemies to Lovers RomCom

Royally Kissed
Book 4

KATE O'KEEFFE

Royally Off-Limits is a work of fiction. The characters and events portrayed in this book are fictitious. Any similarity to real persons, living or dead, is purely coincidental and not intended by the author.

All rights reserved, including the right to reproduce, distribute, or transmit in any form or by any means.

Copyright © 2025 Kate O'Keeffe

ISBN: 978-1-991378-30-9

Introduction

❝ Good people of Ledonia! Hold on to your fascinators because your ever-devoted royal correspondent is reporting on the most spectacular display of royal ridiculousness in recent memory!

I'm calling it The Scene of Aquatic Chaos, aka man-child Max getting up and personal with royal carp.

Every royal watcher's favorite, Prince Maximilien, has provided us with enough entertainment to fuel my column for the next

Introduction

century. And trust me, darlings, this story is positively dripping with drama (quite literally, as you'll soon discover).

It's a perfectly civilized palace garden party. Cucumber sandwiches, pots of tea, children politely enjoying a slip 'n slide, and our beloved royal family mingling with distinguished guests beneath the afternoon sun.

So far, so regal.

But then our himbo Max decided to transform this genteel gathering into something resembling a nature documentary gone spectacularly wrong.

After what sources describe as "a martini or two", our Prince McHottie Junior apparently lost a bet with his friends. The stakes? A fully clothed journey down the children's slip 'n slide.

Now, one might think a twenty-seven-year-old prince would possess enough rudimentary knowledge of physics to calculate that about two hundred pounds of royal muscle hurtling down a children's water slide might produce some unexpected results.

One would be mistaken.

What followed, according to multiple horrified witnesses, was nothing short of aquatic pandemonium. Our dear prince launched himself torpedo-style down the slide, landing in an 18th-century decorative fishpond, the very same pond that houses descendants of ceremonial carp gifted by the Thai King to the country of Ledonia over 200 years ago.

Introduction

The result? Seven fish sent airborne in a spectacular display, captured in my trending TikTok (link below), featuring a child's call of "Cannonball". Because let's face it, no quote says 'dignified monarchy' like a fully grown man in a pond.

Fear not, fish lovers among us. Every dislodged fish was scooped off the lawn and returned to the pond unscathed.

So, here's to you, man-child Max, himbo extraordinaire, for reminding us that even princes are human, that aristocratic carp can fly, and even the most sophisticated garden parties can become disasters worthy of trending TikTok fame.

Your ever-devoted royal correspondent,

Fabiana Fontaine xx

#ManChildMax
#RoyalCannonball
#SpiceUpTheGardenParty

Chapter 1

Max

The thing about being the last-born in a family full to the brim of famous royals is that you may start out as everyone's favorite adorable toddler, but somehow you end up as the country's most documented cautionary tale about what happens when privilege meets poor decision-making.

I'm that person. Me, Prince Maximilien, fourth-born child of King Frederic and Queen Astrid of Ledonia, and about ninth in line to the throne these days, last time I checked.

I'm "the problem" that needs to be fixed, allegedly. The wild child. The party boy.

The *man-child.*

I have journalist Fabiana Fontaine to thank for that little gem. But don't even get me started on her.

As far as I can see it, I'm just living life within my gilded cage as best I can. Not that anyone ever asks for my opinion. As far as they're concerned, I've got an image problem that needs to be fixed, STAT.

The palace PR team has devised three possible solutions:

1. Being forced to smile through a televised cake-tasting segment on *Ledonia's Best Bake-Off* to show I am, and I quote, "one of the people"
2. Taking part in a documentary series about my life to show the country that I'm a regular guy who just happened to make a poor decision (or twenty)
3. Enter an arranged engagement with some pre-approved aristocrat to show I'm a new man with serious life goals and a penchant for tweed

I told them I'd rather fight a bear.

Bare handed.

And blindfolded.

I mean, what kind of options are those? None of them appeals in the slightest. A few little slip-ups that somehow managed to make it into the press thanks to that Fontaine woman, and suddenly I have an image problem?

Please.

My antics barely rate on my brother's scandal-o-meter. Alex was the one who had an image problem before he fell in love with the woman he's now married to and cleaned up his act. He had women coming out of his ears. Not literally, of course, but you get the picture.

I'm a freaking monk in comparison.

And really, all I did was lose a bet with a couple of my friends after a martini or two at a boring garden party. Now, Fabiana Fontaine has got the entire country calling me a man-child.

Isn't name-calling the height of immaturity? It's like we're back in the school playground and she's sneering at me by the swings, throwing insults my way to impress her gaggle of friends.

And sure, in hindsight I can see diving on the children's slip 'n slide in my linen suit while balancing a martini in one hand wasn't the smartest decision of the day. But to be fair to me, overshooting and landing in an 18th Century decorative fishpond, sending carp flying into the air as they flapped their fins in desperation was never part of the plan. I thought I'd come to a stop at the bottom of the slide, just like the children had, not get launched like a torpedo as some nearby child yelled, "Cannonball!"

It's now become a trending TikTok sound, along with Fabiana Fontaine's video, of course.

How did she even get the footage? It's not like she was an invited guest.

I blow out a breath.

"So? What's it going to be, Maximilien?"

I look at my father's grim face, his mouth down turned, his nostrils flared. He's got one eye twitching in irritation. I've taken things too far this time.

"Look, Father. Be reasonable. It's not me who's the problem here. It's that Fabiana Fontaine woman. She's the one who broke the story. Not that there really was a story."

"No story? We nearly lost seven carp thanks to your little show. Those fish are descendants of those given to our family by the Thai King over 200 years ago," Father says, his nostrils flaring to widths never witnessed before.

"I feel bad about the fish. Really, I do. But in my defense, I never thought I would end up in the pond. None of the children did."

"None of the children are twenty-seven years old and weigh 200 pounds, my dear boy."

"205," I correct. "I've been lifting more weights recently."

Father glares at me, and I'm pretty sure some smoke begins to emit from his nostrils.

"What your father is trying to say, darling, is that not only did you re-home the carp to the lawn, but you could have hurt yourself," Mummy says in a far more conciliatory tone.

"Yes, that and the fact you made a spectacle of yourself that's now headline news across our country," Father adds.

"As I said, blame Fabiana Fontaine," I grind out, my dislike for that woman growing in intensity with each passing minute. Which I didn't think was possible. I've hated her for years, even before she tried to blow Amelia and Ethan's cover in Monteluce five years ago. "Why did she have to make a big deal of my minor mishap? It's hardly newsworthy. *Prince falls into pond*. Big deal," I say.

"And now you've become a meme, I'm told," Father says.

"Do you even know what a meme is, Father?" I ask.

"Of course I do," he sniffs, but we both know he doesn't.

"Amelia keeps sending us videos of people falling into toddler's swimming pools with the child calling 'cannonball!' She thinks it's all rather amusing," Mummy says, and a hint of a smile quirks her lips.

"We, on the other hand, do not," Father adds, as if that's not blindingly obvious by the mere fact I've been summoned for this very conversation. "You have become the laughingstock of our family, Max."

I take exception to the term. "Laughingstock? Isn't that going a bit far? Look, I get it wasn't the right thing to do at a garden party, but in my defense—"

"You have no defense, son. You messed up *again*, and now you need to fix it," Father says.

"What do you mean 'again?' It's not as if I make a habit of diving onto slip 'n slides, you know," I say in protest.

"Oh, this isn't your first mess, my boy," Father quips. "There was the time you were photographed partying on Prince Nicholas's yacht with popstar twins, wearing nothing but your swim trunks and drinking from a champagne bottle," Father says, continuing to catalog my less than stellar decision-making over the last couple of years.

"Doesn't everyone need to cut loose every now and then?"

"Not while dancing to a very inappropriate remix of the Ledonian national anthem, my dear boy," Father grumbles.

"Trixie and Tallulah hit number one with that song." My protest falls on deaf ears as my parents continue to count off my failings, all with alarmingly accurate details.

"Didn't you auction off a kiss as well?" Mummy asks, even though it's clear she already knows the answer. "To that female TV presenter who gushed about your 'superior lip action' on national television?"

"That was for charity. I raised a lot of money with that one kiss. And besides, Lorena Samboni was rather a good kisser, so all in all, it wasn't a bad outcome."

My parents are not listening.

"And then there was the time you donned a Hawaiian shirt and mustache, borrowing your friend's yellow Ferrari to visit your sister while she was hiding out at a Malveauxian lake with an actor," Father says.

"By 'actor' you mean Ethan Roberts, aka her *husband*?" I say pointedly.

"The fact of the matter is you were in a yellow Ferrari. You may as well have circled Amelia's location on maps and personally handed them out to the paparazzi!" Father says.

I hold my hands out, palms up, willing this rather too lengthy list of my poor choices to end. "All right, I get it. I'm a mess-up of epic proportions. I should be thrown in the dungeon and fed gruel and water for the rest of my life. Not that I know what gruel is, exactly, but I'm sure it's appropriately horrible."

"Sadly, that option isn't open to us in the 21st century," Father says with a smirk on his face that makes me wonder if he means every word.

"What your father means, darling, is that we've laid out the options to you. You need a reputation rehab, as Amelia puts it, and you need it immediately."

Thanks for the support, Ami.

Father fixes me with his stare. "Son, you're no longer a rebellious teen. Your brother and sisters are all happily married with families of their own, working on their various enterprises and experiencing much success, not once diving on a child's slide and landing in a pond. Isn't it time you grew up?"

I chew my lip. Don't get me wrong. Part of me agrees with them, as much as I won't admit it. As the last born, I've led a carefree existence without the pressure of being the first-born son, without the discipline of being my sister, Sofia, and without the need to do much at all. Playing the fool, taking my friends up on their dares, never worrying about the consequences of my actions, has been a way for me to enjoy my life. To try to forget that everything I do is recorded and analyzed.

When you're the last-born in the Ledonian royal family, there's no set role for you. You're never going to be the monarch, but you can't have a career outside of the military. You need to support charities, but you can't stand out too much or it looks like you're making it all about yourself.

Some days I wonder if I'm just an expensive insurance policy with a pulse, kept around in case something happens to the others, but otherwise expected simply to smile, wave, and try not to embarrass the family name too spectacularly.

I'm even failing at that.

I clasp my hands in my lap and level my parents with my gaze. "You win. I'll do one of the things you suggest."

Mummy beams. "An arranged marriage would be marvelous! I can think of several young ladies of the aristocracy who would be more than happy to marry you."

I shake my head. "I'm not doing that one."

"Are you quite certain?" she asks.

"Quite."

"The baking show?" she suggests.

"The only time I go to the kitchen is to chat with the staff and eat cake."

"The only option left is the documentary."

I let out a defeated sigh. "I suppose."

"That's settled then," Father declares. "The documentary it is. We'll invite Ms. Fontaine to work on it with you."

That gets my attention.

"Wait," I say, my brows pulling together. "What does Fabiana Fontaine got to do with making a documentary?"

"Absolutely everything, my boy," Father replies, regarding me as though I'm a cucumber sandwich short of a garden party. "She's the one who writes about you with razor-sharp precision. Convince her you're not the hooligan the Ledonian people think you are, and you'll win the country over."

"Hooligan? That's hardly fair."

"We'll invite her to the palace with immediate effect. And you, my dear boy, will smile and acquiesce with every bone in your body, charming her so that she thinks you're the best thing since monarchy was invented."

"But *Fabiana Fontaine*? Are you serious? She's the worst," I complain.

"Ms. Fontaine is the perfect person for this role, my dear boy. She's the one writing these stories about you. Wouldn't it be wonderfully clever to show her the real Maximilien?"

"But Father—" I complain, sounding exactly like a whining seven-year-old who's been sent to his room for being naughty.

"You'll change her opinion of you, Max. You have to," Father says plainly.

I cross my arms over my chest, slumping back in my seat. "She hates me."

"Darling, listen to yourself. She doesn't hate you. She doesn't even *know* you," Mummy soothes, her hand on my arm.

Father rises to his full six feet, his features hard and uncompromising. "Can I trust you with this, Max?"

And just like that, any fight I have left in me is sucked right out. There's no point in arguing with him.

I never win.

"You can trust me, Father," I reply, my tone flat.

Chapter 2

Valentina

LIVING in a house that's slowly collapsing around you, eventually, you stop noticing the small disasters. The shutter that hangs at a jaunty angle like a wonky eyelid? It adds character. The electrical outlet in the kitchen that occasionally shoots sparks when you plug in the kettle? Ambiance. The stack of final notices by the front door that's reached architectural proportions? Abstract decor.

Okay, maybe the last example is taking it a step too far.

Over the years. I've become remarkably skilled at

creative problem-solving. It's why I excel in my profession. When you've spent years figuring out how to shower when the hot water heater subscribes to the "heat erratically" school of thought, writing commentary about people who've never had to choose between hot showers and food becomes surprisingly therapeutic.

"Morning, Nona," I say as I push through her door and step into the darkened room. "I've brought your tea and a slice of toast."

"Thank you, my love," she replies as she pushes herself up in her statuesque four-poster bed, a relic of an aristocratic past. "Breakfast in bed. What a treat!"

"Anything for my favorite grandmother on a Sunday morning," I say as I place the breakfast tray on the dressing table and pull the heavy drapes back to let the morning sun pour in.

"I'm your only living grandmother," she replies with a smile.

"And being alive gives you a distinct advantage in my affections." I place the tray across her lap and lower myself onto the end of her bed.

She eyes the envelopes on the tray, her white brows pulled together. "More final demand notices, I suppose."

"We'll need to pay the electricity bill, but the others will have to wait. Now, you enjoy breakfast. I'm going to get some writing in before I tackle that leaking tap under the kitchen sink."

"It's leaking again?"

"Nona, the whole place is falling around our ears. The leaking kitchen tap is the first task on my rather lengthy to-do list for today."

"You're such an angel, my darling Val. What would I do without you?"

I smile at my grandmother. "Hold house parties with frat boys?"

"I mean it."

"I'm just trying to hold it all together, Nona. That's all."

She takes a sip of her tea. "Lovely cup of tea, Val. While you write, I'm going to tackle the weeds in the garden."

"Just be careful. I don't want you breaking a hip or something."

"I might be getting old, but I'm not frail, thank you."

"You've still got it, Nona." I place a kiss on her forehead. "See you downstairs?"

"In a bit. I'm going to revel in the luxury of breakfast in bed." She reaches for me, her crepey hand clasping my wrist. "You don't deserve to have to live this way, Val."

"Nona, we've been through this. It's not your fault what happened, and we're fine. Right?"

"Your father always said he was innocent."

This old tune.

"The evidence was overwhelming. We both know that."

"What I would do if I met that man in a dark alley…"

I choke out a laugh. "Because the King of Ledonia is always lurking around in dark alleys."

"It's an expression, darling. He's to blame for all this."

I let out a deep sigh. Nona will always defend her son's honor, disregarding the evidence against him. Not me. I've accepted it. What happened is done. History. And we all know you can't change history.

I place my hand over hers. "Drink your tea before it gets cold."

I leave her door ajar and make my way back down the creaking stairs, avoiding the broken step my foot went through last week. I make a mental note to search for a piece of wood in the garden shed later to patch it up.

With my morning brew in hand, I sit down at my desk and crack open my laptop. I'm greeted with an avalanche of emails. This morning's entertainment provides my daily glimpse into the collective psyche of humanity. Nestled between the usual lottery winnings notifications and urgent pleas from African royalty requiring my immediate financial assistance—does that tired ploy ever work?—I discover a gem. Someone claims they made sourdough last week, and the crust formed what they swear is Prince Maximilien's face.

Well, at least that's amusing.

The attached photograph looks remarkably like a poorly formed loaf of bread to me, but if I squint and tilt my head at just the right angle, I can almost make out a rather happy-looking Prince Max. Which, to be fair, captures his default expression nicely.

I could make a fun TikTok with this.

Next there's an email entitled "Royal Aliens." T.K. Ross presents a theory that the royal crest includes a constellation of stars not visible from Earth, which he firmly believes shows their extraterrestrial origins, and he fears they may soon summon their cosmic relatives to enslave us all.

Filing that one in the bin.

Not that I'm in a position to complain. I make my living from information, fed to me by a cultivated network of sources who trust me with their gossip, T.K. Ross notwithstanding. My sources come from all walks of life, but one thing they all have in common is access to the royal family, which is why I'm always the one to break the stories first.

From upstairs comes the sound of Nona's voice, raised

in what I prefer to think of as "spirited discussion" with someone about a bill. It's probably the electric company, though it could be the council about property taxes, or the heating oil supplier.

Our house—Nona's house, technically—is the image you'd see if you looked up "faded grandeur" in the dictionary. It boasts no less than twelve bedrooms, seven bathrooms, a library, and the most useful of rooms in 21st Century Ledonia: a ballroom complete with a sprung floor.

Not a lot of use for that one.

Our heating works in two bedrooms; the plumbing is questionable in all but one bathroom, and even that's a lottery if you'll get a water torrent or a mere dribble; the library roof has developed what we optimistically call "ventilation," requiring a host of buckets to catch drips every time it rains.

Lap of luxury? More like the lap of disrepair.

My workspace occupies what was once an elegant study, complete with floor-to-ceiling bookshelves packed with musty books, and a window overlooking gardens which have long-since been claimed by a terrorist organization of weeds. Nona will need industrial-grade machinery to locate the plants this morning—and a medical degree to resuscitate them.

The house reflects our family's trajectory rather poetically—once grand, now crumbling, hanging onto dignity through sheer stubborn determination.

Sometimes I wonder if I'm doing the same thing.

As I pad across the study floor, the photograph on the mantelpiece catches my eye. My father, looking impossibly young and happy, captured during what I didn't know at the time was our golden period.

I remember it as if it was yesterday, even though it was fifteen years ago now. My world ended with a knock on my dormitory door. The headmistress wore the expression adults adopt when they're about to obliterate a child's world with a handful of words.

"I'm afraid there's been some trouble with your father, Valentina," Mrs. Walters had said, her expression more pinched than usual. And that was saying a lot. The woman closely resembled a prune.

The "trouble" was splashed across every newspaper and media site in the land the very next day, labelling my father as a traitor. Using his position to steal money from royal charities. My sweet, kind, quirky dad, who, with my mother passing away when I was only four years old, had done what he could to be both dad and mum to me. He sent me care packages to my boarding school as regular as clockwork every week, always sneaking in some extra chocolate. He taught me how to ride a bike, how to throw a cricket ball, and how I should expect to be treated by a boy.

I still have the letter he sent me, telling me he was innocent. I believed him. Of course I did. He was my dad. But the evidence against him was too strong, and over the years, I've lost my previous conviction. I love my dad, but everything pointed to him having done it.

We email. Stilted, careful messages where he asks about Nona and I tell him she's fine. I've never told him I'm working as a journalist, that I write about the royal family. Some truths are easier left unsaid.

The last email came two months ago. He called me "piccola", his childhood nickname for me. Little one. It still has the power to make my chest ache.

I want to forgive him for leaving me behind. I want to believe he's innocent, like Nona does so vehemently. But mostly, I'm just angry that he chose exile over fighting for his name.

Over fighting for me.

He fled Ledonia in the dead of night, leaving behind a scandal that was talked about for years. I was twelve, suddenly notorious, unwelcome in the world I'd been born into with one brush stroke that sent me to Nona in Villadorata.

The bullies at my new public high school had been creative with their taunts. "Disgraced Daddy's little princess" was the kindest thing they'd call across the schoolyard. I won't mention the others. I'd learned to keep my head down.

I adapted. I had to. There was no other choice.

So, I became someone new, someone no one could connect me to.

Change your name, and you can change your life's trajectory.

The beauty of anonymity is freedom. I can attend events, cultivate sources, write commentary about behavior I understand all too well, and nobody connects me to anything except the byline I've created.

My phone rings. Unknown number. It usually means either somebody wants to sell me insurance I can't afford, or someone has information.

I answer it using my alter ego, hoping for the latter.

"Good afternoon. This is Ronan Clementine, the Director of Communications for His Majesty, King Frederic."

It's clearly a prank call.

"Uncle Bertie, I'm busy, you know," I reply, a smile in my voice.

The man at the other end of the line repeats, "I am not your Uncle Bertie. I'm Ronan Clementine, Director of Communications at the palace. His Majesty requests your presence this afternoon at three o'clock."

"You're very good, Uncle Bertie. You sound just like you've got a carrot stuck—"

"Miss!" The prim and proper voice cuts me off. "I was told to invite you to the palace today at three o'clock to meet His Majesty."

I narrow my eyes, moving the phone from one ear to the other. "You're not my uncle?"

"I am not."

"And this isn't some kind of joke?"

"It's deadly serious."

"What does the King want to talk to me about?"

"His Majesty would like to meet with you regarding your recent articles about a particular member of the royal family. This afternoon at three. We've spoken with Judith Giovanni, and she gave us the green light to talk directly with you."

My stomach hollows. They've cleared this with my boss.

As if declining an invitation from the King of Ledonia is something people do.

"We can send a car to your residence if you require transport."

"No, no. That won't be necessary," I reply rather hurriedly. The last thing I want is for the royal family to figure out who I really am.

"That's settled then. Mention your name at the gatehouse. The guards will let you in. Good afternoon." The line goes dead, his words sliding over me like ice water.

I stare at my phone as though it's personally betrayed me.

The King wants to talk with me at the palace, a place I haven't set foot in as my true self since I was twelve years old. Where people probably still whisper my family's name there as a cautionary tale about trust and betrayal.

This is it. It's all over. Someone's figured it out. Someone's connected the dots between my insider knowledge and my actual inside experience.

The King's going to have me prosecuted. Exposed. The country will know who I really am.

My hands shake as I set the phone down on my desk. Years of building a new identity, of avoiding recognition, and it could all be about to crumble at the hands of the man who destroyed my father.

My phone rings once more, and I almost leap out of my skin.

"Judith, hi," I say into my phone.

"You've spoken with the palace?" she asks.

"I have."

"And?"

"I'm meeting with them this afternoon, but I'm not sure what they want with me."

And I'm terrified they've worked me out.

"You won't know by sitting at home on your thumbs. Go, meet with them and find out. They've singled you out. It's an honor."

Or an execution.

I look around at the water-stained wallpaper, the photograph of my dad and me in our golden moment.

I've done what I've done to survive, to eke out an existence amid the rubble of my family's downfall.

It's time to discover what the King wants with Fabiana Fontaine.

Chapter 3

Valentina

THE PALACE GATES loom before me like something out of a fever dream, wrought iron and foreboding. My hands shake as I show my ID to the guard, and for one terrifying moment I'm convinced he'll take one look at my face and declare, "Lady Valentina Romano, you're under arrest for impersonating Fabiana Fontaine!"

Yup, I'm as melodramatic as a soap star right now. That's what you get from years of hiding behind a fake identity, who happens to write about the royal family.

But of course he doesn't know who I really am. No one does here at the palace.

And that's the way it needs to stay.

The guard simply nods and waves me through, and I shoot him a tight smile before I park my rattling pile of rust in a space beside one of the palace's sweeping lawns.

My car door creaks as I close it, and I half expect curtains to twitch at windows as staff and family startle at the sound.

I take a deep, steadying breath and smooth down the skirt of my suit. Squinting in the bright summer sun, I try to throw a lasso around my thoughts that are running like wild horses.

Is the King going to sue me for libel?

Could he have me deported?

Is he going to ban me from ever writing about the royal family again, which would mean the end of my career and my income? And most importantly, Nona and I will be out on the street: homeless, hungry, and desperate.

Or perhaps he's going to have me flogged at dawn in front of an audience of everyone I've ever written about, all of whom will be baying for my blood?

I push an errant hair behind my ear.

There's an outside chance I might be catastrophizing right now.

A woman in her forties, with her hair cropped, wearing sensible shoes, with a no-nonsense demeanor, approaches me. "Ms. Fontaine, I presume?" she asks, her eyes gliding over my car in obvious judgment before they land on me.

Show time.

"That's right."

"I'm Nadia Aloni, your security escort today. Please, come with me." Her face is severe; her light blue eyes are otherworldly.

"Sure thing," I reply.

She leads me through a stone archway and into the palace through a service entrance near the kitchens. Not the entrance I used as a child as a guest of the palace for garden parties and the like.

Oh, how the mighty have fallen, and fallen *hard*.

We make our way through whitewashed corridors until we enter the part of the palace I've seen before. Marble columns, high ceilings, gilded edging. The entire place reeks of wealth and privilege.

"His Majesty will see you in the library," Nadia Aloni says as we approach a familiar set of double doors.

My stomach drops to my charity shop designer shoes. The King's library? That's where my father brought me several times to show me first edition children's books that smelt of dust and wonder. I remember marveling at the rows and rows of leather-bound books with gold detailing in the bookcases that seemed to stretch right up into the sky. I remember climbing a ladder on wheels, wishing it would whisk me around the room as if I were Belle in *Beauty and the Beast* in my very own library.

The irony is not lost on me that I'm about to be lectured about my career choices by none other than the King himself in the same room where I once dreamed of my own fairy tale ending.

But that was the old me, the starry-eyed child who no longer exists.

The doors open, and there he is, King Frederic of Ledonia, the man who destroyed my life.

He's sitting behind a grand wooden desk, flanked by a middle-aged man in a suit as he concentrates on some papers, looking every inch the monarch who could have me tossed in a dungeon for treason.

Do they still do that in the 21st century?

I clasp my hands behind my back and squeeze until my joints turn white.

You've got this.

"Ms. Fontaine," the man at the King's side begins. He looks like he's in his forties, with perfectly styled but thinning hair, and a smile that could sell ice to penguins. "I'm Ronan Clementine. We spoke on the phone."

The guy I thought was my Uncle Bertie making a prank call.

"H-hello, Mr. Clementine," I stammer, wishing I had the bravery of a woman who hadn't just stepped out of the staff corridor and into the royal firing squad.

"May I introduce His Royal Majesty, King Frederic," he continues with a respectful bow of his head—for the King's benefit, not mine—and in return, I glide my gaze over the king's familiar face.

He's a tall and imposing, a handsome man, even in his advancing years, "the silver sovereign", as I once referred to him on a TikTok.

It went viral.

"Your Majesty," I manage, doing what I hope is an acceptable curtsy despite my knees threatening to buckle beneath me. Every crazy thought I've had about why I'm here buzzes around my head. Should I make a run for it? I mean, who willingly meets their executioner?

"Pleasure," the King replies, although the way he says the word suggests it's anything but. "Please sit, Ms. Fontaine." He gestures at a chair across from him, and I lower myself onto it, every muscle in my body rigid.

This is the end. The end of my career—or worse.

He places his clasped hands on the table, his dark eyes trained on me in unflinching directness. "I imagine you're curious why I've invited you here today," he says.

Ummm, yeah?

"I'm sure you have an excellent reason," I reply.

I wonder if they have room service in the palace dungeons.

"You recently published an article about my youngest son, Prince Maximilien."

"That's right." That hollow feeling claims my belly once more.

"It was a little… *harsh*, shall we say."

So, I'm going to be rapped over the knuckles for reporting on man-child Max.

"With all due respect, Your Majesty, I simply reported the facts. Your son made some interesting decisions that ultimately resulted in his landing in a pond."

"You're absolutely right, and your sources, whoever they may be, reported the events accurately."

His words surprise me.

"They always do," I reply, sounding one hundred percent more confident than I am.

The King and Ronan Clementine share a look.

If he's going to bring out the firing squad, now would be the time. My eyes dart nervously to the door, half wondering if there's a row of soldiers with rifles waiting for their cue.

King Frederic leans toward me. "Ms. Fontaine, I'm sure you'll be surprised to learn that I greatly admire your work."

I blink at him in shock. "You are?"

I mean, *what the heck*?

"Of course I am. Although you tend to dwell on the negative traits of both my family and me, your writing can be insightful and well informed. On top of that, you have a sharp wit I appreciate."

Huh. The row of armed soldiers marches away.

"Thank you very much, sir," I reply, my muscles

relaxing for the first time since I climbed into my car to drive here.

Who knew the king admired me?

Or…is this a trap?

"I have a proposition for you," he continues.

And here it is.

"We would like to work with you on a project."

Wait, what?

This meeting is getting weirder by the minute.

"Work...*with* me?" I'm fairly certain my expression resembles that of someone who's just been told gravity no longer exists and we're all about to float around the room.

"That's what I said," the King replies evenly.

"I'm sorry. What do you mean you want to work with me, sir?"

"Ms. Fontaine, my son, Maximilien, has found himself in something of a public relations predicament."

That's one way to put it.

"You're referring to my most recent report about him diving onto the slip n' slide and landing in the pond," I say, cringing inside.

He might just be a prince to me and the rest of the country, but he's the King's son. He can't love that I've written that story, or any of the other stories I've written about Max and his siblings over the years, despite the fact they've all been true.

"That was the latest incident in a string involving the prince," Ronan Clementine confirms. "Although we have had concerns about Prince Maximilien's choices for some time now."

Choices is a nice way of saying horrible decisions that have landed him in all sorts of pickles, including a pond.

"Look. I'm sure you didn't like that I reported on that, but I have a duty to my readers. They love to know what members of the royal family are up to, and Max—I mean Prince Maximilien—does provide me with rather a lot of material."

The king presses his lips together as Ronan Clementine replies, "There's no need to be defensive. We know you have a duty to report, which is why we've invited you here."

"Meaning?" I ask.

"We'd like to offer you exclusive access to document my son's efforts to rehabilitate his image. A behind-the-scenes look at the real Prince Maximilien, if you will," the king says.

I stare at him. Is he seriously asking me to help Prince Max look better in the eyes of the public by making stuff up?

"You want me to write a puff piece? Something that will compliment him and make him look good?" I ask.

I might be masquerading as my alter ego, but I've got to draw the line somewhere. My journalistic integrity is that line.

"We want you to share the truth about the prince," Ronan corrects smoothly. "You only hear about his mistakes. We would like you to present a documentary about him, showing all aspects of his personality rather than just his less-than-optimal choices."

"I'm confident that you'll find my son to be more than simply your attention-grabbing headlines," the king says.

"Which is why, as previously discussed, you will get all the access to the prince that you will require. We can provide you lodgings here at the palace to make things easier for you," Ronan Clementine adds.

My eyes widen to the size of royal dinner plates. "You want me to move into the palace?"

The thought of living behind enemy lines is unsettling

to say the least, let alone the fact I'll be under the same roof as the ridiculously handsome and charming Prince Max.

An unwanted tingle shoots down my spine.

I might have labelled him a himbo and a man-child, but I've never denied how attractive the prince is.

"We do," Ronan Clementine confirms. "That way you can have untethered access to the prince, both here and when he travels north for a personal project later in the month."

"North?" I squeak, because the idea of not only living in the palace when I'm hiding my real identity, but travelling with him has my insides tying in elaborate knots even a sailor would be proud of.

"My son has various commitments through the rest of the summer. If you accept this offer, you will need to shadow him on all his commitments, which includes travelling to the northern palace with him," the king replies.

"Why me?" I ask.

"Because you're the one writing all the articles and posting all those videos to social media, Ms. Fontaine. You seem to have an uncanny ability to know what the members of my family are up to at any given time."

It's called sources.

"You're perfectly positioned as the journalist who 'tells it like it is', as they say, only you'll get the whole picture by shadowing the prince for a month," Ronan Clementine says.

"A *month*?" I guffaw.

A full month behind enemy lines would test me to the limits.

"Of course we will provide you with generous compensation for your time, Ms. Fontaine," he adds.

My brain nearly short-circuits. *Generous compensation?*

"How generous is generous exactly?" I ask.

Could it be enough to fix Nona's house, pay the bills, and maybe even afford the luxury of heating this winter?

Without saying another word, Ronan slides a piece of paper across the desk toward me like he's a spy in a movie.

I lift the edge of the paper and glance at the figure.

I nearly fall off my chair.

Holy guacamole. They mean business with a capital B.

I see a toasty warm winter in mine and Nona's future, a fully functioning kitchen tap, and maybe even a new water heater for that price.

"I take it from your expression that the sum is amenable to you?" Ronan Clementine asks, one eyebrow arched in my direction.

"It's…err… amenable," I reply. "But I do need to say one thing."

"Which is?" the king asks.

"I'm not going to create a glowing account of your son simply because you're paying me well. I will need to be honest, showing the world who the prince is behind the headlines. Warts and all."

A muscle in the King's jaw twitches. "I'm confident that you will find my son is a truly decent fellow, despite some of his choices, and almost entirely wart free."

My journalistic integrity wars with my bank account. On the one hand, this seems dangerously close to propaganda. On the other hand , that number on the paper could change everything for Nona and me.

And if I'm being completely honest, the opportunity to get inside access to the royal family, to see how they really operate behind closed doors? It's every royal journalist's dream.

It could make my career.

"Can you guarantee that I will have full editorial control?" I ask.

"Complete control," Ronan confirms. "We must proceed swiftly with this project. So…"

So, it's me or someone else. As difficult as this will be, as personally challenging to keep up my Fabiana façade, I want to be the one to take on this project.

"I'll need to speak with my boss."

"Of course," Mr. Clementine replies.

"When exactly did you have in mind for this to start?" I ask.

"Tomorrow would be perfect," the king replies.

I press my lips together, my mind racing. This is the kind of opportunity that could send my career into the stratosphere, change Nona's and my life forever.

Or this could be the most spectacular disaster of my life.

But really, what choice do I have?

"If my boss agrees, then I will accept," I say, before I can talk myself out of it because there's no way Judith won't agree to this. She lives for this sort of thing.

The King smiles—actually smiles—and for a moment I remember why my twelve-year-old self once thought he looked like a handsome king in a fairy tale.

He rises to his impressive height, tall and broad, just like his sons Alex and Max, and shakes my hand. "An excellent choice, Ms. Fontaine. Ronan will handle all the contract details."

"All right," I say. "Thank you."

"No, no, no. Thank *you*," he replies, his dark eyes trained on mine.

I turn to leave when a thought occurs to me. "What does Prince Maximilien have to say about this arrangement?" I ask.

"He's totally on board with it," the king replies smoothly.

"And he's aware it's me who'll be working with him?"

King Frederic's smile widens, and I swear there's a playful glint in his eyes. "He's looking forward to it tremendously."

I very much doubt that.

Chapter 4

Max

"Come on, Toffee. Time for some more training," I say as I click the leash onto the collar of the household's newest addition, a brown lab with paws better suited to a creature five times her size. She's got delightfully gangly legs, a rich, chocolate-y coat, and a pink tongue that's constantly trying to lick my face whenever I'm near. She's totally captured my heart.

The elder statesmen labs, Lemon and Pepper, cock their heads in my direction.

"Not you two. You're going out with Marco and Sofia shortly," I tell them, and my sister looks up at me from her spot snuggled up against her husband on the sofa.

"My feet are sore from being on them all day. You don't think you could take them out for me, could you, Max? Please? Be a good brother," she says.

"Three dogs are a lot to handle on your own, you know. Particularly with Toffee's four-month exuberance," I reply, watching as Toffee gnaws at her leash as though it's a chew toy.

But better that than one of my shoes, which she did yesterday, leaving it looking like vintage fashion, if "vintage" means "partially digested by rabid canine."

"Your brother can handle three dogs. Can't you, Max?" Marco says, grinning at me. "While you're there, take a look at the flower bed by the south tower. I planted it only last week, and already it's taking off."

My brother-in-law is totally delusional if he thinks I'm going to look at a bed of flowers. Gardening is his jam. It's definitely not mine.

Toffee tires of chewing the leash and begins to tug on my trouser leg in a not-so-subtle way of telling me that it's time to get a move on.

"All right, you two. Let's go for a walk," I say, and both Lemon and Pepper rise from their beds. They look positively sloth-like in comparison with their younger counterpart.

With a total of three tails wagging, one like a windscreen wiper in a driving blizzard, I tell Sofia she owes me one, and together we leave the room, heading for outside.

It's a warm and sunny afternoon when we reach the garden, and I collect a couple of tennis balls from the tub by the stables and hurl them out onto the lawn for Lemon and Pepper. Toffee immediately bolts, yanking on my arm and coming to a sudden stop when she reaches the end of her leash.

"Sorry, Toffee. You're not long enough in the tooth to run with the big dogs yet." She looks up at me with a questioning look on her adorable puppy face. "Quite literally, cutie."

I trudge across the lawn, trailing after the older dogs, who have now secured a tennis ball each, making their way back to me to repeat the exercise. They drop the balls at my feet, and as I lean down to pick them up, Toffee, little minx that she is, worms her way out of her collar and darts across the lawn.

Hastily, I throw the balls for the dogs and rush after her. "Toffee! Come back here!" I call, doing the one thing you're never meant to do with a dog—chase her. Of course, my puppy thinks this is a great game and goes careening through an open gate in the garden wall with happy abandon, her tail wagging like it's trying to power a small wind turbine.

And then I lose her.

"Toffee! Toffee! Come back here, you furry little maniac!" Fear grips my chest. The staff carpark is behind this wall, and that means frequent comings and goings. At only four months old Toffee is small and could easily... No, it doesn't bear thinking about.

With my heart pounding, I sprint through the gate. "Toffee! Come here, girl!"

The parking lot is packed with cars. She could be anywhere.

I sprint between vehicles only to come to a crashing stop when I see a stunning blonde woman in a skirt suit leaning down to pick Toffee up in her arms.

"Hello there, gorgeous," she coos in a soft, melodic

voice. "What are you doing running wild through a carpark? Don't you know that's dangerous?"

Relief washes over me.

She's safe.

I slow my pace, my fear over Toffee's brush with death evaporating as I make my way over to the woman.

They say having a dog is good for your health, and perhaps it can also be good for your love life, too.

Toffee wriggles like an excited brown bundle of limbs in her arms, her long tongue trying desperately to lick the woman's face.

"Thank you so, so much," I gush as I approach her.

She looks up at me, a smile on her face, and I come to a sudden stop as recognition hits me.

Icy cold rushes through my veins.

"You," I accuse, my tone as cold as I now feel.

Her smile falters, but only for a fraction of a second before she pulls her lips back into place. "Your Royal Highness," she says as she curtsies, bowing her head enough that Toffee manages to plant a slobbery kiss right on her nose. She brushes it away with her fingertips, nuzzling my dog.

My dog.

The enemy is holding Toffee in her arms as though she might run off with her. And considering she's Fabiana Fontaine, judge and executioner of my character, I would not be surprised if she did.

I narrow my eyes at her. Of all the people to rescue Toffee from imminent death, it had to be *her*. The bane of my existence, the thorn in my side.

The woman Father has instructed I spend the next month with.

Wow. A month with this woman and her acerbic wit.

Give me strength.

Something flickers at the edge of my memory, but I push it aside. I've met hundreds of journalists over the years. They all blur together.

"Please hand over my dog, Ms. Fontaine" My voice is commanding, but I can't keep the irritation from my tone.

Instead of simpering and blushing like women often do around me, she looks me square in the eyes, unflinching. "Who? This furry missile? You're lucky I caught her, sir," she says with a thoroughly mocking tone. "There are a lot of cars here. The poor little thing might have ended up squished if I hadn't caught her."

I'm in no mood to humor this woman, who's done her best to make me a public laughingstock. I throw my gaze over her. Dressed in a blue skirt suit and pair of shoes that have seen better days, her blonde hair catches the afternoon light, creating a sort of halo effect around her face. But she's no angel. She is in fact essentially a professional assassin armed with a laptop.

Or in this case, a puppy.

My puppy.

And not only that, but Toffee seems more than pleased to be held in the arms of this woman who relishes sharing my every mistake with the country, questioning my very character. She casually throws around terms like "himbo" and "man-child" as though for sport, not caring how deep her words can cut.

And now here she is, standing right in front of me, smiling as though she isn't the devil incarnate, and me, her favorite victim.

"Hand over the dog, please, Ms. Fontaine," I repeat through gritted teeth.

She's looking at me with the greenest set of eyes I've ever encountered, her lips twitching in amusement as Toffee licks her cheek like she's a lollipop.

But darn it all, the way she's looking at me like she's one half amused and the other half challenging me to a duel, makes something twist in my chest that has nothing to do with irritation and everything to do with the fact that Fabiana Fontaine is absolutely, undeniably, and completely gorgeous.

I don't think I've ever seen eyes that impossibly green, like emeralds. Clichéd, but it's the best word to describe them. The *only* word to describe them.

And they're trained on me as though a gauntlet has been thrown down, the corners of her mouth tipped upwards.

This collaboration's going to be torture.

And then I note with more satisfaction than I ought that my puppy got some dirt on Fabiana's lapel.

Good work, Toffee.

And yes, I'm being petty.

I'm fine with it.

"Are you under the impression that I've kidnapped your dog, sir?" she asks, her tone light. "I *rescued* her. She came barreling around the cars as though chasing something, but now it would seem she was in fact running *away*. From you."

"She wasn't running away," I snap, utterly wrongfooted.

I'm used to women simpering and flirting. My royal title makes me an instant hit wherever I go.

This woman? She's rude and snarky and…and still holding my dog.

"You're trespassing on palace grounds," I blurt before I have the good sense to stop myself.

There's a flash of something on her face as her veneer drops, and even if it's short-lived, I wonder if I've somehow got under her skin.

Good. She's gotten under my skin too many times to count. It's about time we redressed the balance.

"Actually, *sir*," she replies, the word dripping in sarcastic deference. "I've just had a meeting with your father. He's invited me to move into the palace, which I'll be doing tomorrow. And now I'm on my way to my car. But thank you so much for the very warm welcome."

My scowl deepens. Of course I knew she was here to see my father, and the topic of conversation was none other than me. Me, "the problem".

The real problem here, however, is the fact that this woman now has the power to make or break me with what she chooses to report over the coming month. Father has made it painstakingly clear that he wants me to go about my everyday life with her shadowing me, confident that she'll learn I'm more than she reports on.

But what if she's right? What if I am as immature and unworthy of my position as she already believes?

The thought clutches at my chest like a fist that won't let go.

Because I *have* done all the things she's reported on. I have been irresponsible and reckless, just as she's said.

Even though my decisions are not me, they're a part of me, and admitting that is hard enough to do to myself, let alone my harshest critic.

Perhaps I should be a little less direct. Bring out some of the famous Prince Max charm.

"Look. We got off on the wrong foot," I begin, despite the words catching in my throat. "Thank you for rescuing Toffee, Ms. Fontaine. I really do appreciate it." I flash her the smile that usually has the effect of softening the heart of even my sternest judge.

But all she does is pull her full lips into an amused smile, her big eyes dancing with mirth. "You're welcome."

She places a soft kiss on Toffee's head before she passes her to me, and as I take my dog in my arms, she squirms with delight at the prospect of licking someone else's cheek.

Fabiana reaches into her purse and pulls out a set of keys. "I believe you and I are going to be spending quite a lot of time together."

"That's correct," I grind out, the prospect hanging over my head like a storm cloud.

She notices the dirt on her lapel and brushes it. But it doesn't budge.

Is it terrible that I have a small sense of victory?

Probably.

Giving up on the dirt, she lifts her chin and turns her green-eyed gaze to mine. "I'll see you tomorrow to start on Project Prince Maximilien."

I arch an eyebrow. "That's what we're calling this?"

She pulls the door open of a car that looks more like it belongs in a junkyard than on the road, and it makes a terrible grinding noise of metal on metal. "That's what I'm calling it, sir. You can call it whatever you wish." She slides inside the car and then pulls the door over. She starts the engine and begins to back the car out of the space.

She comes to a stop beside me, winds down her window—which she actually manually winds, the car is so old—and says, "Bye, Toffee. Sleep well, sir."

And then she turns the wheel and drives off, gravel flicking up behind her wheels.

"This is going to be a nightmare," I mutter as she disappears from sight, her gaze lingering in my thoughts. "A complete and utter nightmare."

Chapter 5

Valentina

THE BATHROOM in my room at the palace is larger than my entire bedroom at home. It's all marble surfaces and gold fixtures that probably cost more than I make in a year.

But then, this is the palace, the seat of power and wealth in this country. If anyone's going to have gold fixtures, it'll be the royal family.

I lean toward the ornate mirror, my hands in rubber gloves as I carefully apply dye to my roots with the precision of a surgeon performing delicate brain surgery. I can't have Valentina's dark hair showing through Fabiana's blonde, particularly not here at the palace.

As far as disguises go, dying my hair and throwing on a pair of non-prescription glasses are about the most basic things I could do. But the fact that I've not been anywhere near the palace as Valentina Romano since I was a tween has given me a certain level of anonymity that I've used to my utmost advantage.

My hands shake slightly as I work, and I force myself to take deep, steadying breaths. I've spent my entire adult life maintaining this identity, and now I'm doing touch-ups in the very palace where the need for it began.

The irony would be enough to make me laugh out loud —if it weren't so freaking terrifying.

I'm behind enemy lines. I need to keep my wits about me at all times.

I set a timer for my hair, kick off my shoes, and sink into the four-poster bed, with its silk comforter and enough scatter cushions to sink the Titanic, careful not to get any of the dye on the covers. Of course, there's a monogrammed cushion with the Royal House of Canossa seal, just in case I forget I'm in Frederic Canossa's house.

I fling that one across the room, watching as it lands on the floor by the sweeping velvet curtains that frame the window.

Don't judge. I've got to get rid of my pent-up emotions in some way, and doing it on a cushion is pretty tame, let's face it.

My phone beeps, and I see my boss's name flash up on my screen.

JUDITH GIOVANNI:

> This is the chance of a lifetime, Fabiana.
> Don't mess it up.

You're telling me. This is my moment. My shot. And I'm going to do my darnedest to take full advantage of it.

ME:

> I won't. I'll get the inside scoop on him, warts and all. You can count on me.

JUDITH GIOVANNI:

> Good girl. Nail this project and you're off the royal beat for good. I'm thinking investigative journalism, political commentary, whatever direction you want.

My heart leaps. I've been pushing my boss for this for years, but she's kept telling me that I'm invaluable with what I do.

The idea of no more royal weddings, no more charity galas, no more writing about what Prince Max wore to a nightclub? It's a dream come true. Real journalism.

Carrot officially dangled.

ME:

> I won't let you down.

I place my phone beside me and marvel at how fast this all happened. Yesterday, I was summoned to the palace, expecting dungeons, firing squads, or at the very least, a rap over the knuckles for calling his son names. Today, I'm the palace's newest resident, with my very own rooms consisting of a bedroom, bathroom, living room, and a fully stocked kitchenette, where I can't imagine anyone ever cooks.

Even though I need to play nice in the royal sandbox, I'm not going to play their game. They might be paying me to front this Prince Max PR stunt, but I'm going to report him as I find him—which yesterday was as a mixture of a petulant child and just about the most handsome man I've seen in my life.

But no matter what, I won't be swayed by the prince with his handsome looks and broad shoulders, as so many women before me have been. No matter how much his height lends him an enviable presence someone my size can only dream of. The way his rich, smooth voice rolls over me, tickling my belly. The way his chestnut eyes bore into me as though he can see into my soul.

I clear my throat.

Prince Max can be as charismatic and handsome as he likes, but I'm absolutely determined to remain impervious to his charms.

He might not have been the one to force my parents to flee Ledonia, but he's guilty by association.

I check my roots. A few more minutes should do it.

Drumming my fingers on the windowpane, I gaze out at the royal gardens, the very gardens where I remember playing hide-and-seek with children at garden parties.

I remember racing through these very gardens with Prince Max when I was about eight or nine. I was only a year older than him, although he was always taller. Sofia had organized games for us younger children, already taking charge, even back then. She was always meant to be queen. Alex had slunk off with a friend, not enjoying being bossed around by his sister, and Amelia, with her infectious giggle, was so friendly and fun.

Back then, my biggest concern was whether I would get to sneak an extra helping of dessert.

Now? Well, let's just say extra helpings of dessert sit way down my priority list.

I didn't come here often, perhaps only a handful of times, but the times I did are seared into my memory. The royal children. The formality of the events. The way my father was always so confident and capable, and knowing everyone.

I push out a breath. It's not the least bit helpful to take a walk down memory lane right now, not while I'm literally behind enemy lines. I need to focus on the project, aka Prince Maximilien and his less than stellar choices.

The palace must be gambling on me finding more than a man-child in Prince Max. That all his antics that have provided such marvelous fodder for my articles for the last five or more years aren't the real man.

Only time will tell on that front.

I return to the window that looks out at the gardens. A couple of dogs come into sight, trailed by a woman in a pretty summer dress, her long dark hair falling down her back. My heart leaps at the sight of her, the woman who will one day be queen.

Princess Sofia.

She picks up a tennis ball and throws it with an impressive arm, the ball sailing toward the palace, pursued by two labs, determined to capture it.

She looks in my direction, and instinctively, I pull back from the window. It's an old habit, trying to keep my distance from the very people I write about, quietly using my network of sources to get the inside scoop.

I pick up my phone again and send a message to Nona.

ME:

I'm all settled in at the palace. It's so strange to be back here again after all this time.

NONA:

Hold your head up high. You've done nothing wrong.

ME:

I know, but I'm not me, am I?

NONA:

You're always you, no matter whether you're Fabiana or Valentina.

I smile at the phone. My grandmother always knows what to say. I'm going to miss seeing her smiling face each day.

ME:

I'm being taken on a tour of the palace soon, and I'm having a meeting with the PR team tomorrow. How are you? I hope the tap in the kitchen isn't leaking again. I followed the YouTube clip frame by frame, and it seemed to be working fine before I left.

NONA:

Stop fussing over your old grandmother. I will be just fine.

ME:

Call me anytime. I'm only twenty minutes away. Promise me?

NONA:

You forget I have Rudolf to help. Between you and me, he's rather a good tea maker.

So, Mr. Beckman has already been over to see my grandmother, and I've only been gone for an hour and a half.

ME:

Don't you dislike our neighbor?

NONA:

He's not as bad as I'd thought.

ME:

High praise.

NONA:

Go. Learn all about your prince. And don't forget to enjoy yourself while you do so.

Enjoy myself? Has Mr. Beckman's tea gone to her head? There's going to be nothing enjoyable about the next thirty days.

But I don't want Nona worrying about me, so I tap out a reply.

ME:

I'll do my best. Love you XOXO

NONA:

Love you too, Val XOXO

I fire off a quick message to our neighbor, Rudolf Beckman. He surprised me with his eagerness to check in on my grandmother, his face positively glowing when I told him I'd be away for a while, only able to come back every now and then.

ME:

Thanks again for being there for my nona, Mr. Beckman. Please message me if there are any issues. I'm not far away.

RUDOLF BECKMAN:

It's my pleasure. Violetta is doing well and says to tell you the roses are blooming beautifully.

I arch a brow. First tea and now he's calling her Violetta. He's always called her Lady Romano.

ME:

> It's good to hear the roses are winning the battle against the weeds. Thanks again.

Twenty minutes later, my roots are successfully blonde again, I've dried my hair and scooped it up in my Fabiana ponytail, and I unpack my pitiful belongings in rooms that could probably house a Vegas casino.

There's a knock at the door, and I make my way across the expensive Persian rug in my bare feet. Swinging it open, I expect to see some uniformed member of the palace staff to take me on the tour of the palace the King insisted I take on my arrival.

Instead, it's Prince Maximilien himself, looking both handsome and about as enthusiastic to see me as someone attending their own tax audit.

He's changed from his puppy-wrestling attire of yesterday into trousers and a crisp white shirt that shows off his tan skin and dark eyes—and does absolutely nothing to hide the fact that he's attractive in a way that should probably be illegal under international law.

And then I remember that he's the entitled prince who demanded I hand over his puppy yesterday like I was some sort of dog-napping criminal mastermind, and *wham!* His good looks instantly reduce to a minor irritation I can readily ignore.

Instinct kicks in and I bust out a curtsy, which probably looks rather ridiculous, dressed as I am in a pair of light cotton shorts and the once blue T-shirt I always wear to dye my hair, complete with peroxide patches and a frayed collar. "Your Royal Highness."

His lips quirk in obvious amusement as his eyes sweep over me, and I wish I were in my Fabiana Fontaine armor.

A simple skirt suit and heels, with my glasses firmly in place. "I see I've caught you at a disadvantage."

"Not at all," I say without even a hint of a smile. Why should I smile? It's clear neither of us are exactly thrilled to be working together, even if we both have something to gain from the endeavor. Plus, he's being rude about how I'm dressed. "To what do I owe this pleasure?"

Pleasure, aka, why are you darkening my door when we will both have to endure one another's presence in a meeting tomorrow?

"I've been asked to show you around the palace, Ms. Fontaine," he says with grudging politeness.

He was asked? Sure he was. More like ordered by Daddy under threat of having his allowance revoked.

Man-child indeed.

"No need. Apparently, someone called Rita will be here soon to do just that."

"Rita has been called away, so I've had to take on the task."

The way he says the word "task" makes it blatantly clear how thrilled he is about being here.

"How lovely. Although I wonder, can you really spare the time from your busy schedule of princely duties?" I ask.

His jaw tightens. "I can."

"There's no slip n' slide you need to hurl yourself down? No fish to dislodge from a royal pond somewhere?"

Yes, I'm being rude back. Much like my treatment of the scatter cushion earlier, I'm good with it.

A muscle in his jaw leaps, his eyes narrowing a fraction. "Shall we begin the tour?"

We shall, Your Royal Reluctance.

"Give me two minutes." Without waiting for his reply, I close the door over—which feels better than it probably should—and quickly change into my Fabiana armor of a skirt suit, a pair of pumps, and my fake glasses. I apply my preferred shade of lipstick, aka Battle Red, and then swing the door open once more.

"I'm ready," I pronounce...to an empty hallway.

What the...?

I glance up the hallway, and then down it. There's no sign of him.

I chew my lip. Where is he? Is this a case of the great disappearing prince? Or maybe he's just playing a game, royal tit for tat as it were: I closed the door on him so he disappears.

Despite my irritation, I laugh. Because really, this is the most ridiculous situation we find ourselves in. Neither of us likes the other, neither of us respects the other, and yet here we are, about to embark on a lengthy project together.

I'm going to need to find a way to get on with this man, or else the next month will seem like an eternity.

"What's so funny?" asks a deep, velvety voice and I almost leap out of my heels.

I place my hand over my heart, which is hammering like it's at a rave, and turn to see the man-child himself, returned from wherever he'd scurried off to in this game of one-upmanship we both seem to be playing.

"Nothing, sir," I say brightly. "Now, this tour. Lead the way." I gesture down the corridor, and naturally Prince Max walks in the opposite direction.

This man!

I follow him through the corridor, doing double steps for each of his long-legged strides.

"If I'd realized this was going to be a cardio workout, I would have worn some running shoes," I say as we turn a corner and enter the public area of the palace.

"As you mentioned, I have other duties I must attend

to," he says over his shoulder, and he actually speeds up his pace, so now I'm tottering in my heels at a potentially dangerous speed just to keep up.

"What would they be? Your duties?"

"The usual. Champagne on super-yachts. Partying in VIP sections of the city's most exclusive nightclubs. A private jet trip with a supermodel." He comes to a sudden stop, and I almost slam right into him.

"So just a regular Monday for you?"

He glares at me. "These are the state rooms where we receive foreign dignitaries." He gestures at ornate double doors. "The throne room is through here."

He pushes the doors open briefly, and I see sparkling chandeliers, red carpet, portraits of monarchs dating back centuries. The atmosphere drips with privilege and power.

I hold my phone aloft. "Okay if I film?"

"Be my guest."

I pan the camera around, capturing both the room and his bored expression. "What can you tell me about this room?"

He manages a smile for the camera. "This is where the king and queen knight people and hand out honors."

"And who is that?" I ask, looking up at an oil painting of a woman in elaborate period dress.

I expect him to at least name his ancestor, maybe even throw in an interesting tidbit. Instead, he simply shrugs. "No idea."

I almost drop my phone. "You don't know which of your ancestors this woman is?"

Without glancing at the painting again, he replies, "Queen Bertha. Shall we move on?"

"You just made that up, didn't you? There's no Queen Bertha."

His dark brown eyes sparkle with mirth. "Queen Bertha happens to be my favorite of all the Ledonian queens," he deadpans, but the corners of his mouth twitch.

"Now that you mention it, I do remember a Queen Bertha. 1574 to 1599, if I'm not mistaken. She forged the first friendly relationship with Malveaux."

Yep, I'm making it up.

Sue me.

He narrows those sparkling eyes at me before he harrumphs, dismissing my fabricated story without bothering with actual words.

"Shall we move on to the Blue Drawing Room?" Without waiting for my reply, he strides away toward another set of double doors, and once again, I trail after him. He pulls the double doors open, and we step into another resplendent room, this one living up to its moniker of the Blue Drawing Room. It's decorated entirely in a deep, royal blue, which of course is thoroughly fitting, considering its name. The rugs on the floor are silk Persians, the wallpaper is blue with gold detailing. Just as the throne room had large windows overlooking the gardens, so too does this room, each window framed by—you guessed it—blue drapes.

"When was this room last decorated?" I ask, my phone trained on him.

"I believe it was sometime in the late 19th century."

"Do you know that, or does it come from your vault where you keep facts on Queen Bertha?" My smile is all teeth and zero warmth, more of a challenge than anything genuine.

A muscle leaps in his jaw.

This is fun. Dangerous, but fun.

I'm meant to be showing deference to this man simply because of his birth, but he's so irritating, it's hard not to want to get one up on him. And really, the look on his face of being one-upped by a lowly journalist is one I'm sure will keep me warm as I fall asleep on my plush royal bed tonight.

Of course, I don't mention that I remember this room. I remember hiding behind that very sofa during a formal reception. I watched the adults in their finery while my nanny searched frantically for me, probably wondering how one small child could vanish.

But Fabiana Fontaine is seeing it for the very first time, so I ask, "What happens in this room?"

"It's another reception room used for official visits and functions. I've been thoroughly bored in this room on many occasions. When I was a child, that is."

"Fascinating," I reply. I pan to the incredible ceiling molding, remembering how I hid behind that sofa and gazed up at it, getting lost in the story it told. "The ceiling molding is absolutely exquisite."

Max looks up. "Yes, it's very...molding-y."

I press my lips together to stifle a laugh. "Molding-y. Is that the technical term?"

He shrugs, looking as bored as he claimed he once was as a child in this room. "How would I know? I'm not an architect."

The prince glances at his watch with all the subtlety of a person trapped in an elevator with someone they despise. I suppose this is our equivalent. We're trapped in a monstrously large palace together with nothing but our sarcasm and mutual dislike to keep us warm.

We move through the state dining room, with its impressively long dining table that seats sixty, and I take some more video and photos, even managing to capture Max smiling.

Well, almost.

It's as we leave the official, public areas and move into the staff corridors when something shifts in his demeanor. His features, once tight, relax, his jaw loosening, and he begins to look like the man I regularly report on. Happy, confident.

I click my camera with curiosity.

"Morning, Timmy," he says to the elderly man polishing silver.

Timmy peers over his glasses. "Your Royal Highness. Miss," he says, rising to his feet.

"I've told you before, Tim. There's no need to stand on ceremony when we're in the business end of the palace," Max says.

Timmy chuckles. "Years of training."

Max clasps his shoulder, the first genuine smile of the day on his face. "How's your grandson's summer football team doing? They had a big game at the weekend, didn't they?"

"That's right, sir. They made it to the semifinals!" He beams. "My Hamish scored the winning goal!"

"That's brilliant! Tell Hamish I said well done, won't you, Timmy?"

"I certainly will, sir. He'll be chuffed."

I watch this exchange with grudging interest, like a scientist observing an unexpected chemical reaction. The prince is genuine, engaged, and seems to know about this elderly man's life.

"And who would this pretty lady be?" he asks, looking my way.

I open my mouth to reply when Max jumps in with, "This is Fabiana Fontaine. The journalist."

Timmy's demeanor immediately changes, his spine stiffening. "What?" he asks, aghast. "Sorry, sir. It's just she's *Fabiana Fontaine*."

I suppose I deserve it. I bet I'm Public Enemy #1 around here.

"I'm covering a story about the prince. Sort of an 'insider's scoop' on all things Prince Maximilien." I offer him a smile, but his face tells me he's not convinced.

"I see." He turns his attention to Max. "I'm sure you know what you're doing, sir," he says, his tone suggesting otherwise.

Max shoots him a look I cannot read. "Tell your grandson congratulations from me. Take care, Timmy."

"Have a good day, sir. Miss."

"Nice to meet you, Timmy," I say as Prince Max gestures at another door.

"The kitchens are through here," he says, holding it open for me to walk into a hive of activity. Delicious aromas emanate from pots on the stove, being stirred by people in white chef coats, others buzzing around, hard at work.

A few faces look our way, and I notice more than one person smiling at us.

Well, at the prince, I suppose.

I take a few shots to use in a video.

"Chef Margot runs things with military precision around here," Max says, gesturing at a woman in her fifties in a chef's hat with a round, pink face.

"I bet she's a marvelous cook," I say, and he startles me by leaning closer and saying in a low voice, "Be warned. She can be absolutely terrifying, but she makes the best chocolate souffle I've ever tasted."

As if summoned, Chef Margot, wielding a large metal spoon like Excalibur, approaches us. "Prince Max!" she exclaims with obvious delight, her stern expression melting into maternal fondness. "What brings you to my domain?"

"I'm showing our guest around, Margot. This is Fabiana Fontaine, the journalist I told you about."

I blink at Max. He mentioned me to the palace chef. Why? And what exactly did he say?

Chef Margot's eyes narrow as she studies me. "Ah. I've read your articles. You're the one writing about our Max and his shenanigans."

Our Max?

"I simply report the facts," I reply smoothly.

She arches her eyebrows. "Facts, you say?"

I tighten my jaw. "Yes. Facts."

"Hmm." She throws an appraising eye over me, and I shift uncomfortably.

I decide flattery is the best approach. "It smells amazing in here, Chef Margot. My breakfast today was delicious. I'm sure I'll love whatever you whip up while I'm here."

"I'm sure you will," she replies coolly.

I eye a pan behind her on the table. "Is that apple pie I smell?"

"It's tarte tatin," she sniffs, naming the French dessert. "Prince Max's favorite."

There's unmistakable fondness in her voice.

She cuts a slice, slides it onto a plate, and offers it to the prince, beaming at him like a fond mother. "Prince Max loves all my desserts. Don't you?"

He takes a bite. "Absolutely exquisite, as always," he says around his mouthful. "You're going to make me fat." He pats a non-existent belly I'm fully aware from photographic evidence is in fact washboard abs.

As I watch him chat with Chef Margot, I try to figure him out. The man who gave me that obligatory tour that so clearly bored him, is not the same person who asks about servants' grandsons or gets indulged by kitchen staff.

The question is: which version is the real Prince Maximilien?

And why do I have the sinking feeling that finding out might be more dangerous than I bargained for?

Chapter 6

❝ Friends! I'm reporting to you from within the palace, where I'm shadowing none other than everyone's favorite royal rogue, Prince Max. That's right, I'm now officially a guest of His Majesty the King.

Call a prince a man-child and suddenly I'm living in the lap of regal luxury.

Who knew?

So, what have I been up to? First order of events was a tour of the palace, given by none other than Prince McHottie Junior himself, Max.

I'll be honest, I expected the usual royal dog-and-pony show. You know, *this is where my great-great-grandfather received dignitaries*, delivered with all the enthusiasm of someone reading the tax code.

What I got might have started out that way, but then it took a turn for the interesting.

The Max who showed me the state rooms was perfectly polite, perfectly distant, and perfectly bored, probably wishing he was on a private island somewhere, sipping champagne and downing caviar.

So far, so predictable.

But then we hit the kitchens, the staff quarters, places where actual humans keep this marble monument functioning. Suddenly, I wasn't looking at the same man anymore.

He became someone else instead.

He remembered that a footman's grandson was playing on a soccer team. The palace chef practically glowed with genuine maternal fondness when she saw him.

Darlings, I nearly got whiplash from the change in this man.

We all know he's dashingly handsome. We all know he has a zest for life that makes even a confetti cannon seem understated. But which is the real Prince Max?

I have a month to figure it out. A month of unprecedented access to unravel the mystery that is Prince Maximilien.

Lucky, lucky me.
Stay tuned. This is going to get interesting.
Yours always,

Fabiana Fontaine xx

#SpoiledOrSincere
#RogueRoyal
#RoyalConundrum

Max

HERE'S the thing about me. I've never responded well to being forced into doing something I don't want to do. Call it a last-born thing, or whatever you like, but I don't deal well with being hemmed in. Having attended boarding school and later, entering the Royal Air Force after I graduated from Cambridge, I've had enough of being told what to do to last a lifetime.

And now I've been told to play nice with a woman I despise. What's worse, she's a woman who's reporting on my every move.

Don't get me wrong, I get it. My parents are trying to change the perception of me that has hung around my neck like a bad smell since I first hit the headlines as a 15-year-old who had no idea that drinking vodka neat would make me quite as drunk as I ended up being.

On a rooftop.

In January.

Naïve? Sure. But then no one ever said 15-year-old boys are known for their smart choices.

Royally Off-Limits

My whole group of friends had thought it was a great idea at the time. What could go wrong, they asked? Try one of my mates falling off and breaking a leg for starters, and then the press finding out about it—which made zero percent difference to my mates, and one hundred percent difference to me.

It was the beginning of my "choices" becoming headline news, and soon enough the press expected me to mess up, which I did, rather too often.

A few years later, Fabiana Fontaine arrived on the scene, a journalist who somehow gets the inside track on everything I do. And she loves name-calling. McHottie Junior, Mad Max, himbo, and her most recent jibe, man-child.

The public laps it up, and I've had more trending hashtags than Father has rules carved into stone, and that man sure loves his rules.

It's only 9:17 AM, and we've been stuck in a conference room, which I've rapidly concluded was designed to make uncomfortable situations even more excruciating. Despite the padded seating and rich mahogany of the table, it's like the conversation is on repeat. And that repeat? An endless discussion about my so-called "public image rehabilitation."

Apparently, the woman who's been talking for years about how vapid and ridiculous I am is the one who's going to resurrect my image.

The irony of the situation is not lost on me.

When Fabiana steps out of the room to take a call, I let out a breath. It's just me, Ronan, and Pippa Chen, the palace's concession to modern times, who was hired to help "connect with younger demographics."

Ronan shuffles through his papers. His controlled

demeanor hasn't slipped once during today's torture, which is more than I can say for mine.

"Remember, sir," he says, adjusting his glasses. "We want to maintain an air of dignified cooperation here. Admittedly, Ms. Fontaine is sharp-tongued—"

"Aka rude," I interject.

"The key is not to let her, shall we say, get under your skin," he says.

I harrumph. *Too late for that.*

"It's not as though she's the first journalist I've ever dealt with. I'm sure I can handle her."

"But she is the first journalist who's made 'man-child Max' a trending hashtag," Pippa adds helpfully.

My jaw tightens. "Hmm."

"I like her," Pippa declares.

Of course she does. Pippa's so oblivious to people's hidden agendas, she'd happily invite Darth Vader and his entire army of stormtroopers to brunch for a nice chat.

"I've been following her for years. She's smart and got some really good ideas. Her social media strategy is absolutely brilliant. Have you seen her hashtags?" Pippa enthuses.

"I'm rather too familiar with her hashtags," I grind out.

But Pippa is on a roll about Fabiana. "She understands how to create authentic engagement without sacrificing journalistic integrity. Her reels and TikToks are—"

"I'm not doing TikToks," I warn.

"Why not?" Pippa asks.

I lift an eyebrow. "The King and Queen wouldn't approve, as Princess Amelia will attest."

"I say let's hear her out," Pippa declares, and Ronan and I share a look that says *let's not.*

The truth is, yesterday's palace tour with Fabiana left

me strangely unsettled. She's exactly how she comes across in her articles. Sharp, sarcastic, and thoroughly unimpressed by me. What I hadn't expected was the way her green eyes flashed when she was teasing me about "Queen Bertha".

Or the attractive curve of her cheek when she pulled her lips into a smile.

Or the way she held herself with a quiet confidence, even when Timmy showed his distrust of her.

And then there was the time I leaned closer to her to tell her about Chef Margot, and I caught a hint of her scent. Something soft and sweet and completely disarming.

It was…inconvenient.

Of course I knew she was an attractive woman. I'm not blind. But it's one thing to know someone is attractive; it's quite another to feel it in their presence.

And I did feel it. I felt it in her quips, in the way she looked at me, in the way she moved.

Dang it! Developing a thing for my arch-nemesis? Terrible, *terrible* timing, particularly when we're about to embark on a full month together.

Because as pretty as she is, as alluring as her scent may be, I refuse to be seduced by her womanly charms. Fabiana Fontaine is the enemy, and I must keep her at arm's length.

The door flies open, and Fabiana steps back into the room, her signature ponytail swinging, her face flushed, rendering her even more attractive.

Get it together, Max.

"Sorry about that," she says as she lowers herself onto the chair opposite me. "Where were we?"

"You were telling us about your brilliant social media strategy," Pippa says eagerly.

"That's right. I was suggesting how you could drag the monarchy into the twenty-first century," she says.

Ronan's eyebrows climb toward his hairline. "That's one way to frame our objectives, Ms. Fontaine."

"You might have noticed that in the interests of saving time, I prefer directness, Mr. Clementine." She glances around the room, her eyes landing on mine, and utterly against my will, my belly does something that seems suspiciously like a flip.

Settle it down, Max. She's the enemy, remember?

Pippa practically vibrates with excitement. "Directness is fantastic!"

Ronan slides a thick wad of paper across the table to Fabiana. "I suggest we put a pin in the whole TikTok idea for now. I've prepared an outline for the documentary series we believe will effectively showcase His Royal Highness in a comprehensive light. If you'd care to take a look?"

She eyes the document as though it were an incendiary device in need of expert detonation. "With all due respect, Mr. Clementine, I believe TV documentary formats have about as much relevance today as a coop of carrier pigeons. Except for David Beckham's series, that is."

So, she's got a thing for Beckham, has she?

And if that's a small stab of jealousy I feel, I'm not going to give it the time of day.

Ronan's impassive face tightens. "Ms. Fontaine, while we appreciate innovative thinking, the dignity inherent in royal representation must be considered."

Fabiana wastes no time in pouncing on his words. "My point exactly! Isn't it time to try something new? Something fresh? And besides, dignity doesn't trend."

I find myself leaning forward despite my best intentions. "What exactly are you proposing, Ms. Fontaine?"

She turns those impossibly green eyes on me once more and I will my belly not to repeat its preposterous flip.

Fail.

Geez.

"I'm proposing we meet your audience where they actually are, sir. YouTube vlogs, Instagram reels, TikTok videos. Footage that shows who you really are instead of the carefully curated version your PR team has been peddling for generations."

Ronan scoffs. "You're suggesting His Royal Highness becomes a social media influencer?" His lip curls in disgust as though Fabiana has just suggested we use eBay to auction off the crown jewels.

"No. I want to turn him into a relatable human being," Fabiana replies with a smile that could cut glass.

Pippa nods enthusiastically. She's drunk Fabiana's Kool-Aid and is coming back for a refill. "The engagement rates on authentic content are absolutely amazing compared with traditional media. Gen Z in particular responds to unfiltered content."

"Unfiltered," I repeat, tasting the word like it might be poisonous. "Define unfiltered for you and Gen Z, Pippa?" I ask, sounding like I don't belong to my own generation.

Fabiana takes the opportunity to dive in. "Unfiltered means showing you doing normal, everyday things. Like walking your new puppy, for instance." She gives me a meaningful smile, and I tighten my jaw.

"I'm not sure my doing 'normal things' is what the Ledonian people want to see," I reply.

"Oh, but they are, including imperfect moments. People connect with vulnerability, with humor, not with perfection," Fabiana says.

"Totally," Pippa agrees.

Ronan looks like he's developing a splitting headache. "Ms. Fontaine, certain royal standards must be maintained. We cannot simply abandon decades of protocol so you can make TikTok videos of His Royal Highness brushing his teeth."

Fabiana leans back in her chair, her fingers steepled. "I hate to tell you this, Mr. Clementine, but protocol isn't serving the royal family anymore, particularly Prince Maximilien. If you want to change his public perception, you need to deliver content where the people are. And that's not sitting on their sofas in front of a TV. It's on their phones. It's on their tablets. And it's short, bite-sized content that's both fun and real."

"I've got some stats on royal approval ratings among the younger generations," Pippa says, tapping on her tablet.

Ronan waves her comment away. "That won't be necessary, Ms. Chen."

"No, Ronan. Let's hear her out," I say.

"They don't paint a positive picture, I'm afraid. Ratings were super high back when Prince Alexander and Princesses Sofia and Amelia were getting married and having their first babies, but now that everyone's more focused on Prince Maximilien—" Pippa trails off, and a sinking sensation claims my chest.

Fabiana leans forward, placing her hands palm down on the shiny mahogany table. "Look. You brought me into this project for a reason. My approach to this is to be transparent with the content we share. If I'm not the right person, tell me now and I will walk away."

The room falls into a tense silence. This could be my opportunity to be rid of this woman I'm beginning to find more interesting than I should. This woman who's been determined to report on every poor choice I've ever made as though it's a national sport.

But as tempting as it is to see the back of her, something tells me she'll deliver exactly what she promises, and as long as I play along and keep my distance, she'll be more help than hindrance.

"What about things I don't want to share, like private conversations? Or my bathroom habits?" I ask.

"Oh, I'm quite sure the public would want to see you in a shower cap," Fabiana quips, and traitor that she's become, Pippa giggles.

"Ms. Fontaine," Ronan warns.

"All right," she concedes, with a clear twinkle in her eye. "No shower cap footage."

"Or private conversations," I add.

"Or private conversations," she agrees, and it feels like a victory, no matter how small.

"We could work it out as we go," Fabiana replies.

She means *argue it out as we go.*

Ronan says, "I suggest we outline some specific ideas. That way we can get a sense of what this might look like in practice."

Fabiana's eyes light up, and she swipes to another screen on her tablet. "One step ahead of you, Mr. Clementine. I've got 'A Day in the Life,' including behind-the-scenes context. 'Unexpected Skills', which would showcase the prince's talents or interests the public isn't aware of. Things like whether he can juggle or hold a tune."

I raise an eyebrow. "Juggle?"

"Can you?" she asks.

"Of course I can."

"Great! Are you any good at karaoke?" she asks, and once again, Pippa lets out a giggle she immediately tries to style out as a cough.

"I'm terrible," I reply.

"That's definitely going on the list then," she says as she taps at her tablet.

"Hasn't the country already seen my, shall we say, playful side?" I say.

"They love it! Man-child Max is still trending," she says.

"Exactly."

"Lean into your strengths."

"Being a man-child is my strength?" I question.

"Clearly," she replies.

Pippa claps her hands together, breaking the mounting tension between Fabiana and me. "This is going to be totally amazing! When can we start filming?"

"What you're describing requires a considerable amount of trust on my behalf, Ms. Fontaine," I point out.

"Yes," she agrees without a moment's hesitation. "Trust works both ways. I'm trusting you to be genuine, and you're trusting me to represent that genuineness fairly."

"Fairness hasn't exactly been in your toolbox when it comes to me," I say, and yes, I sound like a child, stamping my foot and going red in the face when my siblings got more dessert than me.

She shrugs, the smile on her irritatingly gorgeous face not faltering for a moment. "All I can do is give you my word that I will represent you as you are."

Ronan and I share a look. There's no point in looking at Pippa. She's already signed up to be the president of the Fabiana Fontaine fan club.

"What do you think, sir?" Ronan asks.

I tighten my jaw. Not only does this woman seem to be impervious to my charms, but she actively dislikes me. "As long as I get to see the posts and articles before they're published."

She nods.

"In that case, we have a deal," I say.

"Good, good," Ronan says. "Now, let's discuss your

itinerary. The prince is due at his youth outdoor leadership program at Belladonna Palace this week."

"Belladonna Palace." Fabiana repeats, her professional mask slipping.

Huh. Interesting. I wonder why?

"The summer palace," I say, not knowing what's discomfited her—but enjoying it, nonetheless.

It's the little things.

"Is there a problem?" Ronan asks.

"No problem," she replies smoothly.

Ronan closes his compendium over. "That settles it, then. The Palace will make arrangements for you to accompany His Royal Highness to the north. In the meantime, let's begin this project here at the palace. You can shadow His Royal Highness for the next couple of days, attend the state dinner, and then leave for the north."

As the meeting breaks up and everyone files out, I remain seated, watching Fabiana pack up her tablet with brisk efficiency. Pippa fawns over Fabiana as Ronan nods his farewell, and then it's just her and me and suddenly the conference room seems too quiet, too intimate.

"See you later for our first official filming, sir," she says, slinging her bag over her shoulder.

"Looking forward to it," I lie.

She pauses at the door. " I meant what I said about representing you fairly."

I hold her gaze. "Thank you."

She disappears from the room, and I let out a heavy breath.

I'm not the least happy about it, but the fact of the matter is I'm attracted to Fabiana, and not just physically. She challenges me. She isn't afraid to stand up to me. She's razor-sharp. She doesn't react the way most women do, all simpering and blushing, hanging on my every word.

This could be a disaster in the making. A month of serious levels of proximity with someone who isn't impressed by me.

I need to keep my head. I need professional distance. That's what I have to maintain with her, even if something tells me Fabiana Fontaine could turn out to be the most dangerous thing that's happened to me in a long, long time.

Chapter 7

Valentina

I CHEW on a piece of toast topped with the creamiest scrambled eggs I've had in my life. I run my eyes over the schedule I was sent yesterday after the meeting. Prince Max's day is packed, that's for sure. But then that's what you get when you're born into royalty. Endless public engagements, parties, public adoration, and smiles for the cameras.

My heart bleeds for the guy.

Today kicks off with a 9 AM meeting with the Minister

of Education in the Blue Drawing Room, followed by something called a "correspondence review"—code for reading his DMs from adoring women, I bet—then a ribbon cutting at a new library wing across town. Finally, there's a dinner welcoming heads of states from no less than three European countries.

Lots of chances to get both video footage and material for my next article.

I pop the final bite of my breakfast in my mouth and wash it down with barista-level coffee. With all the breakfast options offered to me today, I'll be leaving the palace in a month with tighter clothing, that's for sure. It all looks so good, and I've already planned what I'm having tomorrow: blueberry pancakes topped with maple syrup with a compote of raspberries and blueberries and a side order of clotted cream.

Today's scrambled eggs on toast felt so restrained in comparison.

I pull on my blazer, scoop my hair up into a high ponytail, and slip on my glasses.

It's Fabiana go time.

Gathering my camera equipment, phone, and notebook, I check my watch. It's eight-forty, which is perfect timing to set up in the Blue Drawing Room before the Minister of Education arrives. And who knows? I might even get a couple of moments alone with the prince before she arrives. Not that our time together so far has been exactly great. "Frosty" is probably the softest word I could use to describe it, although "outright hostile" would probably be more appropriate. The prince has made no bones of the fact he thinks I'm a despicable human with no redeeming features.

It's not exactly the start of a beautiful relationship.

My heels click on the marble floors as I make my way

Royally Off-Limits

to the meeting place. Arriving at the doors to the Blue Drawing Room, I wait and listen. With no sounds emanating from the room, I push inside to find it empty.

I'm the first one here.

I position myself near the large windows with my phone ready, my camera on its tripod, and my notebook turned to a fresh page.

I wait.

And I wait.

The time creeps along until it's well after 9 AM and still no one else has arrived—not even the hyper enthusiastic and overly bouncy Pippa Chen.

I pull the doors open again and look up and down the corridor. It's empty but for a couple of palace staff scurrying about their business.

Where are these people? The prince being late isn't too much of a surprise. We're all aware he can be an overgrown kid. But the Minister of Education? She's a real go-getter type, right down to her power suits and sharp bob. Surely she should have been on time?

I slump down into my seat and stare out the window at the royal gardens, the greenery of the lawns stretching into the distance. I check and recheck the schedule. It clearly tells me I'm in the right place and here at the right time.

I'm beginning to suspect that both the prince and the minister have been kidnapped by extremists when my phone shows the time is 9:28. I spring to my feet. It's clear no one is coming to this meeting, and time is ticking on me getting my material for the day.

I need to find the elusive Max, and I need to find him now.

I search the adjacent rooms, finding them empty but for the library, where I accidentally walk in on Princess

Sofia reading papers. I back out as quickly as I can, apologizing to the future queen like it's my job.

"Are you lost?" she asks.

"Just looking for your brother, Your Royal Highness."

"Oh, he's unlikely to be in here." She gestures at the book-lined walls.

"You're right. Sorry to disturb you."

I end up in the office wing, where I ask a staff member to take me to Prince Max's rooms, which he does with obvious reluctance.

His rooms are vacant.

Where *is* that man?

The problem is in a place as large as the royal palace in Villadorata, if a person doesn't want to be found, they can virtually disappear.

Prince Max, it would seem, is good at this game.

Arriving at Ronan's office, I'm told that he's in a meeting with the King, so I ask to speak with Pippa Chen.

"Ms. Fontaine!" she says, her face alight as she greets me with an eager handshake that threatens to jiggle my arm right out of its socket.

I thrust the schedule at her. "Do you know why no one turned up to the meeting this morning? I waited for the prince and the minister for half an hour."

She knits her brows as she scans the now dog-eared page. "Prince Maximilien and the Minister of Education completed their business last month. I posted about it."

"That doesn't make any sense."

"And he wouldn't have been there at 9 AM anyway. Not on a Wednesday."

"Why not?"

"Because he has a personal trainer come to the palace at that time every Monday, Wednesday, and Friday." She leans in, her dark eyes darting from left to right. "I know because I've met him and let me tell you, he is *hot*."

I blink at her. Is she really referring to Prince Max as hot? "Who?"

"The personal trainer."

"Right." I'm not here to discuss the alleged hotness of some PT. "So, this meeting at 9 AM—"

"Could never have been on the schedule for today," she finishes for me, shaking her head. "As I said, hot personal trainer time."

I'm not sure what to think of this. Did the prince have an old schedule sent to me by accident? And if it was on purpose, why would he do something like that? It makes no sense.

Unless…? *No*. It can't be. The prince wouldn't have intentionally had an out-of-date schedule sent to me to avoid having to see me. Would he?

The label "man-child" never felt so appropriate.

Heat climbs my neck. "What about this?" I say, pointing at the next scheduled appointment of the day. "Will he be in the library at 11 AM?"

"The library? I don't think so. His PT session lasts an hour in the palace gym, and then he goes for a run through the grounds." She lowers her voice, her eyes darting around. "There's a group of us girls who watch out of the windows on the top floor."

"You watch the prince run?"

"The PT. Chase is his name. Chase Johansen. He's from South Africa."

I'm not thinking about some South African called Chase. There's only one conclusion here. Max somehow got a false schedule sent to me with no intention of being at any of the day's events. He deliberately sent me on a royal goose chase—and Prince Max is that royal goose.

Preferably cooked.

The conniving, manipulative, absolutely infuriating—

I twist my mouth and scrunch the schedule up in a fit of frustration, flinging it into a nearby rubbish bin. "Where does he run?"

Pippa's eyes light up. "Come with me."

I follow her up to the third floor, where three female members of the palace staff are already staring out the window at the garden below, coffee cups in hand. Some are even munching on chocolate cookies.

"Everyone, this is Fabiana Fontaine," Pippa announces, and the three women turn to look at me.

"As in the journalist?" asks one of them, a pretty young woman in a black and white uniform that tells me she's likely a lady's maid.

I open my mouth to respond when Pippa replies for me. "The very same. But don't worry, she doesn't bite. She's terrific!"

Three sets of eyes assess me.

"I only bite if something really annoys me," I say.

"Hmmm," replies the lady's maid, her eyes scanning my outfit.

"No, really. Fabiana's great!" Pippa insists. "She's come to watch Chase and the prince." She indicates between the four of them. "This is the Chase-slash-Max Fan Club. We're here religiously, every Monday, Wednesday, and Friday. Right, ladies?"

"We are," another of the women replies. She's probably a year or two older than me, and by her jeans and T-shirt, smeared with dirt, my guess would be she's on the gardening team. "But don't tell anyone. This isn't exactly our jobs. Got it?"

"Got it," I reply.

"This is Theresa, Hetty, and Isadora," Pippa says as she gestures from one of the women to the next.

"Hi, everyone. You do this three times a week, every week?" I ask.

"We sure do!" Pippa replies.

"Only when I can," Theresa replies. "I work for Princess Amelia and sometimes have to travel, so I miss this."

"We video those times for her," Isadora explains.

"And I so appreciate it," Theresa replies.

"And you're all here to watch the PT?" I ask, wondering whether some of them have a thing for Max. For purely research reasons only, of course.

"I'm here for Prince Max," Hetty says, her cheeks blushing. "Chase is too perfect for me."

"And Prince Max isn't?" Isadora guffaws. "Face it, Hetty, they're both gods among men."

"Preach it," Theresa agrees.

Gods among men? *Wow.* This really is a fan club.

"Ooh, look. I can see them!" Pippa declares, and everyone clamors around her, peering out the tall window.

There are two male figures rounding the rose garden in the distance, moving with speed and impressive athleticism. They're both in shorts and sneakers, their shirtless torso's glistening with sweat.

Wait. Shirtless?

Oh, come on! No wonder there's a fan club for these guys. They're out there flaunting their ripped bodies as though the palace has no windows through which people can see them.

They may as well have a gigantic neon sign above their heads yelling *Half naked men right here!*

I watch as they stride towards us, their long, athletic

legs pounding the ground. I'm not going to lie, they're both good looking men. Strong. Muscular. In great shape.

The women are enraptured, never pulling their eyes from them.

I click on my phone and begin to film. For content only, you understand.

"It's like they're two Greek statues that have come to life to do cardio together," Isadora says.

"A slow-mo montage of male perfection," Theresa says on a sigh.

Greek statues? Male perfection? *Please*.

Yes, I'll admit, they're a couple of good-looking guys. Objectively, there's no denying that. But Greek statues come to life? Male perfection? From what I understand of Prince Max he's about as flawed as they come. Arrogant, rude, shallow as a puddle.

Even if he does look particularly sexy with his torso taut with muscle, glistening in the late-morning sun.

Not that I'm staring or anything.

It's my job to observe him. To learn everything I can about him.

But there's nothing professional about the way my pulse quickens as I watch him. I have to consciously remind myself to breathe. Because if I'm honest with myself—truly, truly honest—seeing the prince's muscles ripple, his jaw held in strong determination, *does* things to me. Things I shouldn't be feeling for a man I'm not only meant to be working with, but a man I actively dislike.

Well, at least I did actively dislike him before I began to see glimpses of someone beneath the suave, playboy exterior. Glimpses of someone real.

Dang it! I'm supposed to be immune to this man's charms, not standing here like some lovesick teenager ogling the popular boy.

Get it together, Valentina.

I've been so focused on Max, I've barely noticed Chase, until his movement catches my eye, snapping me out of whatever trance the prince has put me in.

Reality hits me like a sharp slap to the cheek. I'm wasting time admiring the view—because as much as I hate to admit it, I am most definitely admiring it—when I should be getting my story.

They're right there in front of me, only three levels down.

This might be my only real chance today.

"Bye, ladies." I dash across the floor, heading to the door.

"Where are you going? They haven't started stretching yet!" Pippa calls out after me.

"Out!" I call back as I fly around the corner, and down the stairs, nearly tripping over my own heels as I traverse the expansive staircase that leads to the ground floor.

Once there, I call on my childhood palace knowledge to locate my nearest exit, bolting through it and out into the gardens.

I gulp in air, my heart hammering from more than the exertion as I search the gardens for the two Greek statues in motion. I come to a stop, and my heels sink into the grass. *Dang it!* I pull them off, hopping on one foot and then the other before I clutch my shoes in one hand and dash around a fountain in hot pursuit.

It's not until I reach the veggie gardens and fruit trees at the back of the kitchens when I let out a defeated breath. They're nowhere to be seen. Somehow, those half naked exercisers slipped through my fingers.

A couple of gardeners have stopped to stare at me, and I give them a brief, embarrassed wave before I smooth back the hair that's loosened from its ponytail and pad across the grass in my now dirty bare feet.

A brown bundle of fur bounds over to me.

"Hello, Toffee," I coo despite myself, leaning down to pet her, and she plants her dirty paws on my skirt once more.

My dry-cleaning bill is going to bankrupt me in this place.

"Oh, hello," a woman's voice says warily, and I look up to see Princess Amelia. She's in a pair of dungarees over a T-shirt, her long dark hair in a messy bun on top of her head, holding the hand of one of her children.

I drop into a curtsy. "Your Royal Highness."

She waves her hand in the air. "Don't bother with all that here. I'm Amelia, and this is Jamie."

I smile at the toddler's rosy cheeks, his hair lighter than his mother's but with her beautiful brown eyes. "Hello, Jamie. It's a pleasure to meet you both."

"Toffee!" he replies, pointing at the puppy and showing no interest in this frazzled woman in the garden.

"What happened?" Princess Amelia asks as she slides her gaze over me.

"I was, err, chasing someone."

Her eyebrows ping up to meet her hairline. "In a skirt suit?"

I shrug. "Needs must, I suppose."

"It was my brother, wasn't it."

I press my lips together. As much as I don't love what Max is doing, I'm not going to rat him out to his sister.

"He's always been the naughty one. Wonderful but naughty."

"Mama," Jamie says, pulling on her arm.

"I must go. I promised Jamie he could feed the chickens."

"Do you want me to take Toffee?"

"No. She needs the run, and Max has been trying to train her. Between you and me, he's not very good at it."

I smile as I watch Jamie try to reach for the dog, who's too busy sniffing the ground to notice.

As she moves away, I rush after her. "Amelia, can I say something?"

"What?"

"About what happened with you and that reality show."

"If you're going to tell me you had nothing to do with it, I already know. The inquiry told us as much."

"Thank you," I reply. It's always played on my mind that she and her husband, Ethan, thought I was part of the plan to illegally film their every move. I may have said many things about the royal family over the years, but I've never gone to those kinds of lengths.

Her eyes dance when she smiles. "Now go, find that brother of mine and tell the country what he's really like."

I return to the palace and march up the stairs to the PR office in my bare feet, where I'm met with more curious gazes from the palace staff.

Prince Max may have eluded me once more, but it's my job to spend time with him, and I'm not going to let him get the better of me.

By the afternoon, I've had words with a confused Ronan, who provided me with what is Prince Max's actual schedule, and after freshening up in my room, I head to his office. Apparently, he's reviewing some documents there after lunch.

He's not getting away with this. I'm not just some mouse for him to toy with his big cat paws. I'm a serious journalist, here to document his life. Here to do him and his family a *favor*.

Doesn't he realize I could publish horrible things about him? Tell the country he's worse than a man-child? Worse than a himbo?

And you know what? I might just do that.

I'll give him one last chance, and then that's it.

With my jaw clenched so tight I might crack a molar, I arrive at his office a handful of minutes early. It's a stunning room, with wood paneled walls, the obligatory high ceilings, and a large desk. I make my way over to the fireplace, where I squat behind one of the high-backed leather chairs. I have a clear view of the entrance, and I'm ready.

This is what that man has reduced me to: hiding behind furniture like some oversized kid.

I push out a frustrated breath. I'm supposed to be documenting his daily life, providing intimate access to the real Prince Max. My career cannot become a series of failed ambush attempts with Ledonia's most elusive prince.

And I'm going to do my darndest to make sure it isn't.

Finally, after my knees begin to cramp, Prince Max appears.

He saunters into the room as though he owns it, looking all relaxed in his post-shower pair of slacks and white polo shirt that does everything for his broad shoulders—and absolutely nothing for my mental state.

Really, for a guy who's successfully led me down the garden path today, he sure looks relaxed. He's humming a tune as he sets some papers out on his desk.

I spring to my feet, my knees creaking in protest, and his eyes land on mine. With more than a touch of satisfaction, I watch his expression shift from relaxed to something rather closely resembling trapped prey.

"Ms. Fontaine."

"You've sent me on quite the royal goose chase today,

Your Royal Highness," I say in a clipped tone that leaves him in no doubt of my displeasure.

"I did?" he asks as though it comes as a surprise to him.

"Did you purposely send me to the wrong location this morning?"

"The wrong location?"

I narrow my eyes at him. "Please don't play coy with me. You sent me a schedule from last month and I waited in the Blue Drawing Room for half an hour. You're well aware I need access to you to do the job your father is paying me to do."

"Perhaps the schedules got mixed up."

I raise my brows. "Perhaps?"

"These things happen."

"Admit it," I spit. "You did this on purpose."

"Are you being a little paranoid?"

I throw my hands on my hips and glare at him.

He raises his palms in the air. "Okay, I admit it. I had a schedule from last month sent to you."

"What?" My jaw drops open. He *did* send me on a wild goose chase!

"I was being childish."

"You said it," I scoff. "You need this more than I do," I bluff, because a broken-down house and a pile of bills tell me otherwise.

"I suppose you're right. I wasn't playing fair."

"Damn straight you weren't."

The corners of his mouth twitch. "What will you do with me now you've caught me?"

Is his tone…flirty? Because it sure sounds like that to me.

It's so wrong on so many levels.

It's also a little thrilling, in a totally messed up, inappropriate way.

Man. Talk about mind games.

My heart is drumming from both anger and something else I'm not going to label. "Is that an apology, sir?"

He shrugs as though what he's put me through today is no big deal. "It's as much as an apology as I'm likely to give you."

I twist my mouth.

"All right. I'm sorry I did that to you. It was wrong and I should know better. Shall we start again?"

"Why? Do you have a schedule in your papers dating back to 1992?"

"I wasn't even alive in 1992. And no, I'm all out of old schedules." His lips curve into a smile, and in an instant, I know exactly why all those women swoon over this man. Why his poster has been plastered across teenage girls' bedroom walls for years. Why he gets away with his crazy party boy antics.

He's not only handsome, but he has a way about him that can only be described as charming—when he's not scowling at me and treating me like the enemy, that is.

Or maybe especially then, in an Elizabeth Bennet bantering with Mr. Darcy kind of way. But then I am dealing with the playboy prince here, the heir to his brother's Prince McHottie badge.

Max has flirted his way across the globe virtually since he hit puberty, winning people over with his good looks, boyish charm, and easy-going nature. The nation has always been enthralled with the youngest royal sibling, a chubby toddler causing havoc at garden parities; cute as a button as a little boy in a straw hat and tie on his first day at an elite private school; growing into a handsome teenager who began to understand his attractiveness to the opposite sex; a scruffy but nevertheless undeniably hot student during his Cambridge days, all messy hair and thick sweaters; and more recently, a dashing young man in his formal military uniform.

Of course, as a royal correspondent, I needed to reflect the country's fondness of him, remarking on how well he'd grown up, how he'd deservedly become Ledonia's new "McHottie". Just as I had with his older brother, Alex, I acted as though I'd swooned along with the rest of the nation. I talked the two brothers up as though they were something special, when in reality, they were simply born lucky—both to be Ledonian royalty and to win the gene lottery for good looks.

I've always known better. Alex and Max and their sisters may not have been the members of the royal family to destroy my family, to take away everything I'd ever known. They might not have been the ones to prosecute my father, to force him to flee Ledonia. But their parents have blood on their hands, and that's something I can never forgive them for, no matter how charming they may be.

"Can we agree that we're both going to act like adults and put your game-playing aside to work together?" I stretch my hand out toward him.

He looks down at it, and I wonder if he's going to keep me hanging. But then he takes my hand in his, and the touch of his skin sends a strong but nevertheless unwanted bolt of electricity right up my arm and across my chest.

"No more game playing, Ms. Fontaine. You have my word," he says, his eyes dark and intense.

I swallow. Something just shifted between us, and suddenly this coming month has become so much more complicated, and I have a sinking feeling our handshake just changed *everything*.

Chapter 8

Max

As I SLIDE another arrow from my quiver and pull the taut string of the bow back, I try to push thoughts of Fabiana from my mind. I acted like an immature idiot yesterday, sending her off all over the palace. It had felt like a fun thing to do at the time, but I'm not proud of myself. I was acting out. It was my pathetic protest at having to work with her for the next month.

The truth of the matter is I find her presence here at the palace…unsettling. Yes, that's the word. And it's not just because she said all those things about me over the years, although that's bad enough.

It's the effect she has on me.

Yup, the journalist I've grown to hate over the years has gotten into my head.

She should be everything I can't stand. Snarky and smug and totally judgmental, calling me names and looking down her nose at me. But then she walks into the room and, *bam!* my pulse leaps at the sight of her.

Maybe there really is a fine line between hate and love?

Or at least lust.

That moment in my office when we called a truce, when I held her hand in mine, the soft touch of her skin sent something skittering down my spine. Something warm and enticing. Something I shouldn't be feeling.

She's the one woman I should *not* want.

But man, do I want her.

"Come on, Max. You're taking forever! We've all got to practice, you know," Amelia complains as she leans against a post, watching me.

"I think he's got something on his mind," Sofia says.

"More like some*one*," Amelia quips.

I lower my bow and arrow and turn to glare at my sisters, both of whom are looking rather pleased with themselves.

"You two jabbering away isn't helping me take this shot," I complain.

"Oh, of course. It's totally us who are putting you off and not the pretty journalist staying down the hall," Amelia replies. "Isn't that right, Sofe? Fabiana Fontaine's presence here has got nothing to do with Max being off his stride this morning."

"Oh, I'm sure you're totally right, Ami," Sofia replies.

I shoot them both a look. That's the thing with sisters.

They're always up in my business, commenting from the sidelines.

"She's nicer than I expected," Amelia says.

"When did you talk to her?" Sofia asks.

"I met her in the garden yesterday afternoon. She was chasing a certain someone." My sister shoots me a meaningful look. "Fabiana's got the most amazing green eyes, did you know?"

As if I'm not tortured by those eyes.

"Although I haven't loved what she's written about us over the years, she seemed nice," Amelia adds.

"You would say that. You like everyone," I grumble.

"That's not true," she replies, indignant.

I lean on my bow, looking at my sister. "Name one person you don't like, Ami."

She chews on her lip, her brows pulled together.

"See?" I return my attention to the target.

"Greg Smith! I don't like Greg Smith," she exclaims.

"Who?" I ask.

"The one who duped Ami into thinking she was falling for him when all he wanted was her money. You're well within your rights not to like him, Ami," Sofia says.

"I might not like him, but really, if it weren't for Greg Smith, I would never have met my husband," Amelia says with satisfaction. "Now, are you going to shoot that arrow, Max? I need to go and stare at my baby while he sleeps some more."

Since getting married almost five years ago now, Amelia and Ethan have been busy making babies, just like Alex and Maddie and Sofia and Marco. I've become an uncle several times over, thanks to these loved-up couples, and I low-key relish my role as fun uncle in their lives.

"Go watch your baby sleep, Ami. I might be able to concentrate better if you're elsewhere," I say.

"I don't need to be told twice. Catch you both on the flip-side," Amelia says before she walks away.

"All right, you. No excuses now. I expect nothing less than a bullseye," Sofia instructs.

I get myself into position once more, pushing thoughts of Fabiana, my sisters, my nieces and nephews, and anything else that's intent on distracting me, from my mind. My breath is even and controlled as I line up my target, the inner yellow circle my sole focus. I pull back and let go of the arrow, watching with satisfaction as it slices through the air, hitting the target with a satisfying *twang!*

"Well done, Max!" Sofia exclaims, her eyes bright. "You hit the outer red. You're doing so much better than last time. Have you been practicing without me?"

"Why would I want to practice archery without my bossy older sister to tell me what to do?" I throw her a sardonic smile.

"Very funny," she deadpans, barely cracking a smile. "You do realize you wouldn't be this good if I hadn't taught you, don't you?"

I slide another arrow from my quiver. "You just keep telling yourself that, sis."

I wait as Sofia lines up her target and sends her arrow on its trajectory with practiced ease, hitting right in the center of the yellow.

"Stop showing off, will you?"

She shrugs. "I can't help it. I'm good at this *because I practice.*"

"Really? You've never mentioned it," I reply, because if there's one thing you can rely on with my oldest sister, it's that she's a firm believer in the old adage practice makes perfect.

I'm lining up for my next shot when an all too familiar

voice interrupts me. "Good morning, Your Royal Highnesses."

Fabiana Fontaine, the woman who seems to have taken up permanent residence in my mind.

Startled, my fingers release the arrow, which falls short of the target, slicing into the dirt.

"Bad luck, sir," she says.

I turn towards her. Just like yesterday, she looks that particular combination of smug and hot she does so well, completely out of place in her skirt and blazer, like one of those sexy double agents from WWII.

"You put me off," I grumble.

"Max, play nice," Sofia warns. "How are you finding things in the palace, Ms. Fontaine?"

Fabiana does a low curtsy, which is no small feat in her pencil skirt. "It's been a very interesting experience so far, ma'am."

"There's no need for formalities," my sister replies. "We're all off duty here."

I harrumph, and both sets of eyes land on me. "What?" I ask as though I'm entirely innocent of scoffing when we all know I did.

"I suppose you mean Ms. Fontaine is working," Sofia replies pointedly.

Sure, *that's* what I meant.

Fabiana holds her phone aloft. "Okay if I take some footage?"

"Of course," Sofia replies for me. "That's what you're here for."

"Thank you. I'd love to capture both of you if I could?" She steps over a tree root in her high heels. "Ready when you are, sir."

There's something in the way she says the word "sir". It's respectful, sure, and appropriate since I'm a member of the royal family, but it's got a teasing, sexy undertone that sends an involuntary shiver through me.

"Why don't you call him Max?" Sofia asks. "Sir is so formal."

"It's the way I've always been told to address a member of the royal family. Your Royal Highness first, and then sir or ma'am next. Ma'am."

Sofia laughs. "Call me Sofia."

"Only if you call me Fabiana," she replies.

"Deal. And call Mr. Grumpy here Max."

"I rather like 'Mr. Grumpy,' actually," she replies, her sparkling eyes alighting on me once more.

"Thanks a lot, Sofe," I grumble. The last thing Fabiana needs is more names to add to her already bulging arsenal.

"Are you going to shoot, Max? Or just glower at Fabiana?" Sofia asks, calling me out.

Sisters.

I collect another arrow and line up my shot, all too aware that Fabiana is watching my every move.

"Don't forget to breathe," my sister instructs.

I gulp in a breath, hoping Fabiana doesn't notice, and then release my arrow. It hits the target, but only just, slicing into the white outer ring.

I lower my bow as Sofia says, "Better luck next time."

"Were you not aiming for the yellow in the middle?" Fabiana asks, and I'm certain she's mocking me.

"He was. The yellow at the center," my sister replies helpfully.

Fabiana pulls her brows together. "That's a shame. Do you want to have another try, Max? I can film it again."

An idea hits me.

"Why don't you have a go?" I say, proffering my bow. "Let's see which color you can hit, shall we?"

Fabiana places her hand over her chest. "Me?"

"Why not? I'll even film you, if you like," I reply. "You can make a TikTok out of it."

She shakes her head, her ponytail swooshing from side to side, and I do my best not to notice how pretty she is in that girl next door kind of way. "I don't think so. But thank you all the same," she replies.

"Why not? Chicken?" I goad.

She straightens her back, her lips tight. "Not in the least."

"Oh, I think you are. I think you're afraid you'll miss the target altogether."

She lifts her chin, and I note with satisfaction that it seems to be my turn to get under her skin.

Sofia shakes her head at me, her lips pursed. "Why don't you use my bow?" she says to Fabiana. "I need to go anyway, and Max's bow will be far too big for you."

"That's so kind of you."

Sofia hands Fabiana her bow, sliding her quiver of arrows from her shoulder strap. She pauses, studying Fabiana's face with a slight tilt of her head. "Have we met before? You seem familiar somehow."

Fabiana's smile tightens. "You probably know me from my social media posts. I would certainly remember meeting you, Your Royal Highness."

"Sofia," my sister corrects absently, still looking at her with that thoughtful expression. "That must be it. I suspect I'll only be in the way if I stay." She shoots me a smile.

"Thank you, Sofia," Fabiana says.

"And don't listen to Max. He's just annoyed that he missed his last shot while you were filming. Aren't you, brother?" Sofia asks.

Something like that.

"Have fun, you two. And Max? Be nice to our guest."

Fabiana bites back a smile. I'm certain she's enjoying my being bossed around by my older sister.

I'm certainly not.

As Sofia makes her way back to the palace, she turns to me. "Your sisters are wonderful."

I shrug. "They're okay." I gesture at her phone. "You're not going to use that footage, are you?"

"Do you think you can do better?"

It's more of a challenge than a question.

"Of course I can. You put me off, that's all."

"Did I." It's not a question, and I note it isn't an apology either.

"Well? Go on, then," she challenges. "The goal is to hit the yellow in the middle, I take it. Do you think you can do it while I film?"

"Only after you've taken your shot first."

Two can play this game.

"All right." She unbuttons her blazer and slides it off, exposing a form-fitting white, sleeveless top underneath. Coupled with her pencil skirt, all her womanly curves are plain to see.

Another involuntary shiver races through me before I have the chance to look away.

Why does she have to be so darn sexy? I mean, she's not even trying, and she somehow manages to make me incapable of doing anything other than gawking at her like a love-struck teen.

She's just a woman here to do a job. I've got this.

My brain may be shouting *No! Stay away!* at the top of its lungs, but my hormones? They're another matter entirely. My hormones are telling me in no uncertain terms that this woman is sexy as all get out. Sexy and beautiful and smart and totally under my skin.

How the heck am I going to get through the next day, let alone the next month?

She'll be in my face virtually 24/7, filming me, asking me questions, always...*there*. Always looking the way she does. Always with that knowing smirk of hers that does things to me, wearing that sexy business outfit. It's like every one of Ami's rom-com movies I've ever rolled my eyes at have come to life, with *me* in the starring role.

Only this isn't a rom com movie. This is my *life*. And I refuse to allow any misplaced attraction for Fabiana Fontaine to cloud my better judgment.

As she pulls an arrow from Sofia's quiver, something catches the light. It's a necklace with the letter V.

Why would Fabiana Fontaine wear a V necklace around her neck?

Biting her lip, she attempts to attach the arrow to the bow, looking every inch the amateur I hoped she would be.

"Do you need help, Fabiana?" I ask.

"No thanks."

"Are you sure?"

She fumbles with the bow. "I've done this before, but it was a very long time ago."

I raise my hands in the air, stepping back. "Okay."

She holds the bow up and pulls back the string, the arrow bouncing around. I press my lips together to suppress a satisfied laugh bubbling up inside of me.

She has no idea what she's doing.

She releases the arrow, and it glides to the ground in an inelegant arc, landing only two feet away. She looks up at me. "This is harder than it looks," she admits. "It's clear I'm no toxophilite."

"Toxo-what now?"

"It's an old-fashioned word that means 'lover of the bow'."

The word "lover" hangs between us.

I clear my throat. "How do you know that?"

She shrugs a shoulder. "Words are my business."

"I thought you were more into words like 'man-child' and 'himbo' rather than anything quite so technical," I say in retort, and to my surprise she lets out a laugh. It's girly and cute and totally *not* what I expect from her. "What's so funny?"

"I really bothered you with those names. Didn't I?"

"Not in the least," I lie, because let's face it, being called a man-child by her burrowed deep under my skin like a mole.

"Max, I—" she begins and then breaks off.

"What?"

She lifts her chin, pushing a stray lock behind her ear. "I'm sorry I called you those names."

I blink at her in surprise for a beat. "Why?"

"Why what?"

"Why are you sorry?"

"Because I was wrong. You may have man-child tendencies, but you have other qualities, too. I overlooked them."

I look into her big, emerald eyes, half expecting some snarky quip to follow. But nothing does.

"Thank you," I say in reply, not sure what else to say.

She pulls her full lips into a smile. "You're welcome?"

I smile back at her. This concession is like one step closer to us burying the hatchet completely. "What name would you give me now?"

"Oh, Mr. Grumpy for sure," she replies, and I bark out a startled laugh.

"Please don't."

"You have been rather grumpy."

"Fair call."

"But I won't call you it."

I hold her gaze for a beat, my belly going all kinds of crazy.

"See? We can get on, Max. We can do this project together now that you've stopped hiding from me."

"You might be right," I concede, not quite sure what to do with my newfound camaraderie with this woman I've despised for so long.

She holds up Sofia's bow and arrow. "How do I do this?"

"Not that way," I say, gesturing at the arrow she shot into the ground.

"That much I know."

"The first thing you need to understand about archery is that it's not about strength. It's about being precise and controlling your breathing."

"Breathing? I held my breath, but it didn't help."

"You see, that's where you went wrong. Well, that and having no clue how to use a bow and arrow."

She lets out another light laugh, and the tinkling sound makes my belly buzz. It's the strangest sensation, and I don't think a woman's laugh has ever had this kind of effect on me before.

"You're not going to hit your target if you hold your breath. You need to exhale as you let the arrow go."

"Like this?" She holds up the bow with another arrow, pulls it back and pushes out a breath. The arrow flops to the ground as the bow twangs.

She bites her lip as she turns to me, sheepish. "That didn't go quite as planned."

Without pausing to examine any motivation other than teaching, I position myself directly behind her. "May I?" I ask as I hold my hands out.

"Of course," she replies.

I place my hand over hers and adjust her grip on the bow. As our flesh touches, electricity shoots through me, just as it did in the library, and my heart rate kicks up. I'm close enough to catch her scent, something floral and pretty, perhaps with a touch of vanilla.

It doesn't help me concentrate on archery, that's for sure.

"The way you're standing is all wrong," I say, my voice a little gruffer than I intend. I place one hand on her hip to turn her so her shoulders are correctly positioned in relation to the target. "Do you feel how you're aligned now?"

"I do," she replies, her voice suddenly breathy, and it occurs to me that perhaps she feels more than just the right archery position. Perhaps she feels the intensity of our proximity the same way I do.

I lift her elbow, lightly holding it in position. For just a moment, something tugs at my memory. There's something in the way she tilts her head, a familiar gesture I can't quite place. But it's gone before I can grasp it, lost in the distraction of our closeness.

"Now, pull the string of the bow back." I guide her hand with mine, acutely aware of every point where our bodies touch. Her back against my chest, my arms bracketing hers, the way she leans slightly into my guidance when I adjust her aim.

Why did I put myself in this position?

"When do I breathe?" she asks, her voice soft.

"Breathe in as you draw back until the bowstring touches the corner of your lips."

She does as I tell her, the bow creaking into position.

"Now exhale and release."

The arrow jolts as she lets it go, slicing through the air and hitting the target.

"You have got to be kidding me," I say as I gawk at the circular rings.

"Is that a bullseye?" she asks excitedly, spinning around to face me. Standing close enough to me that I can see the light sprinkle of freckles across her nose, she looks up into my eyes, her own eyes gleaming, and I have the sudden urge to pull her roughly into my arms and press my lips against hers, to know how she tastes, this beautiful, feisty woman who's invaded my brain.

My heart is thudding against my ribs like a wild animal, her enchanting scent filling the air, messing with my mind.

No. *Not* happening.

Fabiana Fontaine is the last woman I should *ever* want to kiss.

She's the journalist who called me all those names. She's the woman I'm being forced to spend a month with.

She's the one responsible for rehabilitating my image.

But none of the reasons is enough to stop me wanting it. Wanting *her*.

"So?"

"Yes," I murmur, my eyes sliding to her full, pouty lips.

"Is it a bullseye?" she asks.

I need to break this spell, and I need to do it *now*.

I take a step back.

The right decision. The *only* decision.

Clearing my throat, I gesture at the target. "That is indeed a bullseye. Well done, Fabiana. You're a natural."

Her full lips pull into a grin, her whole face lighting up. "I can't believe it! I suspect we make a good team, Max."

Why is she looking at me like that, like she means what she says, that we do make a good team?

"Can we try again?" she asks, already reaching for another arrow.

I want to say no. I *ought* to say no. I should collect my bow and arrows, bid her *adieu*, and walk away.

But instead, I hear myself saying, "Let's see if we can replicate the same magic, shall we?"

This time, when I position myself behind her, I make sure not to allow my body to touch her back. But despite my care, just as before, my heart rate leaps.

I tighten my jaw.

What kind of a masochist am I that I'm deeply drawn to a woman I hate?

Or at least a woman thought I hated.

Man, this is beyond confusing.

She pulls back the bow at the wrong angle, and I adjust her grip. Then she forgets to hold the arrow against the bow, and it drops to the ground.

"I thought I was doing it right," she says in frustration as she collects the bow in her hand.

"You're overthinking it. Just let it happen."

As the words leave my mouth, they seem loaded, and she snaps her attention to me. "What do you mean?"

What *do* I mean?

I'm talking about archery. That's all. Nothing else going on here.

I press my lips together before responding. "Archery is as much about instinct as it is about your technique. You need to feel the bow and arrow, allow it to become an extension of yourself."

"That's easy for you to say. I bet you've been doing this since you were in nappies."

"You think I started archery lessons as a toddler?" I ask, thankful for the chance to make a joke, to release some of this excruciating tension between us.

"Isn't that what you do when you're royalty? Learn all

the outdated practices that are of no use in the modern world?"

"Such as?"

"Archery, obviously, and how to rock a crown."

I arch a brow. "You think I had actual lessons on how to wear a crown?"

"Why not? You're a member of the royal family. You and crowns are synonymous."

"Ah, but you forget, I'm the last born. The only crown I will ever wear is a paper one from a Christmas cracker."

She looks into my eyes for a beat, and that urge to kiss her slams me, full force.

What is it about this woman that draws me in? Yes, she's beautiful. She's smart and witty. And her body in that outfit? Let's just say she deserves a round of applause.

But this level of attraction is beyond anything I've felt before, particularly for someone I don't even *like*.

I've got no clue how to handle it.

"Does it bother you?" she asks.

"Does what bother me?" I reply, my mind blank. This woman is scrambling my brain, making it hard to think straight.

What were we talking about?

"That you'll never be king."

That's right.

"No. No, it doesn't. Not in the least."

I need to break this spell. Remove myself from the danger zone.

In one brisk move, I step back and collect my things. "I'm sorry, but I've remembered I have an appointment, and I'm going to be late if I don't leave now."

She slots the arrow back into the quiver. "I'll come with you."

Not the plan.

"It's personal. The…dentist," I say as I back away from her like a coward. "I'd prefer you not to document that."

"Of course," she replies, her face looking confused. "Thank you for the archery lesson."

"Anytime," I reply without looking at her.

"I'll see you this evening at the state dinner?"

The dinner. Right.

"Yes, of course. I'll see you then." I throw her a brief smile before I turn on my heel and stride away from both her and the conflicted, growing pull she has on me.

Chapter 9

> Good people! Your intrepid palace correspondent behind palace lines has just experienced something rather unexpected: Prince Max being genuinely helpful without a single theatrical sigh. Alert the press!
>
> Oh wait, I *am* the press.
>
> This morning's adventure began when our beloved royal rogue performed archery with the kind of skill one would expect from a royal prince, aka an impressive display of athleticism with a Robin Hood vibe.

Catch my video on my socials for all the arrow-focused action.

Then, he asked me to try it. What do you think I said? Of course! My first attempt was... well, if hostile forces were attacking from ground level, I'd have shown them who's boss. The arrow achieved what I can only describe as the world's most pathetic arc, landing a mere meter away at my feet.

But here's where things got interesting. Instead of enjoying my incompetence from a safe distance, Prince Max offered to help. Properly help.

Following his guidance, I drew back, exhaled, and released. The arrow sliced through the air with satisfying purpose and hit the bullseye. A bullseye! On my second attempt.

Which brings me to the real story: your favorite royal rogue may be far more complex than any of us realized. The man who patiently taught me archery, who celebrated my success with genuine enthusiasm isn't the shallow party prince I've been writing about for years.

The question remains: which version is real?

Yours,

Fabiana Fontaine xx

#BowAndTellAll
#RoyalAimGame

#PrinceOnPoint

Valentina

I FINISH my edits and check the video, syncing it to a trending sound that works perfectly with the content. In the opening image, Max is holding his bow taut, his eyes focused on the target, his broad shoulders accentuated by the twist in his torso.

He looks good. Very good. Confident, athletic, handsome.

My followers are going to lap this up.

I add the hashtags #RoyalAimGame and #PrinceOnPoint before I publish it to several social media platforms. Within seconds, the views begin, and people start to like and comment.

The first few are super positive.

Robin Hood, but royal 🐭 🩶

Excuse me, who gave him the right to look that good with a bow?

Bullseye? More like heart-eyes 🩶 👀

The comments are peppered with some less than positive, too.

Cute. Now, someone get the man-child a juice box before his nap.

All biceps, no brain.

Someone had better take away the sharp objects.

He might be able to hit a bullseye, but can he hit a day's work?

Something twists in my gut, something I've not felt before when it comes to my coverage of the prince. If I'm not mistaken, it feels a lot like guilt.

Guilt? Why? I can't be responsible for every single member of the country's perception of this man, nor the fact that people make up their minds based on what they see.

But I have been the leading media voice about the prince's playboy ways. It's hard not to think I'm somewhat responsible.

I scroll down through more comments, most of them the usual mix of royal worship and criticism, when one catches my eye. It's from @MThorneThePost.

Great technique demonstration, HRH! @Fabiana_Fontaine has certainly captured you.

At first glance, it seems like an innocent enough compliment, but something about it sets my teeth on edge. I click on her profile and see her name is Miranda Thorne, a journalist from *The Post*. I scroll through her other recent comments on my posts.

Beautiful video of the Blue Drawing Room. You captured the morning light perfectly. You clearly know the best angles at the palace already.

This wasn't your first visit to The Throne Room, was it? Because you look so at home there.

Her comments could be read as professional admiration, but together they feel like something else entirely. It's like she's noting how familiar I am with the palace, how easily I navigate spaces that should be foreign to me.

I click my phone off. I'm being paranoid. I've heard of her, of course—Ledonia isn't exactly huge—but she doesn't know me.

I dismiss it as just my fear of being discovered rearing its ugly head.

Sliding my dress on, I reach behind myself to zip it up. I slip on my heels and turn to the full-length mirror in the corner of my room. Its gilded edges scream wealth and history along with everything else in the room. But then royalty isn't exactly known for its decorative restraint.

I slide my gaze over my dress. Probably because they assumed I'd neither have the right kind of clothing for tonight's function nor have any clue how to actually dress for it, a member of staff materialized with a selection of beautiful dresses, wheeling a rail into my rooms this afternoon.

I was like a kid in a candy store, choosing between the jewel-toned dresses and sparkling accessories. I chose an elegant, deep-blue silk strapless dress. It skims my curves and makes my skin look luminous. It's sophisticated and a touch sexy, tasteful and expensive, the kind of dress I used to dream about wearing when I was twelve and still believed in fairy tales.

But happily ever after only happens in stories.

I smooth my hair, twisting and pinning it into an appropriate low bun. I pull a few tendrils from the sides to frame my face before I slide on my glasses. Without them, I'm exposed, more like Valentina Romano than Fabiana Fontaine.

The woman staring back at me right now is somewhere between the two.

Tonight, I've got to retain my Fabiana edge, no matter what happens. Here, it's more important than ever that I fly under the radar. I can't have anyone looking at me sideways, trying to place me from my past.

But the woman looking back at me through her fake glasses? She looks put-together and confident. Beautiful even. Nothing like the frightened twelve-year-old who fled this palace in disgrace.

You've got this.

Only… have I?

Because I'm finding being here in the palace, spending time with Max, there's something building, something new. Something entirely unexpected. Not only am I being forced to face my demons by being in this palace, which is hard enough, but now every time I see the man I'd once written off as a shallow party boy, I feel this undeniable pull to him.

A pull that's growing stronger and stronger with each passing day.

Back when I first met him with his puppy in the carpark, he was rude and abrasive, clearly unhappy about having to work with me. His disdain for me is about as discreet as a prince at a nightclub.

That's the Max I could handle. That's the Max I knew. The Max I expect.

Since then, I've seen a different side of him. Firstly, as he spoke with staff on the palace tour. Then in his office, when I finally tracked him down and we called a truce. The intensity of his gaze, the touch of his skin against mine…

My breath hitches at the memory, and I close my eyes.

I barely got through the archery lesson this morning. It took what I feel for him to a whole other level. It was hard to keep my head together. His touch as he guided my arrow, the low rasp of his voice, the smell of him, his warm, firm body so close behind me? It was almost too much, and I had to force myself to focus on shooting the arrow and not on…*him*.

And the scary thing? The way he acted made me wonder if he felt this thing between us, too. Could that be why he pulled back from me so abruptly? Why he made up some lame excuse about a dentist's appointment and walked away from me, like he was fleeing a crime scene?

Because that's exactly what it felt like to me.

And you know what? I was grateful he did it. If he hadn't… No, it doesn't bear thinking about.

I cannot go there with this man. End of story.

Brilliant. Just brilliant, Valentina.

I know what the smart thing would be to do. I should pack my bags, tell the king I cannot carry out this project, and hightail it back to Nona. The king would have no trouble believing that the differences his son and I have are simply too great for me to be able to present the country with an unbiased view. And he told me himself he had other journalists vying for the job.

It would be an easy way out. Over with.

Done.

But dang it! The money and the boost to my career are just too good to pass up.

I need this. Nona needs this.

I've got no choice.

I bite down on my lip, my hands clenched. I'm standing here in front of this mirror in this gorgeous dress with my knees wobbling like a newborn foal at the thought of him.

It's ridiculous. Laughable!

I push out a breath.

There's only one option open to me. I need to keep my distance from him, at least physically. I need to ensure I never put myself in the position I was in at the archery lesson again.

Physical attraction is one thing, but the last thing I can do is develop feelings for my enemy's son.

With an application of lipstick—battle-ready red, naturally—I take one final steadying breath before I collect my clutch and make my way down the hallway, with its deep red carpet and high ceilings. The painted eyes of dead royals follow me as I leave the private rooms and enter the formal area. Instantly, my heels click against the marble floor, the sound echoing around me in this hallway.

I pass the entrance to the Red Salon and slow my pace.

Without even thinking about why I'm doing it, I grip one of the door handles and push my way inside.

The room looks the same as it did in my memories, although maybe a little smaller. The red and gold silk wallpaper, the huge Venetian mirror above the ornate marble fireplace, the collection of delicate objects on the mahogany side table by the window. It all combines to create an atmosphere that's both grand and austere, and a cold shiver prickles my skin.

This is where it happened.

This is where I crouched behind these doors all those years ago, watching through the crack as the king announced my father's disgrace to a roomful of officials.

This is where my dad pleaded his case to deaf ears. Where I watched him leave with his head hung low.

It might have been a lifetime ago for me, but it's as raw as though it were yesterday.

I make my way over to the table and pick up an old porcelain music box with a painted pheasant on the lid, the symbol of Ledonia. I remember being fascinated by this music box as a child during those boring adult conversations, watching the ballerina inside spin, her porcelain arms raised elegantly above her head.

I lift the lid, and the ballerina springs to life as a melody sounds out around the room. It's something classical that makes my chest ache for my younger self. And just like that, I'm transported back to a simpler life, a life where I didn't need to pretend to be someone else, a life where I was just me, Valentina Romano, daughter of Lord Romano. Happy. Free.

I watch as the ballerina spins and spins, mesmerized.

"Finding your way around, I see, Fabiana," a deep voice says, and instantly, I snap the box shut, the music coming to a sudden halt. With my heart hammering against my ribs, I spin around to see who it is.

Prince Max.

Of course it is.

He's standing in the doorway, outdoing 007 himself in his perfectly tailored dinner suit and crisp white shirt. His dark hair is neatly styled, and he has a deeply unimpressed look on his face. His eyes are fixed on me with an intensity that makes my breath catch—and it's not just from the shock.

He looks... devastating. Yup. That's the word. *Devastating.*

I grip the music box behind my back as though I'm hiding contraband in my prison cell, an appropriate metaphor for me in this palace.

"I-I think I'm lost," I reply weakly, because let's face it, we're both aware I didn't exactly walk into this room and make it all the way over to this chest thinking this is where tonight's reception is.

The fact that there are no other people in the room might have been my first clue.

"Lost?" he asks as he moves closer to me, and his tone confirms my fear that he doesn't believe a word.

I lift my chin and double down. What else can I do? "That's right. I was lost, and I found myself here."

"And you thought you might look at some priceless artifacts in an empty room to help you find your way?" His gaze travels over me, and something shifts in his expression, something that suggests he likes what he sees.

Although I might be misreading it.

I hope I'm misreading it.

Don't I?

I shrug, aiming for nonchalance. "I figured I was early."

Another bald-faced lie, and not a very convincing one.

I grip the music box tighter in my hands. "It's a big palace. It's easy to get turned around here for those of us not familiar."

He's now close enough that I could reach out and touch him, and the memory of how it felt to be so close to him earlier today has my breath hitching.

He narrows his eyes at me. "What have you got behind your back, Ms. Fontaine?"

I've got a choice here. I can either tell him to mind his own business, surreptitiously pocket the music box, and make a run for it.

Or I can fess up.

I fess up. I don't want to add theft to my list of misdemeanors.

I pull the music box from behind my back and hold it out for him. "I was just looking at this."

"A music box." He takes it from me, and his fingers brush briefly against my palm. It sends a flutter of electricity through me, and I shift my weight, determined not to let him see the effect he has on me.

He opens the lid, and the room fills with the music once more, and my gaze zeroes in on the ballerina's pirouettes.

"She's so beautiful," I murmur, more to myself than to him.

Without warning, he snaps the lid shut, making me jump.

I shoot him a look. His lips are quirked in amusement, and it's clear he did it on purpose.

What is with this guy?

"Why did you do that?" I ask, my hand over my heart.

"Because we need to leave." He places the box gently down on the chest of drawers. "Please allow me to escort you to the correct room for tonight's dinner." He steps aside with exaggerated politeness, gesturing for me to move. "I wouldn't want you to take another wrong turn and end up in the dungeons."

I flick my gaze to his to see his lips quirked in a smile.

He's toying with me. There's no doubt about it.

"Are you admitting there are operational dungeons in the palace? Because I'm sure my readers would be fascinated to know."

"We use them as wine cellars these days, but I'm certain to someone like you, they might as well be dungeons."

I quirk a brow. "Someone like me?"

"Someone who can create a headline from next to nothing, like, say, a slide into a pond."

"That *was* a headline, Your Royal Highness."

"That depends on your point of view."

"You're right. From your point of view, it was just another Tuesday. Wasn't it?"

He darts me a look that's equal parts amused and annoyed.

Is it terrible that I enjoy getting under his skin?

Instead of biting, he replies, "We're back to formal titles now, are we?"

"You're the one who called me Ms. Fontaine. Your Royal Highness felt like the appropriate response."

The temporary closeness we experienced during the impromptu archery lesson seems to have backtracked to snarky banter and one-upmanship.

So, business as usual.

We make our way down the wide, echo-y hallway.

"Did you see the archery video? I posted it not that long ago," I say.

"I did."

"And?"

"And you didn't use the footage of me missing the target."

"You asked me not to."

He slides his eyes to mine. "Is that a sign of things to come?"

"What do you mean?"

"If I ask you not to use some footage or report on something I've done, will you agree?"

"Be careful. You're teetering on the edge of propaganda with that request."

He raises his brows, his eyes sparkling. "And we wouldn't want that."

"No, we wouldn't."

We reach the entrance to the Grand Hall, where a couple of royal guards flank the doorway, with the sound of voices chattering and soft music emanating through the doors.

"Here we are. Shall we go in?" he asks.

My body buzzes with anxiety. "That's what we're here for."

He offers me his arm, and as I hook mine through, I have to fight not to shiver at the closeness.

Fail.

"Thank you for escorting me," I say as the doors swing open, my heart thudding at the prospect of coming face to face with a roomful of people I've made a sport out of writing about. A roomful of people who have no clue I used to be one of them.

Will they turn their backs on me?

Abuse me to my face?

Or worse yet, will they work out who I really am?

He places his hand over mine. "I didn't want you to get

lost again," he says, but there's no sting in his words, and the quirk of his lips tells me he's only teasing.

"It was a very beautiful music box," I reply.

"If you say so," he replies.

I open my mouth to respond, but there's nothing I can say. In entering that room and looking at that music box, I was taking a stroll down memory lane to a time when life was simpler for me, but Prince Maximilien of the House of Canossa is the very last person I could ever tell.

Chapter 10

Max

STEPPING INTO THE ROOM, I glance around at the sea of familiar faces, dressed up to the nines in their finery and sparkling jewels. As the doors are closed behind us, heads turn like a Mexican wave, and words are whispered throughout the room.

Fabiana and I are the talk of the town.

By now, every person in the room will be aware that she's here to report on me, to show the country "the real Prince Max". What they don't know is, standing here with her on my arm, I swell with pride to have this gorgeous woman on my arm—despite the fact I know she's only here because my father's paying her.

When I came across her in the Red Salon, it was hard not to notice how utterly stunning she looks tonight in that deep blue dress. What was she doing in there though? Prying for her articles? But why? What interest can a music box hold for a journalist?

I gaze at her. In the soft lighting of the Grand Hall, without her blazer and with her hair styled differently, there's something almost familiar about her profile. Something beyond her official photo. Something I can't quite pinpoint, but it's familiar.

I shake the thought away. I've met thousands of people at events like this over the years. They all start to blur together.

I smile at the sea of faces watching us, and Fabiana stiffens at my side.

My instinct is to give her a reassuring squeeze, but she'd probably see it as a declaration of war. So instead, I capture her gaze with mine. "You've got this," I tell her, surprising even myself at how protective I sound.

"Thank you," she replies softly, and something shifts in my chest.

She might be the woman I've despised all these years. She might be a journalist here to do a job. But right now, she's a lot like a deer in headlights.

I get it. Being in this room may be second nature to me, but to her, it's probably pretty intimidating.

A waiter offers us drinks on a silver tray, and I snag two flutes of champagne, offering her one.

She takes it with a tense smile.

"Go on. Take a decent slug. You'll feel better when you do. Take it from a professional champagne drinker."

She takes one sip, and then another. "You're right. Much better." Her shoulders relax a notch. "Why are you suddenly being nice to me?"

I almost choke on my drink. "What do you mean?"

"One minute you're acting all suspicious about me looking at a music box, and then next you're offering me a tip on how to get through tonight." She holds her glass aloft. "It was a good tip, by the way."

The thing is I'm not sure how to handle this woman. On the one hand, she's clever and witty and utterly gorgeous, the kind of woman I want to get to know a whole lot better. On the other hand, she's my enemy.

A man whose dinner jacket is straining at the seams approaches us and bows to me.

It's Lord Blackwood. The universe has a twisted sense of humor, presenting me with one of Father's most groveling hangers-on just when I'm trying to navigate my complicated feelings for Fabiana.

"Good evening, Your Royal Highness," he simpers in a reedy voice that doesn't match his frame.

"It's nice to see you, Cyril," I reply. As a member of the royal family, lying gracefully is part of my job description.

His beady eyes swivel to Fabiana, like a predator spotting fresh prey. "And who is this gorgeous creature on your arm tonight, sir?" he asks, his eyes roving over her in a way that sets my teeth on edge.

"Allow me to introduce Ms. Fabiana Fontaine. Ms. Fontaine, this is Lord Blackwood," I say.

She unhooks her arm from mine, extending her hand with the kind of confidence that, despite her obvious nervousness of being in this room, tells me she's capable of handling leering aristocrats. "It's nice to meet you, Lord Blackwood."

Blackwood blinks like an owl. "Fabiana Fontaine? As in *the* Fabiana Fontaine? The gossip columnist?"

"I prefer the term 'royal correspondent,' Lord Blackwood," she replies with a smile that doesn't reach her eyes.

I have to admire her composure.

"I'm sure you do," he says. He's still gawking at her as though he could eat her right up. He pulls on my sleeve, and I turn to him. "Granted, she's a pretty young thing, but why, pray tell, are you entertaining this woman, sir? Don't you know who she is?"

Something hot flares in my chest. He's speaking about her as if she's an object, not standing right here, listening to every word he says.

"Ms. Fontaine is here to document my life for the next month, Cyril. She's a guest here." I hear the edge in my own voice. I've just publicly defended the woman who's spent years making my life difficult.

If someone had told me last week that I would be defending Fabiana Fontaine to a member of the aristocracy, I would have laughed in their face.

That's not something I ever thought I would do.

"But she's—" Blackwood starts, and I already know I don't want to hear the rest.

I open my mouth to respond when Fabiana jumps in. "The enemy?" she offers, and as her eyes flash to mine, my lips twitch.

This gorgeous woman at my side has got more backbone than half the people in this room, Cyril Blackwood included.

"The enemy. Indeed. I couldn't have put it better myself," Blackwood sniffs, his little eyes practically disappearing into his face.

"The king felt I would be best suited to the job," Fabiana adds.

"Lucky you, getting intimate access to Prince Maximilien," Blackwood drawls, and there's something in the way he says "intimate access" that turns my stomach.

"He taught me how to shoot an arrow today," she says as she places a hand on my forearm. "Didn't you, Max?"

"I would have thought in your line of work you were quite adept at shooting. Or am I thinking of mudslinging?" Blackwood says.

"Come now, Lord Blackwood. This is an elegant evening for visiting dignitaries. Let's keep it friendly, shall we?" she replies, not missing a beat.

There's one thing I'll say for Fabiana: she can hold her own.

"I'm quite certain I can. Can you?" he replies.

"As a matter of fact, I can," she says. "Although I've only been here for a couple of days, I suspect I'll learn a lot more once His Royal Highness and I travel north together," she says, and then looks at me and adds, "Isn't that right, Max?"

The way she says my name does something to my belly. "That's right."

Blackwood's eyebrows make an impressive migration toward what remains of his hairline, which is no small feat, considering it's situated halfway down the back of his head. "You're taking her to the summer palace, sir?"

I nod. "Correct."

"Good luck with that." He harrumphs like a disgruntled walrus before excusing himself, and I watch him waddle away with a mixture of relief and irritation.

"Tell me something," I say once he's out of earshot. "Do you make friends wherever you go?"

She drains her glass, the only sign she was rattled. "In my line of work, it's hard to be everybody's favorite."

Something about her matter-of-fact tone bothers me

more than it should, and I find myself saying, "I'm sorry he was rude to you."

The words surprise her as much as they surprise me.

She lifts a shoulder. "I have thick skin."

"I imagine you need it," I reply, and realize I mean it more kindly than critically.

A woman with a razor-sharp bob and calculating eyes approaches us. Unlike the other guests, who've been stealing glances at Fabiana all evening, this one has been openly staring, even when she spoke briefly with Blackwood as their paths crossed on her way to us.

She greets me with a curtsy and then turns to Fabiana. "I'm Miranda Thorne from *The Post*," the woman says, extending a manicured hand toward Fabiana.

Recognition flashes across Fabiana's face as her lips tighten. "Nice to meet you. I'm Fabiana Fontaine."

"Oh, I know exactly who you are," Miranda says, her smile as sharp as cut glass. "I've been following your work for years. You're very... insightful. You seem to have quite the inside track on royal protocol."

"Thank you," Fabiana replies tightly. "I was reading some of your comments on TikTok only today."

"Were you indeed? In that case, you'll know I'm a big fan. Huge." Miranda's eyes dart between us. "I have to say, I'm fascinated by this new arrangement. A journalist getting such unprecedented access to a member of the royal family. It makes one wonder." She pauses for a beat before she adds, "No. I'm being silly."

I narrow my eyes at her. "Wonder what?" I ask, aware I'm walking right into her trap.

"Oh, nothing inappropriate or anything," she says, clearly thinking something inappropriate is going on here. "I'm simply curious about the selection process. There are so many qualified journalists who would love this opportunity, and yet you chose a beautiful young woman."

"My father chose her, actually," I reply.

What's this woman's beef? Is she annoyed she didn't get the job herself?

"I'm sure Ms. Fontaine's background was thoroughly vetted."

There's something about the way she emphasizes the word "background" that has my eyes sliding to Fabiana. Her back is as straight as a rod, her jaw tense.

Miranda Thorne is clearly bothering her.

"Well, I should let you get back to your evening, sir. Ms. Fontaine, I do hope we'll have a chance to chat more. I'd love to compare notes sometime," she simpers.

As she moves away, I say, "You've got a fan."

"You think?" she asks with a sardonic smile as her eyes follow Miranda retreating through the crowd.

We're called to dinner, and I don't analyze my disappointment too deeply when I note I'm not sitting beside Fabiana. She's across the table from me and a couple of chairs down.

Lady Pemberton, seated to my left, is regaling me with stories about her prize-winning roses, and I nod at appropriate intervals, all the while keeping one eye on Fabiana. She's talking with Carrington Belvedere, a philanthropist who seems to have forgotten the "anonymous" part of giving, and Lord Busoni, whose hearing aid I know from experience is more decorative than functional.

"Such an interesting young lady," Lady Pemberton chirps, following my gaze. "Though I do hope she's not planning to write anything unnecessary about tonight's dinner. She does have a habit of doing that."

"You're right," I say as I take a bite of my salmon.

"My grandson showed me how to watch her videos. She's quite clever, actually."

I nearly choke on my wine. Lady Pemberton watches TikTok? "She's very professional," I manage to say.

"I liked the archery one, although I was disappointed she didn't have a try herself,"

"Oh, she did."

"Really? Good for her."

I try to listen in on what Fabiana and Belvedere are talking about.

"The prince looks like a very proficient archer," I hear Belvedere say. Of course he watched the archery video, too. If the eighty-year-old Lady Pemberton can tear herself away from her roses long enough to watch it, I imagine most people in the room tonight did, too.

But they only saw what Fabiana shared. They don't know what transpired between us as I guided her bow and arrow, how I nearly gave in to temptation to kiss her. How being so close to her had messed with my mind.

What started as merely physical attraction seems as though it's building into something more, and I'm not quite sure how to handle it.

"You must remember that what the royal family needs is dignity and respect, not trending hashtags," I hear Belvedere say to Fabiana, loud enough that it was clearly designed for an audience.

I tell myself I'm only listening in out of interest, but it runs deeper than that.

"I'll keep that in mind," she replies smoothly.

Lady Pemberton pats my arm, pulling my attention. "It's rather sweet how you keep glancing over at Ms. Fontaine. Are you quite certain this arrangement is purely professional?"

My brain short-circuits. "I'm sorry, what did you say?"

"Oh, don't look so panicked, Your Royal Highness. I might be a lot older than you, but I know attraction when I see it. The question is whether you've acted on your feelings."

I stare at her, not quite sure how to respond to this woman who seems suddenly more soothsayer than rose enthusiast-slash-TikTok-watcher.

"It's... complicated," I say weakly, even though it's the honest truth.

Developing a thing for Fabiana? That's a disaster waiting to happen, and one I didn't expect. I feel a pull to her that I'm finding increasingly difficult to resist, and now I'm listening in on her conversations over dinner and watching her every move.

What the heck is wrong with me?

Lady Pemberton winks at me. Winks! "Complicated? The best things usually are, my dear boy."

Thankfully, the guest to my right asks me a question about The Games, and my attention is effectively diverted from Fabiana. Before long, the meal is finished, and the guests are mingling in the adjoining reception room. I seize the opportunity for some solitary solace on the balcony.

I've got to do something to try to get my head straight.

The evening air is a welcome reprieve from the suffocating politeness of the state dinner, and of Lady Pemberton's uncomfortably acute observations. The royal gardens stretch out below, fairy lights twinkling in the trees. It's my favorite time of day, that magical hour when the sun has set, leaving behind a soft glow on the horizon.

I'm leaning my elbows on the stone wall when I hear footsteps behind me. I straighten and turn to see Fabiana stepping into the moonlight.

"Fancy meeting you here," she teases.

"Fancy that," is all I can manage.

Why won't my brain function normally around this woman?

She moves to stand beside me, and I catch that scent again—something floral with vanilla undertones that's becoming dangerously familiar.

"Why are you out here on the terrace on your own?" she asks.

"How do you know I'm not waiting for someone?" I reply, challenging her with my eyes.

She glances around the conspicuously empty terrace. "Because there's no one here. Perhaps you have been stood up?"

The teasing note in her voice surprises a laugh out of me—the first genuine laugh I've given all evening. "I just needed some fresh air after all the talk."

"Did you grow tired of flirting with octogenarians?"

The mischief in her tone makes something warm unfurl in my chest.

"I was charming her, Fabiana. Not flirting. There's a difference."

I don't mention Lady Pemberton's wry observations about her and me.

"If you say so." She turns her attention to the gardens, and I find myself watching her profile in the moonlight instead of the view.

"Beautiful," she whispers, almost to herself.

"It is."

"This is my favorite time of day, when it's growing dark, but the last rays of light can be seen on the horizon," she says, and it's like she's in my head, plucking out my thoughts. "It's—"

"—Magical," I finish for her, and when she looks at me, there's something unguarded in her expression that makes my breath hitch in my throat.

"Magical," she repeats.

We hold one another's gaze for a beat too long, until I pull mine away, looking out at the horizon once more. We stand in silence, and it's surprisingly not as uncomfortable as I might once have expected.

"I should let you get some rest," I say, breaking the silence. "We need to be up early to catch the train north tomorrow."

"True," she replies. "Good night, Max."

"Good night, Fabiana." I step away, but I don't leave. I should, but I don't. Instead, I find myself lingering, watching as she wraps her arms around herself against the cool night air, and that now familiar protectiveness I felt earlier stirs in my chest.

I pull off my jacket and place it across her shoulders.

She snaps her attention to me, with a look of surprise on her face. "Thanks," she murmurs.

"You looked cold."

She nods, pulling my jacket closer around herself. It's so much larger than her and she's dwarfed by it.

Tomorrow, we head north together, just her and me and Pippa Chen. The thought should terrify me, and in a way it does.

But as I finally force myself to walk away, leaving her silhouetted against the fairy lights, I can't shake the feeling that everything has shifted irretrievably between us.

I had once thought this was going to be the longest, most difficult month of my life, but now, with these new, uncharted waters we're both wading through, I wonder if it might in fact be the best.

Chapter 11

Valentina

THE ROYAL FAMILY'S train is just as pretentious as I'd expected, with its polished mahogany panels, crystal decanters, and Ledonian red upholstered seating. Uniformed staff move discreetly through the carriage, catering to any need, and the overpriced two-day-old sandwiches and terrible coffee I usually get from the food carriage have been replaced with a silver service three course meal, accompanied by local wines and coffee the best barista in Villadorata would be proud of.

I'm not in Kansas anymore, Toto.

As the train chugs along, I gaze out the window as the Ledonian countryside rolls past, marveling at what my life has become. Only a few days ago, I was lying on the floor of the kitchen, water dripping on my forehead, as I tried to tighten the leaking tap, catching the distinct form of a rat scurrying by. Now, here I am, being whisked north inside a luxurious metal bullet with a prince I've got conflicting feelings for, heading straight for the summer palace in the mountains.

Toffee is sleeping in her crate, and the human version of a labrador puppy, Pippa Chen, is slunk in her seat across from me, her laptop on the table between us. She's reviewing the content strategy we've been working on since we left the city a couple of hours ago.

"I still can't believe we're actually doing this!" she gushes. "Can I call you Fabiana? Mr. Clementine expects everyone to be super formal at the palace, but I'm about 90 years younger than him, and I call everyone by their first names, even my parents."

"Plain old Fabiana is fine by me," I reply as I take another sip of my coffee and resist the urge to purr. Seriously, it's that good.

"There's nothing plain or old about you. You're so amazing! And the ideas you came up with in the strategy meeting and how you didn't back down when Mr. Clementine was pushing for a boring old TV documentary? Chef's kiss." She mimes kissing her fingertips as Max slides his gaze across the aisle at me for what seems like at least the thirtieth time since we left Villadorata Central.

I catch his stare and immediately he pulls it away, running his fingers through his hair as he returns his attention to some papers on the table in front of him.

I take the opportunity to assess him. He's removed his

jacket to reveal a buttoned-up white cotton shirt, the sleeves of which are rolled up to show off his sinewy forearms, a couple of buttons undone at his neck. The white of his shirt contrasts perfectly with the olive of his skin, his thick dark hair slightly mussed up from the number of times he's run his fingers through it whenever I catch him looking at me. As I said, it's at least thirty times.

That's a lot of hair mussing in anyone's book.

And the looks he shoots me, all brooding and intense, would make a weaker woman melt.

Thank goodness I'm not a weaker woman.

I glance at him again and catch his eye, and instantly a shot of electricity courses through me.

Okay, maybe I'm a little weaker than I should be around him.

The thing is, now that I've seen glimpses of a man I didn't know existed, he's wormed his way into my head, and for the life of me, I cannot get him out. I find my mind wandering to him at all times of the day and night.

Especially at night.

As I lay in my huge bed after he left me on the balcony last night, I couldn't stop thinking about the way he'd acted toward me at dinner. The way he took my arm as we entered the dining room, perhaps sensing I was unnerved to be there. It was a little like he was my ally, not the journalist he's being forced to work with.

Perhaps he was just being a gentleman or a good host, but there was something in the way he looked at me, the way he stood beside me, the way he spoke up for me, that made me feel as though he had my best interests at heart.

Which has got to be the biggest U-turn in the history of driving.

"The behind-the-scenes access you're planning alone is going to be absolutely revolutionary for royal digital engagement," Pippa says, pulling my attention from the prince.

"'Revolutionary' might be overstating it a little, Pippa," I reply as I lift my phone to capture Max. He's studiously reading his papers, his brows pulled together in concentration. Judging by the way the fabric of his shirt strains against his arms, a hashtag appears before my eyes: #BicepsAndBookmarks. Even as I think of it, I'm aware Max is so much more than the hashtags I've given him over the years. I vow to come up with more authentic versions over the coming days.

"Are you kidding, Fab?" Pippa says. "You're totally revolutionizing the way royalty will be seen in this country."

I raise my eyebrows. "Fab?"

"Has anyone ever called you 'Fab'?" she asks.

"I can't say they have." I click my phone off.

"It totally works for you. Fab for Fabiana and fabulous." She beams at me.

Well, I've got a new fan.

"What you're doing is going to change completely how people see the monarchy! You've got to understand that!"

In my line of work, I'm not exactly used to being fan girl-ed over. I'm not quite sure how to manage it now.

"Thanks?" I offer, and Pippa laughs as though I've made a brilliant joke.

No more coffee for Ms. Chen.

I raise my phone once more to record Max as he frowns at whatever he's reading, his dark hair falling across his forehead in a way that probably makes women go wild. He looks genuinely engrossed, and I find myself watching him closely.

This man is way more complex than I've ever given him credit for. This is good content. Sitting here, unaware

I'm filming him, he's not putting on a show. He's not performing. He's simply reading, not performing. Not being a party boy prince.

He glances up and catches sight of me filming, and his entire demeanor stiffens. "What are you doing?"

"Fab is capturing authentic content, sir," Pippa clarifies helpfully.

"Fab?" he asks, his eyes sliding back to mine.

I shrug.

"Fabiana, of course! I shortened her name," Pippa declares proudly, as though she's conquered Mt. Everest, rather than removed the "iana" from Fabiana.

The corners of Max's lips tilt upwards.

"I'm capturing the real you, not the public version," I say.

"Perhaps they're the same thing," he counters, but there's something playful in his tone. "If you're going to insist on filming me, why don't you do it from here." He gestures at the empty seat across the table from him.

It's not a bad idea.

I slide over, and he immediately straightens, offering me that practiced royal smile.

"Should I stare pensively out the window?"

"Heck, no. I want the person who was actually reading, not someone performing for the camera."

"You certainly studied me closely," he says, lowering his voice. The comment sends a flutter through my chest. He lowers his voice for my ears only. "Or should that be 'Fab'?"

A snicker threatens to morph into a laugh, and I work hard at not allowing it to escape my lips. "She's super enthusiastic. I like that about her."

He widens his eyes, those lips quirking once more.

"Toffee's having a good long sleep," I say to change the subject.

Max turns to look at his dog, asleep in her crate, her paws twitching.

"She looks like she's dreaming about chasing bunnies across the lawn."

"I imagine she is," he replies. "How did you enjoy the dinner last night?"

"It was very tasty," I reply.

We both know he wasn't asking me about my food.

He places his elbows on the table, leaning toward me, and I try not to notice how the muscles in his forearms ripple as he moves. "Tell me if I'm wrong, but I felt you were a little nervous going into that room last night."

I think of the way he walked in with me as though I weren't just the hired help, there to do a job. He'd been gentlemanly, proud, almost.

But that could have been a figment of my imagination.

"I don't usually attend state dinners," I reply, although that wasn't the real reason I was nervous.

"Some of the guests were, shall we say, less than polite."

"Oh, you mean Lord Blackwood? He's nothing I can't handle."

I remember Lord Blackwood from childhood as a self-interested man my dad didn't like. They had some kind of professional rivalry that I didn't understand at the time but have since learned was around their respective businesses. I remember hearing him referring to him as "a snake in the grass" and my eight-year-old self-wondering how someone so portly could be a snake.

"You held yourself well."

"You've got to when you're a journalist who makes a living out of writing about people's lives."

"I imagine you do."

"How did you enjoy yourself? Have you been DM-ing with your octogenarian today?"

He chuckles, his eyes dancing. "We've got a date next week."

"I bet you do," I tease.

This bantering is easy. Fun.

Dangerous.

"You have a way with people, Max. I've seen it before, but I've not really written about it, other than saying how charming you can be."

"Charming? I thought you said I was flirting."

"I've been told recently that those are two different things."

We share a smile, the intensity in his rich espresso eyes trained on me making my belly perform a somersault.

"Oh, I'm so glad I captured this," Pippa says from across the aisle, her phone pointing in our direction.

We both turn to look at her.

"Captured what?" I ask.

"Your interaction, of course. It's gold!" she says.

"What's gold, exactly?" Max asks.

"You've got this whole 'will they, won't they' thing going on. Like Ross and Rachel from *Friends*," she replies.

Oh, good grief.

"I really don't think—" Max begins at the same time as I say, "That's totally crazy."

"Are you sure? Because my phone says otherwise," Pippa replies, waving her phone in the air.

The surrounding air thickens, and I can't look at Max.

"May I take a look at your footage?" he asks.

"Of course." Pippa hands over the phone, and I wait as Max reviews the video, wondering whether it does in fact have the vibe Pippa mentioned. Because from my perspective at least the only answer to the question *will they, won't they* must be a firm *they cannot*.

But if Pippa can see how I feel about Max—and worse yet, capture it on film—who knows who else can?

Max clicks the phone off and hands it back to Pippa. "It's just a conversation between two work colleagues. Nothing more."

Pippa's eyes swivel between Max and me. "Are you sure?"

"Absolutely sure," he says with a finality that tells her the conversation is now closed.

I still can't look at him. Not now that Pippa has called us out on our chemistry. I turn to look out the window, and my heart nearly comes to a stop. There in the distance, partially obscured by a line of ancient oak trees, is the roofline of Tenuta Fioralba.

My family's estate.

Or rather, my family's *former* estate, since it was seized by the Crown all those years ago when my father's reputation went up in flames, along with everything else we'd ever owned.

The train sails past the vineyards, and I catch a glimpse of the house in the distance. A lump forms in my throat as memories wash over me.

The way I used to "help" the grape pickers at harvest time, trailing behind them and picking up the discarded fruit from the ground.

The way we would eat our dinners on the stone patio in the summer, enjoying the long evenings filled with the sweet, heady scent of jasmine in the air.

The way I would run wild in summer with my cousins, building forts and making mud pies, the days like they stretched on forever.

And now someone else lives in the house, enjoying its views, a stranger who owes nothing to my family.

I swallow, my throat suddenly tight.

I knew it was likely I would see my old family estate when I agreed to come on this trip. But it's one thing to know something and quite another to actually experience it. Getting emotional about my family's lost past isn't going to help anyone, least of all me.

Now is not the time to get sentimental over what's been lost. I've got a job to do, not to take a painful walk down memory lane while I'm sitting at a table with the prince.

I flick my gaze back to Max. He's watching me with a questioning look in his eyes, so I pull my lips into a smile. "I'm going to capture you looking out the window as you suggested."

"Why the change of heart?"

"I think it's a good idea." Before he has the chance to say anything else, I lift my phone and begin to film him, panning from him to the view outside.

"We're not far now," Max says.

I click my phone off. "Tell me about this youth program. It's not something I've heard about before."

"That's because it's nothing particularly newsworthy. It's a leadership program to help disadvantaged young people from families who wouldn't otherwise get the chance to do things like outdoor activities and team-building exercises. We're trying to develop these kids' self-esteem and improve their resilience, as well as give them some practical skills like teamwork and problem solving."

"Is this a palace initiative?"

He pauses for a beat before he replies, "It's *my* initiative. Not the palace's."

"Yours?"

"This probably doesn't fit your perspective of me as a

privileged member of the royal family, who attends parties more often than most people eat hot meals."

That's what I used to think of him, anyway. Now, I can see it's just one of the things he does. It doesn't define him. He's so much more than parties and super yachts and martinis.

"It's something I'm passionate about. I've had a lot of advantages in life, and I'm well aware that most people don't have what I've enjoyed."

I offer him a wry smile. "That's somewhat socialist for a member of the royal family."

He chuckles, the deep sound filling the air, and it strikes me that I want to hear that laugh more often. "I wouldn't exactly call it socialist. More having a social conscience."

"I'm interested in seeing how you interact with the young people. I'll need to get their parents' or caregivers' permission to film them, of course."

"I can do that!" Pippa declares.

I'd forgotten once again that she's sitting right across the aisle, listening to everything we've said.

"That would be great. Thanks, Pippa," I reply.

"If I'm going to call you Fab, you have to call me Pip. It's only fair," she says.

"Pip. Got it," I say.

I don't look at Max.

"I want to ask the kids if they want to be a part of your videos first," Max says.

"Of course. How long have you been running this program?" I ask.

"Three years, give or take."

Huh. That's three years of hands-on charitable work that he's never talked publicly about.

"Why have you never sought media coverage for it?"

"Not everything needs to be a photo opportunity."

"Agreed. Who funds it?"

"Does it matter?"

"Everything matters when you're trying to understand someone's character, Max."

He pauses for a beat. "I do."

"As in you personally?"

"Is that so surprising to you?"

If he had asked me that question a handful of days ago, I would have said yes, it was surprising. Shocking, even. But now that I'm getting to see the real Max, I'm beginning to understand he's a whole lot more than the man I've reported on all these years. He's deeper, more layered, more *real* than I ever gave him credit for.

"Not anymore," I reply, my chest filling with warmth. "Why do you do it?"

"Because my local store ran out of Cristal," he says with a sardonic smile. "Why do you think?"

"That's why I'm asking you."

"Because it seemed like the decent thing to do."

As we enter the familiar picturesque town of Castelvino, the train slows to a stop, and through the window I can see a couple of Range Rovers waiting for us.

"Welcome to my favorite place in Ledonia," Max says as he rises from his seat.

I worry my lip. Max's favorite place is a mere twenty-minute train ride from my childhood home. The universe clearly has a twisted sense of humor. It's going to take all I've got not to let my Fabiana mask slip over the coming days.

Chapter 12

Max

For as long as I can remember, Palazzo Belladonna has been my sanctuary. It's a place where I can kick off my shoes and relax. The palace in Villadorata is more like a museum, with all its formal rooms and oil paintings of my ancestors judging me and my choices. This place, nestled in the mountains, covered in snow in winter and now, at the height of summer, surrounded by wildflowers and beauty everywhere I look, is like an actual home.

I'm not on show here.

I can be me.

The small number of staff at the palace have known me since I was knee high to a grasshopper, many of them still calling me Maxie. It should make me cringe—I'm a man of twenty-seven—but secretly, I love it. They know who I really am, and that's what matters.

By the looks of things, Toffee adores this place just as much as I do. The moment she's out of her crate, she gets a serious case of the zoomies, bolting the moment I open her door, only to come careening back when I whistle for her. Her tail wags like a windscreen wiper in a storm, her tongue flapping as it hangs out of her mouth, her big brown eyes glistening with excitement.

I bend down and ruffle her fur. "This is your new favorite place, isn't it, girl?"

Her answer is to take off once more.

Fabiana strides over to me. She looks all business in her high heels, so out of place here in the country, as they crunch across the gravel, her ever-present notebook clutched against her chest as she films. She's removed her blazer in the heat of the afternoon, and I allow my gaze to trail over her curves, encased in a slim-fitting skirt and blouse.

My belly clenches at the sight of her.

Man, she's hot.

"Someone's happy to be here," she says as she films Toffee madly sniffing the plants, darting between them like she's never smelt anything so wonderful in all her life.

"She told me she prefers the country to the city," I say.

"A talking dog? Royalty really does get all the good stuff."

We both watch as Toffee begins to dig a hole in the

middle of the lawn, dirt flinging through the air like little missiles.

"Is she allowed to do that?" Fabiana asks.

"Not exactly. Father would have a stroke if he knew."

She clicks her phone off. "Good job he doesn't, although I would have thought you'd be bothered by it. Don't you have a thing for lawns? Sloping ones, covered in slip n' slides, that is."

I let out a laugh. Once I would have taken it as a jibe, now it's more like her teasing me.

She grins. "It had to be said."

I shake my head. "Did it really?"

"This place is amazing! And it's so warm here. I'm roasting!" Pippa exclaims as she wanders over to us. "I thought it would be cooler in the mountains, sir."

"It usually is. It's unseasonably warm," I reply.

She plunks herself down at the edge of the fountain and dips her fingers in the water. "Smell that fresh air! I bet you can drink this water; everything's so fresh here." She cups a hand and lifts it to her mouth.

"I wouldn't do that if I were you, Pippa," I call out.

It's too late as she takes a long sip and dips her hand in the fountain for more. "Why not? It's so refreshing!"

"Is that water safe to drink?" Fabiana asks.

"We can but hope Pippa's digestive system is made of stern stuff."

"Let's hope, for her sake."

I whistle, and Toffee immediately stops her digging, turning in my direction, her ears pricked up. "Come on, Toffee!" I call, and she comes bounding over to me, only to leap at Fabiana as though she's the one who called her.

By now, Toffee's dirty paws are all over Fabiana's skirt, but she doesn't seem to have noticed as she leans down to pet her, or even care. "Hello, little Toffee," she says as she strokes her fur. "Aren't you having a marvelous time already? And look at your dirty paws. Your daddy will need to give you a bath."

I arch a brow. "Daddy?" I question.

She looks up at me. "Should I have referred to you as His Royal Highness?"

I laugh again as I watch her nuzzle Toffee, my chest filling with warmth. Only a few short days ago, her holding Toffee enraged me. Now? Now, watching how easily she interacts with my dog makes me all the more drawn to her.

Don't they say dogs are great judges of character? Fabiana sure seems to have Toffee's stamp of approval—quite literally, all over her skirt.

"Oh, no, Fab! Your skirt!" Pippa exclaims.

To my surprise, Fabiana looks down at her skirt and simply shrugs, not appearing the least bit concerned. "It comes with the canine territory. I had dogs growing up, so I understand."

Pippa gasps. "But your skirt is ruined!"

"It's just a skirt, Pippa."

I'm so used to women preening themselves around me, always trying to look like their idea of perfection. Fabiana is a breath of fresh air.

"Where's my room, please, Max? I'll go and unpack my things, change out of these clothes into something more appropriate for the country."

"I'll take you there. You too, Pippa."

"Thanks, sir, but I think I might take a little wander around the gardens first. I thought I saw a funny-looking baby goat when we arrived," Pippa replies.

"That'll be one of Dolly's kids. She gave birth a few weeks before I was last here. She's a very proud mum of new triplets," I say.

"Triplets? Oh, how cute!" Pippa replies. "What sort of goats are they?"

"Shami goats, which is why they have white faces and those long black ears," I reply.

Pippa's eyes are bright. "You could use them in a video, Fab. People adore baby goats."

"Great idea," Fabiana replies.

"I'll catch up with you both later. It's baby goat time!" Pippa bounces away and disappears around the house toward the stables in search of Dolly.

Fabiana arches a brow as we make our way into the house. "Dolly?"

"Dolly Baa-ton," I say.

Her eyes dance with amusement. "Did you name her?"

"One of the kids from the program a couple of years back. You should hear what we've called her triplets."

"Let me guess." She taps her chin. "One of them has got to be Baa-bara."

"Amateur hour." I shake my head. "They're Taylor-bleat, Rihabaa, and Ariana Goat."

"All female pop stars? I'm not sure if that's utterly adorable, or completely hilarious."

"Couldn't it be both?" I whistle for Toffee, and she bursts into the house before us, immediately clambering up the stairs as though she knows where we're headed.

Moving inside the house, Fabiana looks around at the arched doorways, the terracotta-painted walls, and the high beamed ceiling. "This is just lovely," she exclaims, and sunshine blooms in my chest.

"It's my favorite place," I say simply.

"I can see why."

"It's a lot less grand than the palace in Villadorata. That's something I like about it. Which suitcase is yours?" I gesture at a couple of suitcases that have been placed by the wall.

She raises her eyebrows. "Don't you have people for that?"

"I'm pretty sure I'm capable of carrying a suitcase up a flight of stairs."

"The burgundy one, but I'll carry it." She marches over to the suitcase and picks it up.

"Why when you have this hunk of testosterone here, willing to do it for you?" I gesture at myself with my thumb.

"Because it's mine," she says simply. "And 'hunk of testosterone'? I couldn't let that one go." Her eyes dance.

"My PT calls me names like that. He thinks it's motivational."

She snickers. "I see."

"Don't make a hashtag out of it."

"Would I?"

"We both know you would."

She holds two fingers aloft. "I promise I won't. Scouts' honor." She lifts her case.

"You're sure I can't take that?"

"I'm fine," she insists.

I lead her up the wide staircase, keeping an eye on her. By the time we reach the first landing—some twenty-three steps up—she's gone all red in the face from the exertion.

I reach for her bag. "I'm not taking no for an answer."

Letting out a heavy breath, she raises a hand in surrender. "I'm not quite as fit as I thought. So, here you go, self-named hunk of testosterone. Be my guest."

"My PT, remember?"

We make our way up to the third floor, where I take her to the room that's usually Amelia's. The door creaks as

I push it open, and as we enter the darkened space, I pull back the drapes and light floods inside.

"This is so pretty," she says, looking around at the floral wallpaper, the wrought iron bed, and the writing desk by the window.

"It's my sister Amelia's room."

"The princess has good taste. I can work at the desk, too." Turning to me, she adds, "I'll be very happy here for the next two nights."

"Three," I correct. "Then we need to be back in Villadorata." I place her suitcase on the ottoman at the end of the bed as Toffee appears, sniffing her way across the room.

"Should I tip you?" Her luscious lips are curved in a smile, the green of her eyes pronounced by the flush in her cheeks.

And then it hits me. The room may be pristine, yet untouched by her, but knowing it's *hers* makes the surrounding air suddenly seem different. In a few short hours she'll be here, alone, brushing her hair or removing her glasses or pulling the sheets back to climb into bed.

It's a glimpse into her private side I should not be having.

As much as I prefer this version of Fabiana, as much as I feel this increasingly strong pull to her, I should have no business thinking of her as anything but the journalist here to do a job.

And now she's looking the way she looks, her easy smile lighting up her beautiful face, the outline of the curves of her body visible under her slim-fitted clothes, and it's clear what I must do.

Get out of here before I say—or do—something that would be wildly inappropriate, possibly even jeopardize the entire project with her.

"I'll leave you to it," I say, my lips tight as I turn to leave. "Come on, Toffee."

Toffee darts past me into the hallway.

Fabiana places her hand gently against my sleeve. "Thank you, Max," she says, her voice softer than it was a moment ago, making me want to turn around and collect her in my arms, to tell her how much I want her, how the feelings I have for her are growing and growing.

I can't.

We may have entered a new kind of relationship over the last day or so, but she's responsible for showing the country the real me. I can't act on the way I feel about her and throw all of that into jeopardy.

I Was Seduced by Playboy Prince Max.

The headline appears in neon lights right before my eyes, and it won't matter that what I feel for her is stronger than I've ever felt in my life before. All anyone would know is that I've lived up to my reputation once more. That I'm all about having a good time. That seducing a journalist, here to do a job, is just part of my shallow, good-time-boy character.

She'd almost expect it of me.

"You're welcome," I reply briskly, as I step out of the uncomfortably intimate space into the relative sanctity of the hallway.

She follows me, casually leaning her shoulder against the door jamb. "The kids arrive for the program soon, right? The human variety, I mean. Not the goat."

I press my lips together. "They do."

"I'll come out to meet them. Say hi."

I nod my head as rapidly as one of those bobble head figurines. "All right."

Before she has the chance to say another word, I say goodbye and rush down the hallway to my own room.

I wish I'd put her further away from me. The stables would have done the trick nicely.

I close the door and let out a breath, leaning up against it, my heart drumming.

I can allow her to film me and ask her questions, all the while projecting the version of me my parents expect.

I can do this. I'm strong.

All I need to do is keep my head.

Chapter 13

Max

LESS THAN HALF AN HOUR LATER, the members of my team arrive, and I greet them at the house entrance as Toffee darts across the driveway toward the gardens once more. Rocco Mansoni and Dante Brownley, a couple of my Ledonian Royal Air Force buddies, greet me with handshakes, smiles, and backslaps.

They're as passionate about this program as I am. They live locally and leapt at the chance to be involved when I set the program up three or so years ago.

"Your Royal Highness," Rocco says with a sarcastic bow, his dark eyes sparkling.

"There's no need to stand on protocol, my man," I tell him.

"My mama would kill me if I didn't show you the appropriate respect," he replies with a wink.

That's one of the weird things about being royal. Even your oldest friends are meant to call you by your official title, despite the fact they've seen you in less than royal situations in the past.

"I haven't seen you since that garden party at the palace. Still a man-child, I hope?" Rocco asks.

A laugh rips out of me. "Actually, I have something to tell you about that."

"You've moved your slip n' slide game up a notch?" Rocco asks.

"Eyeing the Olympics, I bet," Dante agrees.

I arch a brow. "Is there an Olympic slip n' slide event?"

"There should be," Dante replies. "You'd win, hands down."

Rocco nods. "You've got that right."

"How's married life suiting you?" I ask Dante, whose wedding I was best man at in the spring.

"She sends her best, and these." Dante opens a tub of scones. "Freshly baked."

"Cheese?" I ask.

"What else?"

"Tell her I adore her," I reply as I breathe in the delicious scent.

"Who do you adore?" a feminine voice asks behind us, and we all turn to see Fabiana walking down the steps.

Right on cue, my stomach flips at the sight of her. She's now wearing a pair of country-appropriate khaki shorts, sneakers, and a T-shirt, her hair tied up in her usual high ponytail, swinging from side to side.

She looks…well, she looks like she belongs here, there's no other way to put it—not to mention completely hot. Her legs are long, slim, and lightly tanned, and her T-shirt is close fitting enough to show off the curves I've become all too aware of these past few days.

Both Dante and Rocco's brows lift towards their respective hairlines, shooting me meaningful looks.

"Oh, it's not what you think," I say swiftly, before they say something to embarrass me.

"It's not?" Dante asks with a smirk on his face.

"You didn't tell us you were bringing a new girlfriend," Rocco says.

The idea of Fabiana being my girlfriend fills me with a cocktail of emotions that I push away, and *fast*.

"Gentlemen, may I introduce Fabiana Fontaine," I say, and the looks on my friends' faces turn from questioning to *what the heck?!* before you could mutter the words *arch nemesis*.

"Fabiana Fontaine," Rocco repeats dumbly. "As in *the* Fabiana Fontaine? The journo?"

Fabiana offers her hand to my friends. "That's right," she says pleasantly, but then I've seen firsthand how she deals with her haters. All in a day's work for her.

Dante narrows his eyes at her. "You're the one who called Max a man-child, aren't you?"

"Among other things," she admits brightly with her usual confidence, seemingly unfazed. "Max has certainly delighted my readers with his antics over the years. I've simply labelled those antics."

"Labelled? Is that what you call it?" Rocco grinds out. "Tell me, how do you always seem to know what he's doing?"

"I could never reveal my sources," she replies.

My friends share a look.

"So, why are you here? I mean, the two of you… together?" Dante asks.

"I'm working on a project with Max," she replies. "I'm sorry. I didn't catch your names."

I've been so busy worrying about how this will go that I forgot my manners. "Forgive me. This is Rocco Mansoni and Dante Brownley."

"We go way back with the prince," Dante says.

"Royal Air Force," Rocco adds.

"Great," she replies. "So, you're involved in the youth program, too?"

"We helped Max set it up," Rocco says, his eyes narrowed at her, assessing.

"In that case, do you mind if I film you? I'm making social media content as well as writing articles, a kind of 'here's the real Prince Max' exposé. You might have seen the TikTok of Max doing archery. I've just posted a picture of him looking all pensive on the train."

Rocco's eyes dart to mine. "And you're down with this?"

How can I tell them that she and I have come a long way since the time I once despised her? That I've found myself opening up to her in a way I would never have anticipated. That she's not the headline-seeking hack I was so convinced she was.

That I can't stop myself fancying the pants off her—and more, developing some real feelings for her.

"Fabiana has been employed by my father to show the country who I really am," I say.

"Like a soldier behind enemy lines?" Rocco asks.

Fabiana's gaze captures mine. "Something like that."

Toffee scrambles over to us, and I lean down to make a

fuss of her. Dogs are so much more straightforward than women, particularly the one currently chatting with my suspicious, loyal mates.

A low rumbling grabs my attention, and I look down the driveway to see an approaching bus.

"Are they about to arrive, sir?" Pippa asks, arriving at our group, and I introduce her to the men.

"We're about to be swarmed by a bunch of hormonal teens," Rocco announces, and I scoop Toffee up in my arms.

"Brace yourselves," Dante says.

Fabiana shields her eyes from the sun with her hand. "How many teens are there on that bus exactly?"

"About twenty, give or take," I reply.

As the bus rounds the fountain, we can hear the laughter and good-natured shouting through the open windows.

"Sounds more like fifty," she says.

The bus comes to a stop, and the kids pour off the moment the doors creak open, spilling out onto the gravel driveway with backpacks on their backs, greeting Dante, Rocco, and me with high fives.

At first, Fabiana holds back as I chat and joke with the familiar faces. Then, to my surprise, she approaches a group and introduces herself, asking them about the program. She looks totally at ease in a group of strangers—teenage strangers at that.

Is there anything that fazes this woman?

"Yo, Max! When are we going to start the obstacle course challenge?" asks Dean, a sixteen-year-old who has been part of the program since its inception.

That's one of the things I love about the teenagers on this program. They couldn't care less about my title. I muck in with them on all their activities, helping them out, giving them advice, sometimes showing them how *not* to do it.

"Give us a minute. You only just got here," I reply with a laugh.

Over the years, Dean has gradually morphed from surly and disengaged, his top lip permanently curled upwards in distaste, to one of the leaders of the group. It's been an absolute privilege to play a small part in his transformation.

I remember when he arrived at our first session, with arms crossed and eyes fixed on his shoes, his shoulders tight. He radiated teenage resentment. From his file, I knew it was the kind of hostility that came from too many adults letting him down. His social worker had described him as "challenging", which I worked out is code for a kid who learned to expect disappointment and closed himself off as protection against the world.

But something shifted during a rock-climbing session that first summer. He smiled. Not in a sarcastic way, but a real, genuine smile. It was the start of a shift, and one that blossomed over the following months.

Now he's the one organizing equipment before sessions start and explaining knot techniques to newer participants with the same care Rocco had once given him.

Many of the teens here were volunteered by teachers or social workers, initially attending with significantly more reluctance than enthusiasm. But they needed a place where they could be themselves, where they could get involved in activities they otherwise wouldn't have access to. Where they could build friendships, and most importantly, build their self-worth.

"I'm glad you mentioned the obstacle challenge, Dean, because you and Daria can help set it up on the back lawn right now," Dante says, and the already excited group begins to buzz with enthusiasm.

A couple of the kids groan.

"I get it. Obstacle courses aren't for everyone, but it's part of what we do here, so you need to at least give it a shot," I say.

"Don't worry, Max. I've got it," Dean says. He gestures for the groaners to follow him, which they do with the same level of reluctance Dean himself showed that first year.

As we make our way around the house to the back lawn, Fabiana falls into step with me. "Can you tell me a little about the kids in the program?" she asks.

"Off the record?"

"Of course. We already agreed on that. I'm not a monster. I'm just a journalist, trying to do her job."

"I never thought you were a monster."

She raises her brows at me.

"Okay. Maybe a touch of the monster. But I can see you're not."

She pauses for a beat before she replies, "And I can see you're more than some playboy prince." She holds my gaze, and that now familiar feeling in my belly begins to build. "Tell me about the kids."

"That one there in the red and yellow striped T-shirt is Aria," I say, nodding toward the girl with copper curls currently holding some camera equipment, snapping shots as others set up the course. "She started on the program three months ago. She had social anxiety so severe she couldn't even make eye contact, let alone be involved in any of the activities."

Fabiana's gaze follows mine. "She looks pretty involved now."

"She's come a long way. Her foster mum, constantly

apologizing for her behavior, had to practically drag her here. Now she's become our unofficial photographer and shows real skill."

"That's quite a transformation," Fabiana says. "What about him?" She points to where Ant is animatedly explaining something to a cluster of younger participants, his hands gesturing wildly.

"That's Antonia. Ant. He has ADHD, with emphasis on the 'H'. He acted out at enough schools to get expelled from three." I can't help but smile as Ant spots some wild herbs growing nearby and immediately redirects the group's attention. "Put him on a wilderness survival course and suddenly his hyperactivity becomes a total asset. He spots edible plants faster than anyone."

"Do you know all their stories?"

"Of course I do. Many of the kids come from difficult backgrounds, the kinds of situations I can only imagine from my life of privilege." I pause, aware I'm revealing more than I typically would to a journalist.

But then, Fabiana is more than a journalist to me now.

"What do you think they get from this program?"

"I think it's a bunch of things, but mostly a need for purpose. For a space where their worth isn't determined by their circumstances." I look out at the scene. Rocco now has all the kids lined up, ready to start the course, and I can tell many of them are champing at the bit to get into it. "Here they get to be who they want to be."

She looks out at the group. "They're lucky."

I turn back to look at her. She's got a look on her face I can't read. "These kids are the closest thing to a genuine purpose I've got. I'm the lucky one."

"You see that purpose in Aria's confidence behind the lens, or in Dean's leadership."

Her understanding makes something move in my chest. "Exactly," I reply.

Rocco yells for the first group to begin, and we watch as they dive under the low net before popping out the other side, dashing with all their might towards the rope wall.

"I appreciate you opening up to me about this, Max. It's..." She trails off, her eyes on the competitors.

"It's what?"

"It's showing me why your father invited me to do this with you. You're not some privileged rich guy with an easy life who seeks out pleasure at every turn. You're this." She gestures at the kids. "Your father understands who you are, and he wants me to show the country."

The way she's looking at me makes my pulse quicken. Without even knowing it had happened, we're standing closer than we were a moment ago, close enough that I can smell the subtle floral perfume she wears, close enough to once again count the freckles scattered across her nose.

"Fabiana, I—"

"Max! You coming or what?" Rocco's voice cuts through our moment, and it jolts me back to reality.

I gesture with my thumb over my shoulder. "I should go."

"You should."

I turn and jog toward Rocco and Dante. As I help line up the next group for their turn at the obstacle course, I can sense her watching me. I can't shake the feeling that something fundamental has shifted between us, that she understands me in a way no one has before. Part of me wants nothing more than to tell her what she's slowly coming to mean to me.

To tell her that with every passing moment, my heart is beginning to beat more and more for her.

Chapter 14

Valentina

From the starting position on the obstacle course, I glance back at the imposing red brick mansion. Surrounded by picturesque mountains, it looks like it's from the set in *The Sound of Music*, and I half expect to see Julie Andrews prancing through a field, her arms outstretched, singing her song with gusto.

But this isn't a musical. This is my life, for the next few days at least. I'm about to watch twenty or so teenagers compete in an obstacle race that includes a cargo net crawl and rope climb over a wooden wall, before they have to weave through a series of truck tires, balance on a beam, and finally wade through mud before a sprint to the finish line.

Not my usual Tuesday afternoon.

"Is the next group ready to go?" Rocco asks.

"We sure are!" Dean calls back.

"On your marks, get set, go!" Rocco yells and instantly, the next four participants take off at blinding speed, throwing their bodies at the race like they're rag dolls. They crawl under the net as Max and the others yell out encouragement.

I find myself watching Max closely, entranced. He's so different here. So free. He's so absorbed with the activity, showing such a genuine connection with these kids. He's running alongside them, giving them support and advice.

It's hard to pull my gaze away.

I watch as he interacts with the teenagers with easy charm, his smile so relaxed, so genuine. The skin around his eyes crinkles, his face lit up as he cheers on the kids as they dive under the net, sprint to the wall, then fling themselves over and land in mud. He calls each child by name, giving them encouragement, telling them they can do this, that they're more capable than they could ever imagine.

Something warm and a little wonderful unfurls in my chest.

This is a new side of him, a side I never knew existed. He cares about these kids, genuinely interested in getting the most out of them.

Across from me, Pippa is cheering everyone on with her usual heightened energy.

I watch the final group of teenagers hurtle themselves at the net, crawling like oversized ants on a mission, when Rocco sidles up to me.

"Are you going to write about this?" he asks, his tone less than warm.

"Max has asked me not to."

"But does that mean you won't?"

I turn to face him, this man who's clearly in Max's corner—and equally clearly suspicious of me. He's a big guy, probably at least 220 pounds, with short-cropped hair and shoulders that could block out the sun. "I want to show the country that he's more than just a party-boy prince."

"You mean the way you've reported on him for years."

Heat crawls up my neck, shame disguised as a flush.

"Isn't that right, Ms. Fontaine?"

I force my eyes to his. "You're right."

He regards me with surprise but doesn't respond.

I return my attention to Max. He's climbing commando-style under the net to a kid who's come to a stop. "He's so encouraging."

"That kid under the net is new. She came with their older brother, Hudson, for the first time today."

I watch as Max lies next to her, propped up on his elbows, talking in hushed tones with the teen. It takes a while, but eventually, she begins to crawl once more, with Max right beside her, and when they climb out the other end, he gives her a high five, and she beams at him like he's the best thing to happen to her all day.

"The person you talk about in your articles and on your TikToks is just one small facet of who he is, you know."

"Give me the Rocco perspective on the prince."

Rocco's features lift. "He's a good guy. The best. Sure, he has fun at parties. What young, single guy doesn't? But he's got a deeper side, too."

Max calls out to the girl as she tries to heave herself up the rope. "You can do it, Adella! You've got this!"

She tries and tries, sliding down the wall each time, until she lands in a defeated heap. Immediately, Max crouches down beside her, his hand on her shoulder. A few moments later, Max himself begins to climb the wall, his strong, muscular arms pulling him up and over as he calls out instructions to Adella. She follows behind, and when she's almost at the top, he reaches down and hauls her up and over with one strong arm.

"Look, I get it. You love to write about all the stupid things he does, and I'll admit, he's made some pretty dumb mistakes. But you? You've reported each and every one of them. Why is that?"

"As a journalist, it's my duty to—"

"Don't give me that crap," he says, interrupting me. "You know stories about him playing the fool will get people's attention."

It's as though I'm being told off for something I already know I've done wrong. Max is more than the person I've represented him as, and I need to right that wrong, starting from now.

I'm about to respond when Pippa arrives, her phone in hand.

"Fab, have you seen this?" she asks, and Rocco gives me a curt not of his head before he moves away to talk with one of the teens.

"Seen what?" I ask.

She hands me her phone. It's an article from The Post with the headline *Royal Correspondent or Royal Mystery?*

What the…?

I scan the text, my heart beating fast.

Why was it Fabiana Fontaine who won the contract to document HRH Prince Max? How did she manage to work her way into the inner sanctum of the royal family when she herself has been such a vocal commentator on Max's behavior over the years? Did the palace choose her because she's the superior journalist? Or did they choose her because she has the inside track on all things royal? Some may call it uncanny. Me? I call it suspicious…

"I'm sure it's just jealousy, but I thought you should see it," Pippa says. "Other journalists want to get to do what you're doing here."

I pull my lips into a smile, feigning nonchalance as I hand her back her phone. "Or just Miranda Thorne."

But the article has got me on edge. Miranda Thorne isn't just watching anymore, throwing snide remarks my way at a party. She's gone public.

What exactly is she getting at by calling me out on having some kind of inside track with royalty?

A prickle runs along my spine, tiny needles under my skin. I blow out a breath. She knows nothing, I tell myself. My cover is rock solid.

But as the afternoon's activities wrap up and the kids head to the showers, I can't help but worry that Miranda Thorne is on a mission, and all I can hope is that she meets a dead end sooner rather than later.

Chapter 15

Valentina

I find Max on the patio in the late afternoon sun, leaning back on one of the comfortable sofas, reading his phone. I fold my legs under myself and sink down into the cushion next to him.

"I brought you a drink of lemonade," I say, holding up two glasses.

"How do I know you haven't poisoned mine?" he asks, his lips lifting into a smile that tickles my belly.

I let out a surprised laugh. "Poison you? Max, if I were

going to do that, I'd wait until the end of our month together, not do it less than one week in." I hold one of the glasses out for him, and he takes it.

"It's so reassuring to know you've thought about this, Fabiana."

"Murder is probably only my third preferred option right now," I reply

"Dare I ask what your first is?"

Immediately, my head is filled with the idea of gripping the collar of his shirt, pulling him to me, and pressing my lips against his.

I clear my throat. *Not happening, Valentina.*

"Report you as you are, of course." I take a sip, savoring the sweet but tart homemade lemonade. "I want to document the youth program."

He presses his lips together. "We talked about this."

"I get that it's your own project, and that it's personal to you. But the Max I've seen today is so very different from the version of you the country sees. My directive was to show the country the real you. This is you."

Carefully, he places his lemonade on a side table. "I've seen what happens when the media gets involved with programs like this. They either sensationalize the kids' stories for sympathy points, or they turn it into some kind of 'Royalty Saves Poor Children' narrative that completely misses the point. This isn't about me looking good. It's about them having a safe space. That's why I've never publicized this."

I chew my lip. "I get where you're coming from, and I promise you, I don't want to make this into either a media circus or that narrative. We could have whatever conditions you want."

He studies my face. "What do you mean?"

"What if we make it about you leading by example? I

saw you out there with Adella. You didn't just encourage her; you did the course with her."

He shrugs as though doing an assault course is no big deal. "She needed to see how to do it."

"Exactly! You could do the same challenges as the kids. I could film you with your highs and lows, show that you're not this perfect, untouchable prince with the occasional poor decision making." I offer him a wry smile, and when he smiles back, I know I've got him.

"That could work."

I scoot closer to him in my excitement. "I know, right? Ledonia has seen you in the Royal Air Force. They've seen you go through rigorous training. But they've never seen what you're capable of. You're impressive, Max, and not just in your encouragement of the kids. You get your hands dirty."

He looks at me—really looks at me—and I can't help but notice the deep, chocolate brown of his eyes is flecked with gold, like autumn leaves before they fall.

Heat sparks low in my stomach, spreading like lava before I can stop it. I swallow hard, pretending to focus on anything else, but he's already everywhere around me. The scent of him, clouding my thoughts. The way that one look feels like a touch.

All I can think about is how it had felt during our impromptu archery lesson when he was so close behind me, his hands on mine as he guided my arrow, his breath warm on my neck, his voice low and intimate, rumbling through me.

Suddenly, I'm way too close to this man who fills my mind, who's been living rent free in my head, the man who's turning out to be everything I didn't know I was looking for.

But everything I want.

I need to break this spell, and I need to break it now.

So, I do what any sane woman who's dangerously close to catching feelings for an off-limits man would do. I lean as far away from him as physics will allow, bracing my hands behind me, my spine as stiff as a ruler.

Max's dark brows furrow as he takes in my impression of a human pretzel, his lips quirking—those lips I have absolutely no business wanting to kiss.

It does nothing to help the situation. My stomach swoops, hard enough that for one alarming second, I almost topple over.

And then, the worst happens. The seat cushion under my hands slides out from beneath me, and I literally tumble to the ground, falling in a heap of limbs like a woodpile.

That did *not* just happen.

One minute, we're talking like normal adults and the next, I'm falling to the ground like I'm a heroine in a 90s chick flick.

I scrunch my eyes shut in utter humiliation.

"Are you all right?" he asks, and I open one eye enough to see concern written across his handsome face. He reaches for me, pulling me up, and I stand, dazed, my pulse thudding.

"I'm…yes, thanks."

The blood in my veins has now been replaced by thick, gooey mortification. I turn and pick the seat cushion from the ground and slot it back in place, silently cursing it.

"What happened? One moment you were on the sofa, and the next… not."

"I, err…" I search my brain for a plausible excuse. "I was stretching, and I didn't expect the cushion to give way."

"Stretching," he repeats, his tone impassive.

I lift my chin. "That's right."

That mouth quirks once more, his eyes dancing. "Perhaps we should get you a yoga mat next time? I'm sure I can rustle one up for you."

"A mat. Yes. Good idea."

Get me out of here!

I've never been so thankful to see a group of teens begin to spill out of the house and onto the patio. Max tells them they need to start pitching their tents, and a few of them grab onto his arms, hauling him along with them. He looks over his shoulder at me and smiles, and I throw him a quick wave.

After I've regained what dignity I have left, I trail after them. I watch as they work together putting up tents, chatting and laughing together. If I hadn't known these kids were from difficult backgrounds, I would never have guessed it. They seem to like one another, and Max in particular, who chats freely with them, laughing at their jokes and cracking some of his own.

I sidle up to Pippa, who's looking distinctly green around the edges.

"Are you okay?" I ask.

She's holding her hands over her belly, her mouth down turned. "I'm not so good."

Before I have the chance to say anything, she darts behind a tree. I follow after her and find her doubled over on the ground. I crouch down beside her, placing my hand on her forehead. "Pippa, you're burning up!"

Her response is to groan, holding onto her belly some more.

"I'm going to get you out of here." I pull her to her feet and throw her arm around my shoulders so I can support her. She's floppy and unsteady on her feet.

"Thanks, Fab. You're fab. Do you get it?" she says weakly as I lead her across the lawn toward the house.

"I get it but save your strength. Where's your room?"

She tells me, and I walk her up the steps to the patio, pausing only for her to lose more of her lunch in one of the potted plants on the patio.

"What's happening?" Max asks as he jogs over to us.

"Pippa's not well. I'm taking her to her room. Can someone fetch a bowl and some water for her?"

"Of course." Max instructs one of the staff to do just that. "Here. Let me take her," he says, not pausing for my response as he lifts her into his arms like a romantic hero from a particularly romantic episode of *Bridgerton*.

I follow them up the stairs, and once we reach her room, he gently lays her down on her bed. A member of staff appears with a bowl, a glass of water, and a stack of towels.

"Did she eat something that could be causing this?" Max asks.

"I've no idea." I shake my head. And then it dawns on me. "The water! From the fountain. She drank it a few hours ago," I reply.

"That'll be the culprit." He turns to the woman. "Can you keep an eye on her? Report back to me? I need to get back to the kids."

"Of course, Maxie. Whatever you need," she replies with the same maternal smile Chef Margot gave him back in the palace kitchens.

Maxie? I file that one away for another time.

"I'll stay," I offer.

"It's all right," Nicole says. "You go and help the prince."

I give Pippa's hand a squeeze. "Feel better, Pippa."

"You're fab, Fab," she murmurs, her eyes half closed.

I smile. "You'll be fab again in no time. Promise."

With Nicole assuring us that she won't leave Pippa's side, I follow Max from the room.

"That was nice of you."

"You're the one who got all heroic and carried her up here."

"Yes, but you're the one who found her and took action."

"I just hope she'll be okay. Poor thing."

"She'll be bouncing off the walls again soon."

We return to the group, and Max immediately begins to work with the kids as they erect their tents around a central firepit.

"Are you here to help, miss?" asks a boy of about thirteen or fourteen with bright blond hair and freckles.

"Sure. Just tell me what to do. And call me Fabiana, okay?" I reply.

"Sure. I'm Cedric." He bounces on his feet as though he's got too much energy to contain within his young body.

"Great to meet you, Cedric. Do we need to put up a tent?"

"There's one over there." He gestures at a zipped-up bag near a large willow tree.

"Let's do it."

I collect the bag, and together we carry it to where Cedric wants to set it up.

I pull out poles and pegs and what must be the tent. I twist my mouth as I survey all the pieces. Most of the other tents are up already, so it can't be that hard. Can it?

"Okay, Cedric. Where do we begin?" I ask.

"Have you ever put a tent up before?"

"Nope. But there's a first time for everything, right?"

When I was little, our vacations would consist of us visiting my family's lake house, staying in our condo overlooking the Med. We travelled through North America when I was about nine and made it as far south as Australia the following year. I've seen tents, but that was as close as I've ever gotten to one. Right now, I'm hoping I can bluster my way through this.

I mean, how hard can it be?

I stare at the pile of green fabric and metal poles scattered across the grass.

"So, which end is up?" Cedric asks, holding a curved pole at arm's length as if it might bite him.

I grab the instruction sheet and squint at diagrams that look more like someone's idea of abstract art than anything. "Okay, it says here that the first step is to insert pole A into sleeve B."

A quick search for the items shows me nothing is labelled either A or B.

Fat lot of good these instructions will be.

Cedric has somehow managed to thread a pole through what is clearly meant to be the door. The tent now resembles a deflated balloon animal.

"Maybe we should start over?" I suggest, watching him wrestle with the tangled mess.

"Wait, I think I've got it!" Cedric yanks hard on the fabric. The entire structure collapses on top of him, leaving only his sneakers visible.

I search for the opening, lifting it up to see Cedric peering up at me. "We're not very good at this, are we?" I say.

He giggles, his shoulders beginning to shake. It's infectious, and before long, I'm giggling, too, both of us breaking into peals of laughter at our total ineptitude.

Max approaches us, and I do my best to hold in my laughter, but there's something so ridiculous about this situation—the collapsed disaster of a tent, the fact I just fell off a sofa to avoid having to get too close to him, not to mention that he's now looming over us like a giant, silhouetted against the sun.

"We're trying our best here, but it's not quite going our way. Is it, Cedric?" I say.

Cedric's response is to snort-giggle, his face turning beet red. He sets me off again, and the situation isn't helped when Toffee leaps on top of the tent and instantly disappears, only for her head to pop back up a moment later, wild-eyed and excited.

"Do you need some help?" Max offers.

"Do we need help, Cedric?" I ask, and we both snort-laugh once more. Looking back up at Max, I try my best to pull myself together. "We're trying, but it's not exactly going to plan here."

"Fabiana's never put a tent together before," Cedric says.

"Cedric! You're totally ratting me out!" I protest.

"All right, you two. Hop up. Let the tent master sort this out," Max says. He cracks his fingers.

"Tent master?" I question as I help Cedric from the tent.

"I'm a man of many talents," he replies.

We work fast together, the three of us, me handing Max the items he asks for, and soon enough Cedric's tent is standing proud alongside the others. Out of the corner of my eye, I watch Max as he works, his movements sure and competent.

Something shifts in my chest, sharp and unexpected. I tell myself not to read anything into it, but I'm in dangerous territory with him. The man I'm seeing now—patient, kind, great with kids—is the kind of man I could so easily fall for. Not a prince, not a title, just... Max.

But that's the problem. He can never be *just Max*, and I

can never be just Valentina, no matter how much I might want to be. Between us lie years of family history, a web of lies about who I really am, and the simple fact that princes don't fall for journalists who've spent their careers mocking them.

No matter how much my heart wants to forget all of that when he smiles at me, no matter how right it feels when we work together like this, the reality remains: I'm Lady Valentina Romano, daughter of a disgraced lord, pretending to be someone else while developing feelings—real, undeniable feelings—for the son of the king who destroyed my world.

Some chasms are simply too wide to bridge, no matter how much I might want to try.

Chapter 16

Max

"Don't get too close to the fire, Shawnee. You'll burn your stick," I say as I show the fourteen-year-old how to hold her marshmallow over the open fire. Let's just say we've had one too many minor fire incidents involving marshmallows and sticks over the last few years for me not to show a newbie how to do it.

"But then it takes ages," Shawnee complains.

"Good things take time," I say, sounding wiser than I am. "It'll be worth it in the end. Who needs another marshmallow?" I ask the group, and a bunch of hands fly into the air.

I hop off the log to collect a fresh bag when Fabiana beats me to it.

"I'll pass them out," she says. "It's the least I can do, considering my recent tent failures."

"Singular. Not multiple."

"Let's face it, it would have been multiple, given half the chance," she replies with a self-effacing smile that lights up her face.

"Putting up tents is not in your skill set, I'll give you that."

"But making s'mores is."

"S'mores? The American treat?"

She gives an easy laugh. "Are you telling me you've never made s'mores before, Max?" she asks, playfully throwing her hands on her hips.

"I've seen people make them in movies. Why, are they good?"

"Good? They're freaking amazing."

"How do you know how to make them?"

"My family stayed on one of the Great Lakes one summer when I was a kid. We made s'mores over the fire every night."

"S'more skills, huh?"

"Yup. Do you have any graham crackers and chocolate?"

"I know we have chocolate bars because the kids love them, and we have some crackers for cheese, sweet and salty."

"The sweet ones will do nicely. In the kitchen, I assume?"

"That's right."

"Okay. I'll be right back."

I can't help but watch as she walks away, her form illuminated by the glowing fire. Her short-clad hips sway from side to side as she saunters across the lawn, her ever-present ponytail swinging.

It takes effort to drag my gaze away.

Of all the problems this woman has caused in my life, proving to be off-the-scale sexy has got to be the most unexpected.

But she's more than just sexy. She's the whole package. Funny, smart, kind, a little mysterious, and as she reveals more and more of herself to me, I'm finding myself in deeper than I ever meant to be.

It's not just attraction anymore. It's something that's starting to feel a lot more real.

A moment later she returns, her arms heavy laden with packets of crackers and bars of chocolate.

"Did you clean the entire kitchen out of supplies?" I ask, eyeing her stash.

She grins at me. "I think so." Laying the food items out on a nearby table, she addresses the group. "Who wants to make s'mores? So much better than just plain old toasted marshmallows."

She's instantly surrounded by eager teens, and I hang back, watching her. She only just met these kids today and already she has a rapport with them. She's at ease, as though she deals with moody, sometimes challenging teenagers every day of her life. And they seem to like her, too. The way she and Cedric got the giggles while working on their tent was… well, it was adorable.

"Once you've toasted your marshmallows, bring them back here and we'll stick them between the crackers and chocolate. See?" She demonstrates how to slide the stick from the toasted marshmallow, held between the crackers and chocolate. All eyes are riveted on her. "*Et voila*! A s'more. I should taste test this, right?" she asks, and I laugh along with the others.

She takes a bite, and her eyes roll back in her head as she savors the sweetness. She grins around her mouthful. "Delib-fuff!" she pronounces.

And there's that word again, springing into my mind. *Adorable*. Adorable and fun and kind and witty and clever and gorgeous and hot. So. Freaking. Hot.

Who knew someone talking with their mouth full of s'more could hit me right in the chest?

I don't want to want this woman, but I do, and it's getting harder not to act on it.

I make some s'mores along with the rest of the group, aware of how Fabiana is constantly on hand to help anyone who needs it, assisting kids when their marshmallows won't slide off their sticks, showing them just the right amount of toasting to melt it so it turns to liquid goo inside the crackers and chocolate.

Once everyone has had their fill, we sit around the campfire telling stories until it's time for the kids to head to bed. Fabiana disappears to check on Pippa, and Rocco, Dante, and I make sure everyone is comfortable, unrolling sleeping bags, providing pillows, and all the things you've got to do to get a bunch of teens high on sugar off to sleep.

"She's not what I expected," Rocco says once the last of the kids is tucked up in their sleeping bags.

"What do you mean?"

"In her articles, she comes across as snarky and rude, sometimes simpering, but I think she's seeing something different in you."

"What's she said?"

"Only that she can see you're not the guy she's reported on all these years. Do you trust her?"

If Rocco had asked me that question only a week ago,

my answer would have been a resounding *no*. I would never have trusted the Fabiana Fontaine I knew from her articles. Not in a million years.

But this Fabiana? The multi-layered woman I'm seeing now? She's a different creature altogether.

"I think I do."

"You think, or you know?" he questions.

And therein lies the million-euro question. Despite everything I thought I knew about her, everything she's written about me, my gut tells me I can. Maybe it's the way she looks at me, like I'm not a headline. Or the way she softens when she thinks no one's watching.

"Just…watch your back, okay, Max?"

"I will," I reassure him.

Rocco and Dante say good night and disappear into their respective tents, and I sit by the fire, lost in thought, when Fabiana sits back down beside me.

"How's Pippa?" I ask.

"Doing a little better. She's sleeping now. I had some electrolytes in my suitcase, so she's been sipping those to rehydrate. Nicole's been doing a great job looking after her."

"She's amazing."

"Is that right, Maxie?"

She's grinning at me, and it makes me laugh. "A childhood name."

"I think it's sweet. It's obvious they love you."

"It's mutual."

A log on the fire drops, sending a shower of sparks into the dark night air.

"Tell me how the program came about," she asks.

"I started it when one of my charities took me to a women's shelter. I met damaged children and their mothers, families forced to escape difficult situations. They showed the kind of strength and resilience I'd never needed in my life."

She nods, allowing me to continue. "There was one kid in particular. Bruno. He was only twelve or thirteen, but his eyes showed experience way beyond his years. He and his mum and younger sister had been living in the shelter for about 3 months. His mum didn't speak much Ledonian, so he took it on himself to navigate the benefit system so they could get what small amount of money the government offered.

"But you know what struck me the most? It wasn't his maturity. It was the way his eyes were constantly assessing adults to work out if they were a friend or otherwise. I got the distinct impression he'd encountered too much of the otherwise."

"Poor kid."

I swallow, remembering how my conversation with him had stuck with me for weeks. How I'd felt compelled to do something, anything, to help him and others like him. "Kids ought to get the chance to be just kids."

Something passes across her face. "You're right. You can never get those years back. Once innocence is lost, it's lost forever."

I watch her for a beat. Is that from personal experience? Did something happen to her in childhood that meant she had to grow up faster than she should?

"Is there a story there?" I ask tentatively.

"No story," she says, and her tone is a touch too light. Forced, even.

It leaves me with more questions than answers.

"You've learned about my past. Tell me about yours."

"Oh, it's all pretty standard stuff really. School, family dinners, the usual. Nothing as exciting as growing up in a palace, that I assure you."

It's as though she's hiding something, but I've no clue what it is. "Are your parents still together?" I ask, wondering if the thing that made her grow up fast was divorce.

"My mom passed away when I was little," she replies, her eyes concentrated on the fire.

My heart aches for her. "I'm so sorry, Fabiana."

She lifts her shoulders. "It was a long time ago. It was just my dad and me." She breaks off. "I spent a lot of time with my grandmother growing up. She taught me a lot about the world."

It's clear she doesn't want to talk anymore about her dad, and I'm not going to push it. As much as I want to know more about her, I want her to open up when she's ready.

"Tell me about your grandmother."

Her features relax. "She's the best. We live in the city together. She's my strongest advocate, always telling me I can do whatever I put my mind to. This is the longest I've gone without seeing her since I was twelve."

"Do you miss her?"

"I've been busy." She takes a breath and turns to face me. "So, tell me. How did you go from a conversation with Bruno to starting this program?"

It's an obvious deflection. I'm not going to press her. I'm hopeful that one day she'll trust me enough to tell me everything about her.

Baby steps.

"I wanted to set up something I could be involved with personally, not just a box-checking exercise or raising money. And let's face it, there are only so many slip n' slides to throw yourself down."

Her laughter is soft, and it warms my belly. "I'll start filming you tomorrow. What's first on the agenda?"

"We're heading out for a climb."

"Perfect." She moves a little closer, and it isn't clear whether it's to take advantage of the fire or to be nearer to me.

Although I know what I want it to be.

We're close enough that I could reach out and touch her, and around us the atmosphere feels charged, like the air before a thunderstorm.

In the firelight, her features soften, and for a fleeting second, I have the strangest sensation that I've known her face for longer than just this past week, not just from her videos and photos.

I shake the thought away.

She looks at me with those impossibly big, gorgeous eyes, and I find it increasingly difficult to remember why keeping my distance seemed such an important thing to do. Because right now, as the dying light of the campfire catches the gold in her hair, I want nothing more than to discover whether her lips are quite as soft and pillowy as they look, whether she would feel quite as good in my arms as I suspect she would.

Suddenly, I don't want to just think about it anymore. I lean towards her, watching her face carefully.

When she doesn't pull away, I have all the sign I need.

I reach out and cup her face in my hands, and she lets out a light whimper, the soft skin of her cheeks making my heart beat faster. Her lips part, her chest rising and falling with increasing speed, her scent filling the surrounding air.

"Fabiana," I murmur, her name slipping out rougher than I mean it to, weighted with everything that's grown between us since the day we met.

She goes perfectly still, her body tense. "I should…the kids might…I've got to…" she stammers before she springs to her feet, this usually articulate woman suddenly incapable of completing a single sentence.

What just happened?

Dazed, I look up at her.

Did I read the signs wrong? Does she not feel this thing between us?

"Of course," I say, my voice hoarse with desire. I clear my throat. "I'm sorry, Fabiana. I…overstepped."

"It's fine. Really. But I should head to bed." She backs away from me before she turns on her heel and begins to march off toward the house.

I'm an idiot. A total freaking idiot. I've pushed her away when all I wanted to do was pull her closer, to show her how I feel about her. To come clean and finally lay it on the table.

I jump up and follow her.

I've never experienced rejection before, and I'm not sure what to do.

"Fabiana, wait," I say, catching up with her in a few short steps.

"It's late, Max, and I have work to do," she says without breaking her stride.

I reach out and place my hand gently on her forearm, and she snaps her attention to me, her face a study in alarm. "Fabiana, I really am sorry."

"About what?" she says with a breeziness we both know is totally forced.

"We almost kissed back there."

"If we had, it would have been a mistake."

"Would it?" I ask softly.

She lifts her chin. "Yes, Max. It would."

"I thought it would have been…nice."

Kissing Fabiana would have been an entire universe

more than just *nice*, but I can tell she's completely spooked, and the last thing I want is to upset her further.

"Nice," she repeats, and for just a moment, her mask slips and I see something that looks like longing on her face. "This can't happen, Max."

I place a hand carefully on her forearm, and she sucks in a breath at the contact. "Is it because we're working together?"

"Yes, and…no."

I make an exasperated sound. "Help me understand, because there is something between us, isn't there? I feel it, more and more each day."

She places a finger over my mouth, her skin briefly brushing my lips. "Don't. Please. There are things you don't appreciate about me."

"You can tell me anything. Anything. I want to know. I want to understand you."

She lowers her head, and I want to fold my arms around her, tell her it's okay, tell her that whatever it is, I can take it.

"I can't," she murmurs. She takes a step back, and I let my hand drop from her arm. "Good night, Max."

I'm not going to fight her on this. She's made it clear that even though I know she wants this, she's fighting it, fighting *us*, even when it's written all over her face.

As I watch her go, I roil like boiling water, restless and ready to spill over, my breath ragged, my heart pounding.

What just happened? One minute we're talking, relaxed by the fire, close enough to kiss, and the next, she's gone, pushing me away as she leaves.

Never in my life before have I wanted a woman so much and then been rejected by her. It's a new sensation for me, and one I have no clue how to deal with.

What is she hiding? What could be so big that she can't

let herself be with me? And why would kissing me, something that's so right, cause such panic in her?

Despite her warnings, I find myself more determined than ever to learn everything about this woman who's utterly bewitched me, body and mind. Because if there's one thing I know for certain it's that I'm falling for her, and no amount of reason is going to save me from it.

Chapter 17

Valentina

THE EARLY MORNING sun creeps across my bed, and I lean back on the pillow, listening to the dawn chorus echo around the mountains as I slowly wake up. It brings back childhood memories of waking up not too far from here, leaping out of my bed to begin my day feeding the goats, baking bread, traipsing around after my papa on the farm.

I stretch my arms above my head and let out a sigh before my mind turns to Max.

My chest tightens.

Last night, he wanted to kiss me, and I was so very close to letting it happen. It would have been so easy simply to surrender to the moment, to give in to my ever-growing feelings for him. To fall into his arms and show him exactly how much he's worked his way into my heart this past week.

If I were just Fabiana Fontaine, journalist, I would have let it happen. No doubt. I find him utterly intriguing. The program he's running, the way he is with the teens, the way his friends show obvious loyalty and love for him, even the way he is with Toffee.

But I'm not. I'm Valentina Romano, daughter of the disgraced Lord Romano, a woman who has been forced to hide her true identity from the world for her entire adult life.

Valentina cannot fall for the son of the king responsible for that.

It's unthinkable.

Impossible.

No matter how much I want it.

I push myself out of bed and pull back the curtains. The blue of the sky is rapidly being taken over by dark, skittering clouds, and there's a distinct smell of rain in the air.

I collect my wash bag and towel and make my way down the hallway. I knock lightly on Pippa's door and then push it open. She's lying in bed in the dim light. I watch her rhythmic breathing for a moment, and not wanting to wake her, I turn and creep out of the room.

"Is that you, Fab?" a croaky voice asks.

"I'm sorry I woke you."

"It's fine."

"How are you?"

"Better than yesterday. I'm so sorry."

"Don't be sorry. Do you think you could eat anything? Maybe some dry crackers?"

"I do."

"I'll get you some once I've had a shower."

"I might sleep some more until then."

I close the door quietly and head to the bathroom. When I get there, the door is closed, so I knock tentatively. When no one answers, I push it open only to become swamped in steam. Through the mist, my eyes land on a lone figure, wearing nothing but a towel, his back to me.

Max.

"I'm so sorry," I mutter, stumbling back.

As Max turns, the steam begins to evaporate, and I can see his hair is damp, and droplets of water cling to his broad shoulders and shapely pecs. He's holding a toothbrush in his mouth, and without giving permission, my eyes roll over him, taking in the sprinkling of hair across his chest, his taut belly, the way his towel is slung low on his hips.

I suck in a breath, rooted to the spot.

He removes the toothbrush. "Good morning."

I should look away. I should *run* away.

But all I do is gawk at this Adonis of a man, wondering what it would be like to be held in his arms, to run my fingers over his muscular chest, the touch of his lips against mine.

Stop it!

"Err…hi," I mutter as I back away further.

The corners of his mouth quirk. "You're staring, Fabiana."

Of course I'm staring. Have you seen *yourself?*

With the strength of Thor, I wrench my gaze away. "I'll come back later when you're…finished."

"I'm nearly done," he calls out, but I'm already

dashing back down the hallway, my cheeks flaming hot, closing the door behind myself as I reach my room.

I scrunch my eyes shut, humiliated, willing the image of him to disappear from my mind. But there he is, looking all tall and muscular and sexy, his body glistening, his lip curving into a soft, teasing smile.

Now that he showed me what he feels for me last night, resisting him is going to take a will of steel.

I pull on a pair of shorts and T-shirt. I'm not going to risk heading back to the bathroom. Instead, I make my way down to the kitchen where Rocco is cooking breakfast.

"Morning, Rocco," I say brightly.

He turns to me, and I wonder how much of Max and my interaction around the fire he heard last night. "Hey."

"Did you sleep well?"

"Up at the crack of dawn, thanks to the birds," he replies as he returns his attention to whisking eggs in a large bowl.

"Can I help?"

Being busy is so much better than thinking right now.

"You can heat up the baked beans."

"I can do that. Are they in the pantry?"

"There's a few big cans on the table behind you."

I turn and spot the cans. I rummage through some of the drawers, looking for a can opener, finally locating one. Rocco works in silence as I set about my task, opening the cans and pouring the contents into a big pot. I light an element on the gas hob, collect a wooden spoon, and start stirring.

"I don't understand why anyone wants to eat this," I say.

"Look, Fabiana," Rocco says, turning to me. "It must be obvious to you that I don't trust you, but I'm willing to try, for Max's sake."

"You're a good friend."

"I don't think it's easy being him."

I turn the heat down and place the wooden spoon on the counter. "How so?"

"He's grown up in the public eye with people judging him." He shoots me a pointed look, clear he counts me in the ranks of those people. "At the risk of making him sound like a poor little rich boy, I don't think it was easy for him to be the last-born son, with certain expectations about what he should do with his life."

"You mean he was never going to inherit the throne."

"Yeah, but more than that, he didn't get a choice about what he did with his life. He was expected to go into the Royal Air Force, just like his brother did, but he can never have a career like you or I can."

"He has this program," I say, looking out the kitchen window at some of the kids slowly emerging from their tents. "Which he's obviously passionate about."

"Don't get me wrong, I think the life of Max is probably pretty good on many levels. But he could never be a lawyer or a scientist or all the things you and I could be."

"Believe me, I could never be a lawyer *or* a scientist," I reply, hoping to lighten the mood. When he doesn't smile, I say, "I get what you mean. He didn't have a choice in who he could be."

"But I do have a choice in what I have for breakfast, and I hate baked beans," a voice says, and we both turn to see Max standing in the doorway. Even though he's now fully dressed in a pair of pants and a polo shirt, his hair now dry, the sight of him makes my whole body buzz, and I quickly turn my attention to the pot of beans.

Toffee bounces in beside him, her tail wagging as she sniffs the ground.

"That's something you and Fabiana have in common," Rocco says. "Isn't that right?"

I chance looking at Max, and I swear my heart skips a beat. "You don't like baked beans?"

I shake my head. "It physically pains me to have to stir them right now."

"Thank you for your service," he says with a grin, and I wonder how he can be so relaxed and easy around me with what happened just now in the bathroom, let alone what happened between us last night.

He rubs his hands together. "I'll feed Toffee, and then shall I get on with cooking the bacon? I'm starving."

"The rabble is awakening, so now's good," Rocco says.

Max places Toffee's bowl on the floor for her, and she gobbles it up. He then slices open packets of bacon and sets about frying it up.

The three of us work together. Whenever Max comes near me, electricity sparks inside, and I do my best to push it away.

"Are you still going to do all the activities today for me to film?" I ask.

"Why wouldn't I?" he replies.

Because you wanted to kiss me last night and I rejected you? Because you laid your cards on the table and I kept mine close to my chest?

I bite my lip. "No reason. Is it okay if I get some footage now?"

"The world needs to see Prince Max cooking bacon," Rocco agrees.

"Be my guest," Max replies, and I pull my phone from my back pocket and begin to film him as he turns the sizzling bacon with a pair of tongs. I pan out to show the kitchen, with Rocco cooking the scrambled eggs, then focus on the attentive Toffee on the floor, hoping for scraps, before I zoom back in on Max as he concentrates on his work, his brows pulled together in concentration.

Why does he need to look so darn good all the time? Even when he's cooking over a hot stove, he looks like he could effortlessly grace the cover of GQ magazine.

He's not playing fair.

My phone rings in my hand, making me jump, and I glance at the screen to see it's Mr. Beckman calling. Alarm bells instantly begin to sound in my head, and I press answer, stepping away from the men for some privacy.

"Hi, Mr. Beckman," I say. "Is everything okay?"

"Valentina, I'm so glad I got you," he says in a rush. "Your Nona is just fine, but she did have a little accident."

My heart leaps into my mouth. "An accident?" I repeat, my voice breathy and thin, like it belongs to somebody in another room. "What kind of accident?"

"She had a fall, and luckily, I was there with her. I called an ambulance—"

"An ambulance!" My shocked voice is so much louder than I expected, ringing around the room, and I clamp a hand over my mouth.

It's too late. Both men are now watching me, and Max has left the stove, concern written across his face.

"An x-ray will tell us more, but she might have broken her ankle. I assure you, she's in good hands, Valentina."

"Where is she?"

"She's at Villadorata Central. But you—"

"I'll be there as soon as I can," I reply, my mind reeling. My nona is hurt, and I wasn't there for her. Guilt twists my belly. My nona needs me. I have to get to her.

"She'll understand that you're working and—"

I cut him off. "Mr. Beckman, I'll be there as soon as I can. Does she have her phone with her?"

There's no way I'm not going to Nona. She's my everything. The thought of her being in pain without me there is too much to bear.

"I'm bringing her phone to her this morning."

"When did this happen?"

"Last night."

"Last night?" I gasp. Why didn't he call me then?

"We were out when she tripped over a curb, poor thing. We iced it and got her comfortable as we waited for the ambulance. She's a tough cookie, your grandmother. Took it all in her stride."

I smile despite my worries. That's Nona. She's where I get my backbone. "Thanks for being there for her."

"You know I would do anything for your grandmother," he replies, which goes way beyond neighborly concern. But I don't have time to unpack that right now. I need to get back to Villadorata, and fast.

I hang up the phone. A warm hand lands on my shoulder, and I turn and look up into Max's face, tight with worry. "What's happened?"

"My grandmother. She's hurt and in the hospital back in Villadorata. I-I need to go to her."

"Of course you do. I'll drive you to the station," he says. "Rocco, can you and Dante hold the fort here?"

"Sure thing," Rocco replies.

Max places his arm around my shoulder and gives me a squeeze. "You'll get to her."

I dash back to my room where I hurriedly throw things into my bag, tearing back down the stairs and out the front door, where the rain that was threatening the sky earlier has now set in full force. Max and Toffee are already waiting for me in one of the Range Rovers, the engine running, and when I climb into the passenger seat, Toffee immediately climbs onto my lap, trying to lick my cheek.

"I can put her in the back," Max offers.

I stroke her warm fur, and she reaches up to lick my ear. "No. Actually, she's comforting."

The tires spray gravel behind us as he takes off at speed.

"What happened with your grandmother?" he asks as the car burns down the long, winding driveway.

"She fell. My neighbor, Mr. Beckman, thinks she might have broken her ankle last night. She's in the hospital."

The windscreen wipers are going at full tilt, and the rain only seems to be getting heavier.

"I'm so sorry to hear that. She means the world to you, doesn't she?"

My chest tightens. "She does."

Max turns onto the main road, and we wind our way further down the hill toward Castelvino, where the train brought us only a day ago, perched high in the hills. "In that case, let's get you to the station as fast as we can."

"Thank you so much, Max. I really appreciate it."

"Of course. I only wish I could do more for you."

"Taking me to catch the train is more than enough."

What almost happened last night hangs between us, but neither of us mentions it. What would be the point? He must feel rejected, and I feel…well, I feel a lot of things, none of which I can share with him.

Even though having to leave to see my injured grandmother isn't ideal, at least it'll give me some much-needed breathing space from him.

He pulls the car into an angled parking space outside the train station in Castelvino. Its station has a small, rustic platform that clings to the mountainside, with goats grazing nearby. Max kills the engine, and I hop out, immediately getting drenched by the downpour. Max materializes at my side holding an umbrella, but it's too late. I'm pretty sure I'm giving my best impersonation of a drowned rat right now.

"I'll come in with you. Make sure you get on the train okay," he says over the sound of the rain landing on the car.

"You don't have to."

"I want to."

I nod. "All right."

He holds the umbrella over both our heads as we make our way into the station. The place is empty but for a woman in uniform at a kiosk. I rush over to her.

"Can I please have a ticket for the next train leaving for Villadorata?" I ask, removing my rain-splattered glasses and giving them a quick clean with the edge of my T-shirt.

"I'm not sure when that will be, dear," she replies, her kindly face lifted in a smile. I notice her name tag says Prunella.

"Isn't there a train timetable?" I ask, confused. This might be a tiny station in the middle of virtually nowhere, but surely, they have scheduled trains.

"There's flooding on the tracks from this rain, dear. All services are cancelled until it lets up and gets the chance to dry out."

I gawk at her in disbelief. "But I need to get to Villadorata. It's vital that I get there as soon as I can."

Her eyes land on Max. "Your Royal Highness," she says with a grin and an incline of her head.

"Good to see you, Prue," he replies. "What's happening?"

"There are no trains running at the moment. I was telling your friend here that the tracks are flooded."

"Surely there's a replacement bus service or something?" I say, panic rising. If I can't get to Villadorata to see Nona, I don't know what I'll do.

"Have you seen the weather? It's raining cats and dogs out there," she says as though we weren't aware.

"Buses can drive through the rain," I retort. "I've been on them plenty of times."

All she does is shake her head. "I'm sorry, dear. You'll need to wait out the storm. I'm heading home myself shortly."

Wait out the storm. I can do that. How long can it last?

Resolute, I reply, "In that case I'll wait."

"All right. I'm closing the kiosk for now. No point being here when there are no trains running." She pulls the sign that says *Closed* from behind the kiosk.

"How long before the trains will be running again, do you think, Prue?" Max asks.

"A day or two, sir," she replies brightly, as though it's no big deal at all. And to her, I'm sure it's not.

To me? Well, that's another story altogether.

"*Two days?*" I repeat, my eyes wide. "I can't wait two days. What am I going to do?"

He places a warm hand over mine. "I'll drive you."

"All the way to Villadorata?" I ask in shock.

"Of course."

I look out at the tracks where the rain is still heaving. "But the rain."

"I've driven through rain before. I'm sure we'll be fine," he says, his voice so warm and reassuring it makes me want to hug him with gratitude.

That's the last thing I can allow myself to do.

"What about the program? The kids? You're needed here, not driving me around the countryside."

"Rocco and Dante can run the program with their eyes closed. I'll message them that we've been called away. I can take you to Villadorata and be back here tomorrow."

To my surprise, my throat heats and tears prick my eyes, and I blink them away.

Spending the next few hours in the car with Max isn't exactly giving me the space I need right now. But I'm not going to look a gift horse in the mouth, as they say. I have no choice but to take him up on his offer if I want to get to Nona.

"You're so kind. Thank you." I shiver, my wet clothes clinging to my body.

"You need a change of clothes," Max says as he takes his jacket off and pulls it around my shoulders, just as he did on the palace balcony that time. It's warm and smells of him, and my heart squeezes.

"Come on. Let's get going." He turns to Prunella. "Thank you for your help. Prue. Send my best to Isaac and the kids."

"I will, sir," she replies with a smile.

We make our way back outside, and the rain seems to be easing.

"Why don't you get a change of clothes? You're a drowned rat."

I give a shiver, right on cue. "Good idea."

Like the gentleman he is, Max walks me to the back of the car, holding the umbrella above our heads, where I collect some dry clothes from my suitcase.

"Here, take this." He offers me his umbrella. "Go back into the station to get changed, and I'll wait in the car."

I dart up the steps back inside, find the Ladies', and then hurriedly peel my damp clothes off. It's never easy putting dry clothes on when your skin is damp, and I wrestle with my jeans, jumping up and down in the stall, before I finally button them up. Then, I pull the dry T-shirt over my head. My hair is damp, so I smooth it back into its ponytail as best I can.

I'm not exactly Instagram-ready, but it'll have to do.

Climbing into the car, I offer Max something from my suitcase.

He eyes it dubiously. "Why are you giving me a pink sweater?"

"Because it's a bit baggy on me and might be the right size for you."

He seems to think it over for a moment before he reaches behind his head and in one swift move, he removed his top to reveal his impressive torso.

As much as my instinct is to gawk at this total Adonis at my side, I pull my gaze away as he pulls the sweater on.

"How do I look?" he asks, and I turn to see what is ordinarily a super baggy and comfy sweater on me, straining across his broad shoulders and sculpted pecs.

I bite back a smile. "You look so pretty."

He mimes sweeping his hair from his shoulder. "That's the look I'm aiming for."

"Well, you nailed it."

"At least it's dry."

"Dry and pretty," I correct, and he lets out a low laugh as Toffee climbs back onto my lap, and we begin to head south along the winding, narrow, mountainous road through the drumming rain.

"You're so kind to do this for me, Max," I say as the small town gives way to trees.

"I'm not exactly going to leave you to wait for a train that's unlikely to come for two days," he replies. "And besides, with this rain, there'll be twenty-odd kids stuck inside back at the house. I'd much rather be here."

He's only being nice. He would prefer to be working on his passion project with his friends rather than traipsing me halfway across the country, the woman who rejected him only last night.

But the fact of the matter remains: he's here with me now, stuck in this car, going out of his way to take me to my grandmother, and it's hard not to let that work its way into my heart.

Max reaches for the radio dial. "Would you mind if I put some music on?"

"Sure."

His arm brushes against mine as he adjusts the volume, and I suck in a breath. The small space of the car seems to amplify everything between us.

Soft music fills the space, a Taylor Swift song I recognize about being in love.

"Toffee looks comfortable," he says as he eyes the puppy in my lap.

I stroke her fur as she sleeps in my lap, curled up like a warm croissant. "She won't fit on anyone's lap soon enough."

"That won't stop her trying," he says with a laugh. "Tell me about your grandmother."

We pass a petrol station with its lights bright against the rain.

"She's my rock. She's always in my corner, no matter what, and I've put her through some stuff."

"Sounds like a story."

"Just usual teenage rebellion types of things."

It's the truth, just not the whole truth.

"You know a lot about me, and we need to address the imbalance."

"You want me to tell you about myself?"

"Anything and everything."

I want to. Oh, how I want to talk to him, as in really, really talk, about everything. About who I am, about my family, about what my life is like, pretending to be someone else. And most of all, I want to talk to him about the way I feel when he looks at me with heat in his chocolate eyes, the way I've got these new, big feelings for the man I once thought was a waste of taxpayers' money.

The man who's reached a part of me no one else has.

"Can we do that another time? Like Toffee, I'm tired," I lie, guilt twisting a knot in my stomach.

"Of course," he replies.

I'm taking advantage of his kind nature, but what can I do? Tell him who I really am? How his family and mine are connected?

Nope. Never.

I lean my head against the window and close my eyes. I'm hyperaware of every small movement he makes in the driver's seat, turning the wheel, slowing the car to make turns.

"Thank you for doing this, Max. You didn't have to."

"Yes, I did."

Something in his voice makes me open my eyes to look at him, but he's focused on the road ahead, his jaw set with an emotion I can't quite read.

As the rain pounds harder against the windshield, I know this journey is going to test every last bit of resolve I have left.

Chapter 18

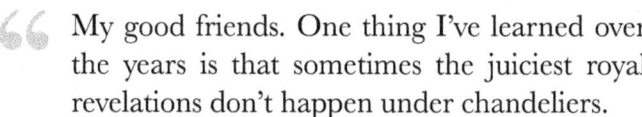 My good friends. One thing I've learned over the years is that sometimes the juiciest royal revelations don't happen under chandeliers.

Picture this: torrential rain, a washed-out road, and your ever-devoted royal correspondent stranded in a quaint inn with none other than Prince Maximilien. When I received worrying family news, he didn't grin his way past it. He simply showed up. He was thoughtful, helpful, and kind. The kind of prince anyone would want sailing to her rescue, looking dashing on a white horse.

Perhaps the storm revealed more than washed-out roads. Perhaps it revealed a side of Max the world hasn't seen before, and one this correspondent isn't quite sure how to dismiss.

Yours in sogginess,

Fabiana Fontaine xx

#StormboundWithaPrince
#MadMaxOrMrDarling

Max

I GRIP the steering wheel as we take a hairpin turn, descending the hill in increasingly treacherous conditions as though we're crawling under the obstacle course's net. We've been stuck behind a truck for the last handful of kilometers with no opportunity to overtake, and the rain seems to be becoming increasingly persistent with each passing minute.

After learning the trains weren't running, driving had seemed like the logical plan. But now, seeing the debris on the road from the storm, the wind whipping around the car as the rain falls, I'm not so sure.

Fabiana has been trying to get a hold of her grandmother, but thanks to the patchy service in the mountains, and the impact of the weather, she's not had any success.

The tension sparking from her is like a fireworks display, the love she has for her grandmother clear.

"Hello? Nona? Oh, thank goodness I've got a hold of you!" She says in a rush.

Her eyes flash to mine and I give her a thumbs up.

"Mr. Beckman told me what happened. Are you okay?" There's a pause as she waits for her grandmother's response. "I'm on my way...Yes, of course I have to come...Because I love you and you're hurt..." She pauses again, listening, and then turns to me. "I'm with him right now, as it happens. He's driving me back to the city because the trains aren't running."

There's another pause, and then she glances at me before she looks away, murmuring, "It turns out I was wrong."

I bite back a smile as I follow the truck around another corner, the windscreen wipers doing double time. She was wrong about *me*. In one short week, she's seen more of who I really am. Yes, she shut me down last night. But there was something in her eyes, in her shallow breathing, that told me she wanted to kiss me as much as I did her. A fire, burning bright.

She has her reasons. She's meant to be working with me, reporting on 'the real Max'. But what I feel for her goes way beyond that, and as we sit side by side, Toffee sleeping on her lap, I can't help but hope that she can see I'm worth the risk.

Because it feels to me that she is.

"You were doing *what*? Nona, at your age?... No, of course. I'm very pleased Mr. Beckman is a wonderful dancer, but maybe try doing something less physical next time? Like playing bingo, or watching a movie..."

I chuckle. Fabiana's grandmother sounds a lot like her granddaughter. A go-getter.

"Nona? Hello?" She looks at her screen. "Dang it. We've been cut off."

"At least you got a hold of her."

"Can you believe she was out dancing with our neighbor?" she says, but there's a lightness in her tone that wasn't there before.

Talking with her grandmother has set her mind at ease.

"Why can't she go dancing?"

"Because she's old," she protests.

"How old?"

"She's seventy-one."

"So, you're going to give up dancing by that age?"

"Maybe?"

I let out a laugh.

"What?"

"I'm not much of a dancer—you've said so yourself in at least one article—but I fully intend to keep on doing everything I do right now for as long as my body will let me."

"You've been planning for your retirement? I suppose you are twenty-seven," she teases.

"Not exactly planning, but you get one life, and you need to live it. It sounds to me that your grandmother has been having some fun while you've been away."

She waves her hand in the air. "Oh, he's just our neighbor. He promised to check in on her for me. She's alone right now and she's not used to me being away for this long."

"Ah."

"What does 'ah' mean?"

"Does your nona dance with all her neighbors?"

She snickers. "I don't think so."

"Then perhaps they were on a date?"

"A date?" she guffaws. "Not likely."

I shoot her a sideways glance. "Because she's seventy-one?"

"Well, yes, that, but also because Mr. Beckman's our neighbor."

"And neighbors don't date."

She opens her mouth to respond, and then closes it again, her eyebrows pulled together.

"I might be wrong," I say.

"You are," she says with more confidence than I suspect she's feeling, by the look on her face.

I slow the car as we drive past an ancient Medieval town wall, crumbling but still intact, and enter a quaint village. The car bumps over the cobble stone streets, passed the solid stone buildings, and I spot a little café with a green and white striped awning through the rain.

My belly grumbles, right on cue.

"Breakfast?" I offer, and Fabiana grins, nodding her head.

"I haven't eaten today. I'm so hungry."

I back the car into a parking space and reach across her to open the glove box.

"What's that?" she asks as I pull out a plastic bag.

By way of answering, I slap on a baseball cap and a pair of sunglasses. She takes in my disguise, and snort laughs, instantly throwing her hand over her mouth, her eyes dancing.

"What?" I ask, a smile busting out across my face at the sound. "Nice snort, by the way. Very ladylike."

"Snorting is perfectly ladylike, thank you. And no Hawaiian shirt this time, Your Royal Highness?" she teases.

I shake my head, smiling at the memory of how I'd turned up in the Malveauxian town of Monteluce in a

Hawaiian shirt and fake mustache to visit Amelia. "Hey! That was a great disguise," I protest.

"Oh, of course it was. Absolutely no one knew who you were," she deadpans.

Sadly for me, Amelia, and Ethan, everyone *did* know who I was.

"So, was it the yellow Ferrari that gave you away do you think? Or the fact you looked like an off-duty prince in a Hawaiian shirt and fake mustache?"

I laugh, enjoying our easy banter. Her wit, once so acerbic and judgmental, is now warm and teasing, and as we sit in the car in the water-drenched town, the rain drumming on the roof, I can't imagine wanting to be anywhere else but here with her now.

"Okay, so maybe that wasn't my finest hour, but when you're recognized almost everywhere you go, you've got to at least try to fly under the radar. Hence the disguise." I hold up the plastic bag.

She throws her gaze over my cap and glasses. "Sunglasses on the wettest day of the year." She shakes her head.

"Just the cap?"

"Just the cap."

"Here." I pull another baseball cap from the bag and position it on her head, and she pulls her ponytail through the back. She's giving off a cute and sexy girl next door vibe, and if it wasn't for my belly reminding me I haven't eaten today…well, as much as I want to kiss her right now, I can't.

I clip a leash on Toffee's collar and climb out of the car, immediately noticing the sweater stops short of my belt, exposing a line of skin.

Fabiana raises her eyebrows at me, her lips twitching.

"You're the one who chose this top."

"And you're the one making it look so fetching," she teases.

I hold an umbrella aloft for Toffee to sniff and do what she needs to do beside a tree, and then the three of us dash inside the café. Instantly the aroma of freshly brewed coffee and baked goods hits my senses, and my belly rumbles once more in approval.

The place is almost empty but for a couple of elderly men sipping espresso, and a woman knitting at a table on her own at the back.

"Is it okay if I bring my dog in here?" I ask a man in his sixties behind the counter, his beard salt and pepper, his hair balding.

He throws his gaze over my pink sweater and cap. "Of course. We can have a bowl of water brought out for him."

"She might want something to eat, too."

The man's bushy eyebrows pull together. "Bacon?"

I'm pretty sure bacon isn't usual canine fare, but Toffee would be more than happy to break with tradition. "She would love that. Thank you."

"Take a seat. Anywhere you like," he says.

We thank him and then find a table by the window. Toffee instantly gets her leash tied in knots around the leg of my chair and then gives up and lies down.

"Do they know if your grandmother's broken her ankle?" I ask.

"She's being x-rayed soon. She's in good spirits, considering."

"I'm glad to hear it. We'll be there in a few hours, if the weather plays ball." I peer out at the storm, which shows zero signs of letting up.

"I hope so, although I'm not as worried as I was, now that we've spoken."

"And she's got her Mr. Beckman."

She twists her mouth. "Hmm."

"What looks good to you?" I ask as I scan the menu.

"All of it?" she suggests, her face lifting in a smile.

"I'm going to start with coffee and a ham and cheese croissant."

"No baked beans?"

I snicker. "Definitely not."

She places her menu back on the table. "Sounds good to me. I'll have the same."

The man from behind the counter approaches our table, accompanied by a woman of about the same age. Both of them are looking at me, an all too familiar look on their faces. I know what's coming next.

"Cover blown," I say under my breath.

"What do you mean?" Fabiana asks as the couple arrives at our table.

The woman urges her husband toward us.

"Err, my wife has something to say," he mutters, looking thoroughly uncomfortable.

"We are honored to have you in our little town, Your Royal Highness," the woman says, dipping into a curtsy.

"I knew I should have worn the sunglasses," I murmur to Fabiana, and she shakes her head, smiling.

I rise to my feet and shake hands with them both. "It's a pleasure to meet you. You have a fine café here, and we're very hungry."

"You're in the right place, sir. I'm Domenico, and this is my wife, Margaux. She does the cooking," the man says, and his wife beams proudly.

"It would be an honor to prepare food for you, sir. Whatever you want," she says. Her eyes slide to Fabiana.

"This is my friend, Fabiana," I say, and as my eyes alight on hers, something passes between us.

"Hello," she says as she raises her hand in a wave.

"Any friend of the prince is a friend of ours," Margaux replies, and her husband nods his agreement. She gestures at my sweater. "Is this a new trend in Villadorata?"

"Something like that," I reply.

"What can I get you both?" she asks.

We place our order, and Domenico and Margaux leave.

"I'm your friend, am I?" she says, toying with a paper napkin.

"I had thought of introducing you as my former arch-nemesis, but that might have caused an uprising in my honor. I thought it safest to go with 'friend'."

She lets out a laugh. "It would have made a great story, though. 'Small town rises up in the name of prince'."

"Are you always thinking of your next story?"

She shrugs. "A girl's gotta eat. It's my job to find stories."

The knitter from the table at the back approaches us and gives a stiff curtsy. "It's a pleasure to have you in our small town, Your Royal Highness."

"That's kind of you," I reply, once again rising to my feet to shake her hand. Soon, the men join us, and I make small talk with all of them, complimenting them on their town and bemoaning the fact it's not a clear day for us to be able to take in all its beauty.

This is not my first rodeo.

As they leave and I sit back down at the table, Fabiana says, "You're good with people, and it's clear they like you."

"Does that come as a surprise to you?"

"It makes me wonder whether I should make a run for it before they work out I'm the one who's written those stories about you. My life may well be at risk here."

I shift in my seat, the question I've wondered the

answer to many times on my mind. "How do you learn about what I get up to? It's not like you're there, recording it all, and if you are, I need to learn your disguise skills to up my game."

"A good journalist never shares their sources," she replies without actually answering my question.

I may have held myself back from pressing her on her past, but this part of her life concerns me personally. "Seriously. How do you get your stories? Although I haven't loved what you've had to say about me, you're always factually right, even if you're sometimes missing the nuance."

She leans her elbows on the table. "Tell me, Max, what was the nuance I missed when you slid down the slide into that pond, dislodging a school of fish?"

She's teasing me, but it's as though she's purposefully deflecting.

Domenico arrives with our food and coffee, interrupting our conversation, placing a bowl of bacon on the floor for Toffee, who instantly chomps it all down, looking for more.

Fabiana and I devour our food like we're competing in an eating competition.

"Oh, my. This is *so* good," Fabiana says as she takes the final bite of her croissant, crumbs clinging to her lips.

"You've got a little croissant here." I point at my own lips.

"Ditto," she replies, and I quickly brush the crumbs away.

"Still hungry?" I ask, and she nods.

I signal Domenico, and this time we order pastries and cake, and a second coffee each.

I make a mental not to tell my PT about this carb-tastic meal.

Once we've finished, I lean back in my seat, totally full. "I may just slip into a diabetic coma after that feast."

"No can do. I need you to drive me back to the city. Can you schedule your coma for after you drop me at the hospital?"

"I'll see what I can do."

Fabiana's phone beeps, and immediately she pulls it from her purse to read the screen.

"Is everything okay?" I ask.

She breaks into a relieved smile. "Nona's X-ray came back clear. No break, just a sprain."

"That's brilliant news."

The door flies open, bringing in a whoosh of rain, and in steps a stocky man in wet weather gear and a police hat, rain dripping from him and pooling at his feet. "They've closed the road!" he announces.

"They've done what?" Fabiana exclaims.

He turns to look our way. "The road. It's closed in and out of town." Recognition flickers across his face, and he does a double take. "Are you...?" the man begins.

"He is!" Margaux beams, her hand held to her chest. "Royalty. Here, in our little café."

The police officer removes his hat and bows. "Hello, Your Royal Highness."

"Pleased to meet you, officer. What have you heard about the roads?" I ask.

Domenico asks, stepping from behind the counter. "What's going on, Terry?"

"I was helping Juan Rogers get his tractor out of a ditch down on Grays Road when it came over the radio. Fallen trees to the north, a flooded river to the south. We'll need to hold tight until the storm blows over," Terry the police officer says.

Fabiana shoots me a look. "But surely there's more than one road in and out of town?" she says.

He shakes his head mournfully. "There is but one road in and out of San Fiorenzo, miss."

"One road?" She knits her brows, her mouth forming an "o". "Are you sure?"

"I've lived here all my life. I'm sure," he replies.

"But—" she begins, and I place my hand over hers.

"Your nona is in good hands. Her ankle isn't broken. If we need to wait out the storm here, then so be it."

She nods, her lips pressed together. "You're right."

"How long will it be before the road is opened, officer?" I ask.

He shrugs, his palms held out. "It could be hours. It could be days."

I blink at him. "Days?"

"We will know when we know. By the looks of things?" He peers out the window, up at the gray sky. "I would say tomorrow or the next day."

"Looks like we'll need to find a place to stay for the night," I say to Fabiana, who gives me a tight nod. "Is there an inn or a hotel nearby?" I ask.

"There's an inn about four doors up the street. It's run by Layla Foramina," Domenico says.

"She's my cousin," Margeaux pronounces proudly.

"Is that the only accommodation here in town?" I ask.

"There's a hotel about one kilometer up the road, but it's full. My brother runs it," Margeaux says.

"We don't have any choice. Do we?" Fabiana says.

"Let's go and see about some rooms," I reply, and she gives a reluctant nod.

Fabiana tries to pay for our meal, but I pull rank, and then the three of us dash through the rain, arriving at the door to the inn. Sheltering under the awning, I knock on the door and read the sign, which says *Osteria Delle Layla* in peeling black paint.

"Thank goodness there's an inn or we might be sleeping in your car," Fabiana says.

The door creaks open, and a woman in a dark blue dress, her white hair cropped short with a pair of purple-rimmed glasses balanced on her nose, greets us. "Margeaux said you were coming, Your Royal Highness." She eyes my sweater, but she doesn't pass comment.

"Word gets around quickly," I reply. "You must be Layla. I hope you've got room for us, and that you take dogs."

"You are all welcome. Please come on in out of the rain, sir, and—" her eyes land on Fabiana "—and friend."

"I'm going to be reported as your latest fling," Fabiana says under her breath as she steps inside.

"Are you going to report that?" I ask.

"Unlikely."

Layla leads us up a narrow staircase, chattering about the storm and apologizing profusely. "The view of the mountains is breathtaking. It's such a shame you can't see them." She comes to a stop outside a door. "I have only one room available. The storm brought in several other travelers, and my inn is small but comfortable."

Wait. Only one room?

She swings open the door to reveal a small but tidy room with a window overlooking the storm-lashed street.

And one bed.

One *small* bed, probably only a double.

My pulse leaps.

Fabiana and I both freeze in the doorway as Toffee pulls on her leash, eager to get inside.

Neither of us looks at the other.

"Are you sure you don't have another room somewhere?" Fabiana asks, and there's a distinct note of panic in her tone.

It doesn't do my ego any good.

"We're full to the gills, miss, but I'm sure you'll find this room very comfortable. It has its own ensuite bathroom," Layla says proudly, as though an ensuite will seal the deal.

"Thank you, Layla. You've been most helpful," I say.

"I'll leave you to get settled, sir," she says before she flashes Fabiana a look and leaves.

"Definitely your latest fling," she mutters under her breath.

"There are no journalists here."

"That doesn't stop people from sending info to the media. Everyone's a journalist these days."

I reach for Fabiana's hand and give it a squeeze. "Don't worry about the one-bed thing. I'll take the floor," I tell her.

"No, I will," she replies.

"Fabiana—"

"What? You're the prince here."

"I'm not going to sleep in a bed while you're on the floor. It would be elitist and wrong."

"There's the socialist in you coming out again," she says.

"I've slept on floors before."

"Don't be ridiculous," she says, a hint of impatience in her voice. "It's a big enough bed for two, Max. I think we can both survive the night."

"Right," I murmur. *Survive.* "We're both adults. We can share a bed without—" I trail off, realizing what I was about to say.

Without what, exactly? Without me wanting to kiss her again, to hold her, to tell her how she makes me feel?

Without noticing how beautiful she looks even when she's drenched in the rain, worried about her grandmother?

If she knew where I was going with that, she doesn't mention it. "We could make a wall of pillows between us," she says, her cheeks flushing pink.

"That sounds reasonable to me."

"It should be only one night."

An awkward silence settles between us as Toffee sniffs every corner of the room. Her little paws click against the wooden floor, the sound far too loud in the stillness.

The bed looms in my peripheral vision like it's taunting me.

It's time to address the elephant in the room. The very large, very plush, double-mattress-sized elephant.

"About last night," I begin.

"We don't need to talk about it. Really. It's fine."

"I think we do." I run a hand through my hair. "Especially now we're here for the night. Maybe two."

She presses her lips together, her eyes flicking briefly to the bed before darting away.

"I don't want you to think I'm the kind of man who would...take advantage of being here with you."

"I don't think that," she says, her voice soft but steady. "I've seen what kind of man you are, Max. Remember?"

Her words land somewhere deep in my chest, and for a second, neither of us speaks. The air hums around us, my mind darting to things I should not be thinking about.

"I'm glad," I manage, but my voice comes out rougher than I intended.

Toffee hops onto the bed, circles once, and flops right in the middle.

"Well, it looks like the dog's claimed Switzerland," I say, hoping to cut the tension with a joke.

Fabiana's lips pull into a tight smile. "You can have the left side. I'll take the right," she concedes.

"You sure?"

"Unless you snore, in which case I'm banishing you to your car."

"No snoring, just endless sleep talking," I shoot back with a grin.

Spending the night with her in this room gives me hope that I can break down her walls, get her to open up to the possibility of us. Yes, she's shot me down. But this night together could be the thing that changes that.

Amusement flickers when she lifts her eyes to mine. "Are you likely to give away state secrets?" she asks.

"You'll have to wait and see."

I swallow hard, because the image that conjures is *dangerous*.

I have no idea how I'm going to close my eyes tonight with her lying inches away from me behind nothing but a wall of pillows. Close enough to hear her breathing. Close enough to remember exactly what it felt like to almost kiss her.

Her phone rings, cutting through the moment. She glances at it, then back at me. "It's my nona."

"Take it. I'll get your suitcase. And no protests this time, okay?"

Her lips lift into a smile before she answers her phone. "Nona, how are you?"

I close the door behind me, hearing the lightness in her voice as she speaks to her beloved grandmother.

Tonight, we're sharing a room, a *bed*. Even if she builds a wall of pillows made of stone, neither of us will come out of this experience unchanged. If I weren't already halfway gone for her before, there's no turning back for me now.

I'm falling for her, and there's not a dang thing I can do about it.

Chapter 19

Valentina

OF ALL THE places my career as a journalist has taken me, never in a million years did I expect to be stuck for the night in a small room with only one bed in a town the size of a peanut with the man I've made it my job to ridicule publicly for years.

The universe sure has a sick sense of humor.

The thought of being here with him makes both my heart and my body sing in a way that is way too dangerous for me.

Yet here we are, trapped by felled trees to the north and an overflowing river to the south.

And to make things worse, my nona's ankle isn't even broken.

This whole crazy scramble to Villadorata has been a giant storm in a teacup.

Max continues to show me how much he cares for others, how he will go out of his way to help a person. I never intended to be someone who needed help, let alone some kind of cliché damsel in distress. But that's what I was today. I needed help and he was the one who gave it to me. Willingly.

Not only that, he's shown genuine concern for my grandmother, checking in with me about her, making sure I'm okay. That's... nice. More than nice. It's considerate and thoughtful and...*Argh!*

He's not playing fair.

He should be this horrible, arrogant, self-absorbed prince with zero emotional intelligence. He should be treating me the way he did on my first day at the palace in Villadorata, doing his best to dodge me, and only responding to my questions with the bare minimum of language possible beyond a guttural grunt.

That Max I can deal with.

This one? The compassionate, thoughtful, sexy, easy to talk to version that I genuinely like?

That version is freaking terrifying.

Max is at the window, looking out at the storm, all casually attractive and relaxed, like this whole situation is nothing but a minor inconvenience to him. "That rain isn't letting up anytime soon. The street is like a river."

I unzip my case and pull out my wash bag. "We just need to make the most of it, I suppose."

He turns toward me. "At least you have your suitcase. I

came with nothing." He collects the damp umbrella that's by the door. "I'm going to head out to pick up some supplies. Do you need anything?"

I place my hand on my case. "I've got everything I need right here."

He pulls his cap down over his head and shoots me an easy smile

"I wouldn't bother with the disguise. Everyone knows who you are."

"It's raining. I can't afford for my hair to get wet."

I snort out a laugh. "Really?"

"No." He throws me a wink before he pulls the door open, calls for Toffee, and the two of them go, leaving nothing but his scent and the memory of his smile in the room, silent but for the pitter patter of rain against the windows.

I push out a breath, chewing on my lip. *I can do this.*

I mean, really, it's all in a day's work as a journalist. And besides, I'm sure I've been in trickier situations. Like the time I spent a full ten minutes interviewing who I thought was a visiting European prince, only to realize he was in fact an actor hired for a charity event. Or the time a palace staff member told me that the then twenty-three-year-old Princess Amelia had announced she was breeding rats to help their dwindling numbers, and believing it, I made a TikTok about it. I later learned that rat numbers are far from dwindling. Quite the opposite, in fact.

But neither of those situations involved sharing a bed with a man who completely scrambles my head. A man I'm meant to have an entirely platonic and professional relationship with. A man who causes a serious butterfly situation in my belly each time he so much as smiles at me. Seriously, it's like they've all drunk too much caffeine and have decided to do the samba *en masse*.

And all this with just a smile.

A smile!

Imagine if I'd gone through with the kiss. Who knows where I'd be now.

We'll need some ground rules. A strictly impenetrable wall of pillows is a start.

Plus, when we do go to bed, we must both be fully clothed. And he can't wear his aftershave, because that would mess with my hormones, lying here in the dark with him next to me.

Yup, definitely no aftershave.

I'm busy hanging up the wet clothes I was wearing earlier today when Max and Toffee return with a rain-splattered paper bag, his cap soaked through. I help him towel off Toffee, who then promptly rolls around on the rug as though she's on a mission to get dirty again.

"I got a toothbrush, some food for Toffee, a change of clothes, and even a pair of PJs." He holds up a box with a picture of a man's torso wearing a white T-shirt. "I can be fresh for our journey tomorrow."

"If we get to leave tomorrow."

"I spoke with the police officer again. Terry. He said they are working hard on clearing the trees, and if the rain eases, they expect to have the road cleared by lunchtime tomorrow."

"That's to the north though, right? What about the flooding to the south?"

"It's still raining hard, so no progress."

"My grandmother may only have a sprained ankle, but I still want to see her. Maybe I could catch a bus or something when the flooding subsides."

"I'm not going to abandon you to some bus, Fabiana. I said I'll take you to Villadorata, and I will take you to

Villadorata. I know it's important to you to see your grandmother," he says softly.

See? He is *so* not playing fair.

He pulls the T-shirt from its package and for a heart-stopping minute, I think he's going to pull off his damp polo to try it on. But instead, he holds it up against his chest. "What do you think? Does it bring out the color of my eyes?"

"It's white, Max. Unless you're a zombie and your eyes are white, too, then no, it doesn't."

He eases himself down onto the bed. "Do zombies have white eyes?"

"Some do. Kind of cloudy. Are you telling me you don't watch zombie movies?"

"Nope. You do?"

"Of course! *Dawn of the Dead*, *The Last of Us*?" He shakes his head. "What about the South Korean zombie shows, like *All of Us Are Dead* or *Kingdom*?"

"Kingdom? I know a little about that, although I can't say I've seen all that many zombies around the palace."

I laugh despite myself.

His eyes are trained on me. "Are you worried about your grandmother?"

"A little."

"Right."

"What?"

"It's just you seem a little...tense, I suppose."

"Who, me?" I squeak, out-mousing Mickey Mouse. "No! I'm good. Great, in fact."

I overdid it. Particularly when he asks, "It's the sharing a room thing, isn't it?"

My shoulders drop. He's hit the nail right on its head. "You've got to admit it's awkward. I'm a journalist doing a series of stories about you. And you're—"

"The story," he finishes for me.

I scrunch my nose. It's only the tip of the iceberg, but it's what I'm running with. "Yeah."

He rises to his feet, and his broad shoulders seem to fill the room. "Let's pretend we're just two friends hanging out together in this seriously soggy town. No journalist. No story. Do you think you can do that, just for tonight?"

Slowly, I nod my head. "I can do that."

"And also, the bed thing?" He gestures at the bed. "I'm happy to sleep on the floor."

"We've already been through this."

"I'm a gentleman. My mother would kill me if I let you do that."

"Your mother doesn't need to know."

My words come out a lot flirtier than I intended.

"Arm wrestle for it?" he suggests with a grin.

My eyes glide briefly to his muscular arms, against which the sleeves of his shirt strain. "I'd say you have an unfair advantage."

He clenches his bicep. "You mean this?" he asks, cocking an eyebrow, and I can't help but admire how his muscles bulge, despite how cheesy he's being.

I swallow. "Exactly."

"How about a pea-knuckle war?"

I snort with surprised laughter. "You're a prince who plays pea-knuckle?"

"I'm a *guy* who plays pea-knuckle," he corrects. "No princes or journalists here tonight, remember?"

"You're on." I hold my hand out, and he grips my fingers with his. The touch of his skin against mine does precisely what I expect it to do, as the butterflies in my belly chug another cup of java.

Holding our thumbs aloft, I count, "One, two, three, four, I declare a thumb war!"

"Five, six, seven, eight, try to keep your thumb straight! Ready, set, go, let's annihilate!

Immediately, we battle it out, both of us straining to hold our thumbs back as the other tries to pin it down. Of course, he has the advantage of having a much larger hand than mine, but this is a battle of wills—one I'm determined to win.

I slam my thumb down, pinning his in place. "Aha! I've got you!" I declare with glee.

"You have," he replies, his tone softer and more intimate than it should be between the friends we're meant to be, and knowing exactly why I shouldn't, I find myself looking up into his mahogany eyes with the little chunks of gold, my heart banging in my chest. "You win, Fabiana," he murmurs softly.

His words are loaded in a way that has risky ideas swarming my mind, my breath shortening.

I pull my hand away. "You let me win."

"You won fair and square. Ami always used to beat me at pea-knuckle. You've obviously got her knack."

I don't believe him for a second.

"You don't have to sleep on the floor," I say after a beat.

"Pillow wall?"

"Pillow wall."

I'm an adult. I can conquer my feelings for this man, even if he's sleeping right next to me.

His lips lift into a smile that tugs at my belly, and I wonder whether I've just made a big mistake.

"By the way, I found a place for us to have dinner while I was out. It's a little trattoria up the street. The menu has about three items on it, but it looks good in a rustic, home cooking kind of way."

"Great!" I say a little too brightly. If he notices, he

doesn't react. Instead, he suggests we shower and change before heading out.

"You go first. I want to get in touch with Nona again to see when she expects to get home," I tell him.

"Sure." He closes the door to the bathroom, and I sink onto the bed, doing my best not to picture water pounding against his broad back and muscular torso.

Not helpful.

Pulling up FaceTime, I call Nona, who answers after only a few rings, showing me an up-close image of her ear. "Valentina, my darling girl! How's your prince?" she asks.

"Shhh, Nona! He doesn't know my real name, remember?" I whisper. "And he's not my prince."

"A man who offers to drive you hours through a storm certainly wants to be yours, my dear."

I grip the phone. What is she, psychic now? "You're wrong, Nona," I say in protest.

"We'll see."

"You need to pull the phone around. You're on video."

"Oh, goodness. All right." She turns the phone for me to see her lovely face. "There you are! Where is he now?"

"He's in the shower."

"The shower?"

"That's why I'm calling you now."

"To tell me the prince is having a shower?" she teases.

"Nona," I warn.

"Shame. I wanted to meet him."

Not a good idea. Nona may forget I'm Fabiana and use my real name, throwing the cat right amongst the royal pigeons.

"The road south is flooded, so we have to stay the night in a little town called San Fiorenzo, but I'm hoping to get to the city tomorrow."

"Oh, I know that place. It's such a pretty little town, nestled in the mountains with its beautiful views. Your papa used to order those delicious pies from a bakery there, remember? It really is the perfect place for a romantic interlude."

"Nona! Seriously," I hiss, immediately taking her off FaceTime and lifting the receiver to my ear.

"Can't an old lady imagine romance?"

"I would have thought you'd had quite enough of that after you went dancing with Mr. Beckman," I reply, switching the focus to her.

She bites. "Oh, Rudolf really is quite something. I never knew! Living in the house next door all these years. I didn't think I liked him, but I didn't really even know him. He's quite the Fred Astaire."

"And you're going to tell me you're his Ginger Rogers, I suppose?"

She chuckles. "Not until my ankle's better," she sing-songs.

"How is your ankle? When will you be discharged?"

"I'm already home. Fred Astaire picked me up earlier today."

"Oh, that's good."

I'm not quite sure what to make of this new development in my grandmother's life. Rudolf has been nothing but a neighbor all these years, and now suddenly he's the man my grandmother is…what? Dating?

An odd sensation twists in my belly. It's always been Nona and me, us against the world. Now, Mr. Beckman seems to have eked his way into her affections.

"Don't worry about me, sweetheart. I'm in perfectly good hands here. You enjoy your time with your prince—who allegedly has zero designs on you—and I'll see you when your project is finished."

"But—" I protest on more than one count. The woman's got romance on the brain.

"No buts, Val. I can manage with a sprained ankle with Rudolf at my side."

"As long as you're sure?"

"I'm sure, my darling girl." She pauses for a beat before she says, "He wasn't the one."

Confused, I reply, "Who wasn't the one? Mr. Beckman?"

"The prince. It wasn't him. It was his father."

"I know that."

"Do you? Because it seems to me you've been holding it against him all these years. He didn't have any part in it, Val."

Her words take me by surprise as my new friend guilt claims my chest. "Where's this suddenly coming from, Nona?"

"It's something I've wanted to say to you for some time now."

"And you think that when I'm stuck in a small town with the guy is the perfect time?"

"Now's as good as any. I don't want you holding something against a man who isn't responsible for what happened to us."

Her words sit heavily with me. She's right. I've known for a long time. I've spent so long hating the royal family for what the king did all those years ago, I'd lost sight of where my true anger lay. It's not with Max. How could it be? He could have only been eleven when it all happened.

I've been punishing him for something he had no part in, not only in my mind, but in my life as a journalist, as well. And it's not been fair to him. *I've* not been fair to him.

It hits me like a blow to the solar plexus.

"It's hard to separate him from it," I reply, my voice quiet.

"But you *can* separate him from it, Val. He doesn't deserve your anger."

I chew on my lip, my emotions swirling around me like a whirlpool.

"It doesn't matter if it wasn't him personally. He's still part of the same system, the same family that —"

"Val." Nona's using her stern tone. She means business. "You think your anger keeps you safe, but it's keeping you from living. That boy drove through a storm for you. He didn't have to do that."

I hang my head, my chest aching. "I know."

"I'm not telling you he's the one. I'm not telling you to fall in love. All I'm saying is let go of that anger. You don't want to be a bystander to your own life."

"What do you mean?"

"I mean, have an adventure. You're stuck in a romantic town with the country's most eligible bachelor. Have some *fun*."

As the steam from the shower wafts into the room, I close my eyes, and suddenly I can see it all so clearly. My nona is right. I've been punishing Max—and all the royal family—for something the king did all those years ago.

The water shuts off, and panic floods through my veins. In a minute or two, he'll be out here in this room with me, and I'll have to look him in the eye knowing that I've been unfair to him from the very beginning.

And that will mean my armor will no longer be my protection, because there will be nothing to protect me from anymore.

It will be just him and me, two people with feelings for one another, sharing a bed in a small town in the mountains.

My heart drums.

"Nona, I have to go," I say, swallowing down a growing lump in my throat.

"I love you, my darling girl. I want only good things for you. You know that, don't you?"

Tears prick my eyes, my chest tight. "I do."

I hang up and sit on the edge of the bed, taking shallow, shaky breaths. I've been wearing my anger like a thick metal jacket, and without it, it's just me, Valentina Romano, a woman who's falling for a prince who could break my heart without even trying.

Chapter 20

Max

I'M NOT GOING to lie: the thought of spending the night alone with Fabiana has my mind roving to all sorts of places it has no business being in. I couldn't stop thinking about it all through dinner, and now that we're back in our room, I can't stop thinking about it now, either.

Sure, we're getting on better than we have ever before, and we've both admitted that we've judged one another based on scant information.

We're good. We're friends.

And therein lies my problem, because friendship with Fabiana Fontaine is rather like trying to satisfy hunger with a single olive. It may technically be sustenance, but it's hardly filling.

Yes, I want to pull her against me, have the soft curves of her body meld against mine, show her how much I want her. How much I *need* her. But that's the simple part, the straightforward desire that a man might have for a woman.

What's infinitely more dangerous is this other thing, this ridiculous, unprecedented longing to get her to open like my favorite book, so I can read every page until I've memorized her completely. I want to know what makes her laugh when she thinks no one's listening. I want to discover what she dreams about in those quiet moments before she falls asleep.

I want to be the person she turns to when the world gets too much.

But equally, I want to open myself up completely to her, to show her who I truly am. Be vulnerable in a way I'm not with most people. Not the prince she thought I was. The man.

The man who lies awake at night wondering if he'll ever be more than his title.

The man who is forced to search for meaning outside of his role.

The man who wants her so badly it hurts, yes, but also the man who wants the connection we've already begun to build to deepen until it becomes something *unbreakable*.

Because there's something magnetic between us, something that's both inevitable and impossible. It's bigger than anything I've felt for a woman before. And trust me, my romantic history hasn't exactly been short. But those were simply attractions. Pleasant diversions. About as deep as Toffee's water bowl.

This? This is like coming home to a place I never knew I was searching for.

Man, when did I become such a sentimental fool?

I already know the answer. It's when I met *her*.

Which is why, when the tension coming off of her is virtually cracking around her head, it's clear as day that she's as affected by our proximity as I am, and my heart leaps at the possibility that it could be because she feels it too.

My instinct is to pull her into my arms and soften her tension, to smooth it away with my touch. But she pushed me away last night by the fire, and I don't want to risk spooking her again.

"Come on," I say, as I pull the creaky door to the armoire open and grab one of the spare blankets I spotted earlier. "Help me with this."

She eyes me. "What are you doing?"

"Building us a fort of course," I reply as though it's the most natural thing for two grown adults to do together. I shake the blanket out and grin at her bemused expression as Toffee bounces about excitedly. "What? You've never built a blanket fort before?"

"I—" She looks genuinely taken aback, and something about her confusion tugs on my heart strings. "Not for a long time."

"Well then, tonight's your lucky night."

"Max," she says, shaking her head. "What will we do with a fort?" she asks.

"Hide. Clearly."

She raises her brows. "From whom? The grown-ups?"

I grin at her. "Precisely."

"You are *so* typically a youngest sibling. Never growing up."

"Why grow up when there's so much fun to have?" I

waggle my brows at her and the tautness in her face relaxes a touch.

"We can't all spend our lives having fun," she replies, and there's something in her tone that tells me there's a reason behind her words. A reason I want to understand, as I want to understand so many things about this woman.

"Come on. Let's get to work."

She throws me an inquisitive look. "Work?"

"Building the fort, of course. Toffee's keen."

We both watch as Toffee turns round and round on the blanket before flopping down.

"You're not serious, Max."

"Try me." I move the chair closer to the bed and drape the blanket over its back. Taking a pillow from the bed, I secure it at one end.

She seems to think about it for a moment. "Come on, Toffee. Off you hop."

Toffee does just that and Fabiana helps me stretch the other corner to the bed.

"I can't believe we're doing this."

"You'll love it. Trust me." I secure the blanket on the bed and hand her the last of the pillows to arrange inside our makeshift shelter. Then I hold back the door flap for her. "After you, *mademoiselle*."

She hesitates, not sure whether to play along.

"Come on, Fabiana. I dare you," I say.

"You *dare* me?"

"Yup."

Without another word, she ducks under the blanket, settling cross-legged on the pillows, followed by Toffee, who thinks this fort is the best thing since the last best thing— because she's a dog and loves any adventure.

I follow, the space around us cozy but somehow less

charged than the open room. Maybe because it's like we're kids playing pretend.

"See? Isn't it like the rest of the world doesn't exist?" I ask, settling beside her, careful to leave some space between us.

Some of the tension has left her shoulders. "Actually, you're right. This is fun. In a totally man-child kind of way."

"Hey! I thought you'd given up the name calling."

"Max, you're a twenty-seven-year-old man who's currently sitting inside a blanket fort."

"You are, too."

The edges of her mouth quirk, and I'm satisfied I've got her to relax a notch.

I pull out my phone from my back pocket and open an app. I place the phone between us.

"You have a candle app on your phone?" she asks as she looks at the flickering candle on my screen.

"You never know when you'll need it."

"Like when? Other than when hiding from non-existent grown-ups in forts, that is."

"Concerts, or when you forget candles for a birthday cake."

She throws me a look. "Are you telling me you can blow the candle out?"

"Watch." I blow on my phone, and the candle blows out.

"That's amazing! What other apps do you have?"

"I've got one called the polite procrastinator," I say as I swipe my screen. "Every time you try to open TikTok, it gently asks if you really want to procrastinate in that way. Listen." I open the app and a sexy American woman's voice purrs, "Do you really want to do that, sweetie?"

"Face it, you just like her voice."

"It has a certain appeal." I waggle my brows at her, making her grin as Toffee curls up at my side, leaning against me.

Fabiana laughs, shaking her head, and any last remnants of tension seem to have disappeared. "Does it actually stop you from using TikTok?" she asks.

"Not in the least."

She snort-laughs.

"I've got to see what certain journalists are saying about me."

"The life of a member of the Ledonian royal family, huh? Spare time to burn."

I turn on the candle app once more and place it between us. "It's light relief."

She leans back against the bed, her legs crossed. In the dim, filtered light, she looks younger somehow. More vulnerable. Definitely more beautiful.

I'm finding it hard to look away.

"Relief from all the garden parties, super yachts, and martinis?" she teases.

"You think that's what my life is all about? Attending functions and getting tipsy?"

"Over our time together, you've shown me it's not, but it's certainly part of it."

I chew on my lip. In this oddly intimate space with her, I want to tell her what life as Prince Max is actually like, to open up to her in a way I never have with anyone. Not even my closest friends are aware of my innermost struggles. Sure, they get that I'm so much more than journalists like Fabiana have portrayed me over the years. But they don't get how I struggle with it. They don't get how exhausting it can be to have to live up to everyone's expectations of who I'm meant to be. They don't understand the pressure I have in representing centuries of tradition while trying to find ways to make my role relevant.

And the truth is, as the fourth born with no clear role, no clear point to my life, I'm not sure how relevant my role really is.

"It's lonely at times to be constantly watched, constantly judged, constantly seen as never quite good enough."

"What do you mean?" she asks, and there's something in her voice that spurs me on.

"I can't make the choices other people can make; I can't live my life the way I might want to. I've got to be Prince Maximilien, son of King Frederic and Queen Astrid, the much-loved monarchs. I've never been able to choose what I do."

"Didn't you choose to go to Cambridge?"

"Where my brother and sisters went and my father before them and his father before him?"

"The Air Force?" she questions. "I suppose you didn't choose that, either?"

I shake my head. "It's tradition. That's not to say I didn't enjoy it. I made friends for life there, like Rocco and Dante, and I learned a lot of useful things about myself and other people."

"And how to fly a helicopter," she adds with a smile.

"And how to fly a helicopter."

"What would you have done if you hadn't been born into the royal family?"

"I don't know. Become a vet? Joined the circus? Picked apples in New Zealand like Marco did?"

"But you never got the choice."

"Nope."

"You do get to do some pretty amazing things though. Take your youth program, for instance."

"You're right. I wouldn't be able to help the way I do if I wasn't a prince." I think of Adella. "That's the first time Adella has made it over that wall on the assault course."

"You're a proud papa."

"It might sound silly, but I am."

"It's not silly. It's—" she breaks off, and I lift my gaze to hers.

"It's what?"

"It's changed my mind about you. That and a few other things."

I arch my brows at her. "So, I'm now a man-child who runs a youth program?"

She shakes her head. "Despite the fact we're sitting in a blanket fort, I no longer see you as a man-child. As I said, I was wrong to call you that."

I widen my eyes at her. "Fabiana Fontaine is saying she was *wrong*?"

"All right. Don't rub it in." She straightens her shoulders. "I'm sorry for calling you a man-child and all the other names. You've shown me that you're so much more than that."

I hold her gaze. "Thank you," I say simply.

"There's really no need to thank me, Max."

"I'm thanking you for saying it, because we both know you didn't have to."

I almost reach for her hand. Almost. I don't. I don't want to scare her the way I did by the fire last night.

Man, was that only last night? It feels like a lifetime ago.

"I can see that you're not the absolutely horrible human I thought you were before as well."

She lets out a surprised snicker. "Thanks?"

I hold a hand up. "That didn't come out quite right. What I meant to say was that I formed an opinion of you based on what you wrote about me, not on who you are."

"Well, to be fair, I was the woman who wrote all those stories about you. The woman who persisted in showing the country the worst side of Prince Maximilien. I didn't know anything else about you. All I saw was the man who wore a bright yellow tutu over his dinner suit to a state dinner."

I shrug. "I'd lost a bet."

She laughs once more, the sound fills the small space and warms my belly.

I chew on my lip. "Since we're taking ownership here, I'm not exactly innocent in all this. I've played into the whole 'Max in Neverland' thing."

"Never growing up."

I gesture at the fort. "What's so great about being an adult, anyway? The kids on the program see me as I really am."

"They love you."

A smile grows on my lips. "They're the best. They show me what's possible. They show me that no matter what life throws at you, you can not only survive, but you can also thrive."

"It's plain to see that you care deeply about them. Do you know what I think? I think you connect so well with them because you had to grow up too fast."

I lift my gaze to hers once more, my heart thudding. No one has ever summed up my life in such a way. No one has even seen the real me. Not really. "What makes you say that?" I ask, my voice small.

"Because you've been in the public eye all your life, at first loved for the sweet but naughty child you were, and then, once you hit your mid-teens, you were scrutinized, your choices put under the microscope. I remember reading about you getting drunk at your boarding school and nearly getting kicked out. Why would you want to grow up when the country made it clear they adored the sweet but naughty boy? And in growing up, you become this person whose life is both privileged and limited by the simple fact of your birth."

I listen as she speaks, my heart thudding like a drum, my mind whirring. As startling as it is to hear my life summed up in a few short sentences by her, the truth in her words is crystal clear.

How did this woman I've always thought of as a headline chaser, my arch nemesis, intent on capitalizing on my less than stellar choices, work me out so fully?

Fabiana understands me in a way I never expected.

She sees me. She *gets* me.

She toys with one of her fingernails before looking back up at me. "What's it like being the youngest son? You've got a brother who is now the king of Malveaux, a sister who will soon be the queen of Ledonia, another sister who jointly runs a wildly successful enterprise with her Hollywood star of a husband. And not only that, all of them are married with children."

I snicker. "Are you purposely trying to make me feel like the underachiever of the family?" I only half joke.

"Is that how you feel?" she asks, her voice low.

I shrug. "In a way," I admit, and when her features drop, I add hastily, "Don't get me wrong. I adore my family, each and every one of them, and I'm incredibly happy that they found love and purpose in their lives."

"But you've found neither."

I snap my attention to her, her words cutting me to the core. "I'm only twenty-seven. I've got time."

"Don't you have to have an arranged marriage if you're not married by the time you're twenty-eight?"

I thin my lips. Of course she's right. It's no secret. It's been the rule for Ledonian royalty for hundreds of years. But I never thought that rule would apply to me. I thought I would have met the one by then, fallen in love, got married.

The stark truth is I've never even come close.

She's the one to reach out and touch me, placing her hand lightly over mine. "I'm sorry, Max. I took that too far. Sometimes I say things without really thinking about the effect they might have on a person."

"No. You're right." As I look into her eyes, my heart tells me that maybe, just maybe, she might be the one I've been looking for. The thought settles into my chest like a warm ember, both hazardous and beautiful. It's the kind of realization that could change everything for me. She's not just someone I want, she's someone I need, someone who makes me want to be the man she sees when she looks at me the way she is right now in this moment.

I want to ask her so many questions about herself, but her words echo in my mind.

There are things you don't know about me.

But I want to know. All of it. I want to learn everything I can about this woman who's bewitched me.

"How do you know so much about having to grow up too fast?" I ask, and instantly her demeanor changes.

"I don't. I'm just observant, that's all. Part of the job description."

She's not telling me the truth. She's hiding something from me.

"What other completely useless apps do you have on your phone?" she asks, changing the subject.

I allow it to happen. I'm not going to force anything with her. "I have many." I scroll through my phone until I find what I'm looking for and then show it to her.

"Sock Matchmaker," she reads. "What is that?"

"You use your camera to scan socks to find their 'soulmate' pair. You can also watch them date other socks if you've lost one." I turn the phone so she can see the app with its bright pink screen and dancing mismatched socks.

"Sounds very useful."

"So useful. Then there's this one. It's a reverse fortune cookie app."

"What does it do?"

"It gives you bad advice, like telling you to text your ex at 2 AM, or to invest your life savings in a Ponzi scheme."

"A reverse fortune cookie app? That is *not* a thing." She takes the phone from my hand, and as she does her fingers brush against mine, sending a ripple through me.

This is torture.

I watch as she studies the screen. Her blonde hair is illuminated by the light from my phone, her big eyes scanning as she pulls her brows together in concentration. She looks impossibly gorgeous.

Suddenly, I'm finding it hard to remember why I need to hold myself back.

She taps something out and then blinks at the screen.

"What did you ask it?"

She works her throat. "Whether I should be alone in a fort with a prince."

"Really? What did it say?"

She clicks the phone off, shaking her head. "I'm not going to tell you."

I chuckle. "Because it said it was a good idea, didn't it?"

"You'll never know, Max."

"Is that so?" I click the phone back on, and as I read the answer to her question, something warm and urgent spreads through my chest, kicking up my heart rate. "As long as you make sure to kiss him," I read aloud, returning my gaze to hers.

The atmosphere around us shifts, and in an instant, this fort we're sitting in is no longer like an innocent game, but something a whole lot more intimate. So much more adult.

I want so badly to reach out and touch her, to pull her against me and press my lips against hers, to learn what it's like to hold this woman who has filled my mind since the moment she stepped into my life.

This woman who has shown me tonight that she understands me in a way no one else does.

She clears her throat, lifting the lips I so sorely want to kiss into a small smile. "The app is clearly living up to its name by giving bad advice."

"Look—" I begin, but she cuts me off.

"Shall we get ready for bed? It must be late, and I don't know about you, but I'm exhausted after today."

Before I have the chance to respond, she pulls back the flap and quickly exits the fort, and I'm left sitting alone with Toffee, my heart still racing.

She feels this thing between us. It's in her eyes when she looks at me with that intensity and fire. It's in the way she smiles at me, soft and sometimes almost shy, completely different from the sharp-edged wit she wields like armor in public. It's in the way she leans closer when we talk, as if drawn by the same magnetic pull that's been driving me wild.

But for whatever reason, for whatever secret or fear that's holding her back, she's too scared to surrender herself to it.

Chapter 21

Valentina

I STARE at my reflection in the bathroom mirror, willing my heart rate to return to normal. It's useless. The way he looked at me when the app told me we should kiss made it hard to remember how to breathe. What started as an ill-advised attraction to him has morphed into something so much more dangerous. Something so much harder to resist.

I feel the pull of him, like an invisible force field that's luring us ever closer together, no matter how hard I resist.

But I must resist. There's no other choice here.

So what if his opening up to me the way he does has made my heart feel as though it's doubled in size?

So what if I can feel his smile in my bone marrow?

I'm here to do a job. I'm here to show the world the real Max.

But now that I've seen him, I want him all for myself.

And somehow, *somehow* with the rain still pelting outside, showing no signs of letting up, we're about to share a bed.

My emotions swirl in my chest, and I heave out a breath. Max is the son of the people who ruined my life, the people who forced my dad from the country. His family is the reason I masquerade as someone I'm not. The reason I can't simply be Valentina.

I have to remember it.

I've got no choice.

Our easy camaraderie is based on a lie. Max thinks he's getting to know Fabiana Fontaine, but she's just a character I invented to survive.

I'm Lady Valentina Romano, daughter of the traitor his father exiled. If he knew that, would he still be scrolling through his apps, making me laugh, opening up to me, looking at me the way he does?

The answer makes my chest tighten.

I wipe the condensation from the mirror with my hand. My hair is wet from the shower, and I've scrubbed off any last remnants of makeup. I pull on my nightdress, instantly regretting the insignia sprawled across my chest. *Commoner by Day, Princess by Night*. A gift from my Nona that at once seemed cute and funny but now? Not so much.

I find an ancient hair dryer under the sink and quickly dry off my hair, the burning smell from years of collected dust filling the air. I collect my things and return to the bedroom.

Max is sitting on the chair, already in a pair of pajamas that I wish were grandfatherly and deeply unattractive. But of course they're not. This is Max we're talking about here. He's in a white singlet, tight enough to show off every single muscle in his possession—which is a frankly ridiculous number—and a pair of plaid cotton boxers that show off his long, athletic legs.

Why didn't he buy an old man's nightshirt that reaches from his neck to his toes with a matching nightcap? That way he'd look way more Scrooge McDuck—and way less hot off-duty prince.

"Your turn," I say, my voice far too bright, and as he looks up at me his eyes darken. It does things to me—unnecessary, tempting things—and so I busy myself with returning my wash bag to my suitcase, placing my glasses on the nightstand.

"I've never seen you with your hair down or your glasses off," he says.

"It happens every night," I reply without looking in his direction.

"You look—"

When he doesn't finish his sentence, I flick my gaze back to him. *Bad mistake.* He's now standing fully upright, his shoulders broader than any shoulders ought to be, all masculine edges and sinew, his eyes trained on me with an intensity that makes my belly somersault.

"What?" I ask, my heart beating against my ribs.

"You look beautiful," he says, and it's like the air has been sucked from the room.

I clench my hands into fists at my sides, willing the ever-growing feelings I have for this man away.

"You're just being nice."

His eyes trail over me, and my body tingles wherever he looks. They land on the insignia on my nightdress. "Princess by night?" he asks, his lips quirking.

"Just a silly gift from my nona." I raise my finger as though to scold him. "Don't get any ideas."

"Ideas?" he asks with a laugh. "No ideas here."

If the look of fire in his eyes is anything to go by, I don't believe him for a minute.

"Good," I say as I pull back the covers and slip between the sheets, noticing the pillow wall he constructed. It's flimsy, but it will have to do.

"I'll use the bathroom," he says, and as he leaves the room, I pull the blankets up to my ears.

I lie in bed, willing myself to fall asleep before he returns. Of course I don't. I'm so tightly wound I'm in fear of bursting out of the covers like a jack-in-the-box, only I'll be wearing a nightdress with a once innocent insignia that now reads as a personal invitation to Max.

Eventually, he returns to the room. As he slips into the bed beside me, I can't help but catch his scent in the air, a shockingly attractive blend of musk and masculinity.

I switch off the bedside light, and immediately we're thrown into darkness but for the dim streetlights, lending the linen curtains a muted glow. I turn my back to him and bunch up my pillow. I take a few deep breaths, trying to force myself to relax. "Good night," I say.

"Good night," he replies.

I lie still, waiting to hear his breath deepen, knowing sleep will elude me until it does.

Eventually, he asks in a whisper, "Are you still awake?"

"Yes," I reply, turning onto my back. "You?"

"Oh, sound asleep."

I smile into the darkness, the sound of the rain reverberating around the room.

"Is this the sleep talking you told me about?"

"Who knows? I'm asleep," he replies. "Can I ask you a question?"

"Sure."

"Fabiana starts with an F, right?"

"There's no silent P, like in pterodactyl, if that's what you're asking."

"So why do you always wear a necklace with a V?"

My hand instinctively goes to the pendant at my throat, the pendant I never remove.

"It was my nona's," I reply automatically, which is the truth. It was Nona's. "V for Violetta."

Also V for Valentina.

It's wrong to lie to Max after what he's shared with me tonight. But what else can I do? I can't blow my cover with this man, not when I'm finally starting to understand who he is beneath his public persona. Not when I've got a job to do.

Not when I feel what I do for him.

"You two are close."

"She's all I've got," I reply before I can stop myself and immediately bite my lip.

Keep your guard up, Valentina.

"You said you've lived with your nona since you were twelve?"

"That's right."

The sheets rustle as he turns over to face me, his scent filling the air once more. It causes my brain to go temporarily offline. "Why? What happened when you were twelve?" he asks, his voice close to my ear. "If you don't mind my asking."

My belly twists at the memories of how my life was

turned on its head, how I was forced to grow up almost overnight. But what can I tell this man whose father I have to blame for my trauma?

I need to tell him something, and a partial truth seems like the safest option. "My dad had to leave Ledonia."

"Why?"

I scrunch my eyes shut. "Can we…not?"

He places a warm hand on my shoulder, and I almost levitate off the bed, I'm so filled with tension. "I'm so sorry. You clearly don't want to talk about this. It's none of my business. It's just…"

"It's just what?" My heart is banging against my ribs.

"I want to know you," he says simply.

We fall into silence, and I wonder what Max now makes of me. What questions must be running through his head? I want to answer his questions, and I'll give him as much information as I can share. He deserves that much from me.

"My family circumstances changed when my dad left Ledonia. He wanted me to continue my education here, so he sent me to live in Villadorata with my nona."

My words fill the surrounding air. Words I've never spoken to another soul. They might not be the full truth, but they're still the truth.

"That must have been so hard for you."

Hard? Try devastating.

"It wasn't exactly a royal parade."

"Do you have any brothers or sisters?"

"It's been just me and Nona for all these years. I see my dad once or twice a year, but it's different from living with him."

He's quiet for a moment, and I can practically hear him processing, trying to piece together the puzzle of my life with the limited information I'm giving him.

Part of me wants to tell him everything. About watching my father's face crumble when he realized we had to leave everything behind. About his late-night escape. About me having to learn in my new life to make myself invisible, because visibility meant vulnerability.

But I can't. Not unless I'm planning on blowing up my entire life.

"What about friends?" he asks softly. "Growing up, I mean. That must have been lonely."

"I kept to myself, mostly. Focused on school."

"And now? You must have colleagues, people you're close to."

I can hear the genuine concern in his voice, and it seems dangerous. When was the last time someone asked about my life like this?

"I have work friends," I say carefully. "But I tend to keep my professional and personal lives separate."

Which kind of goes with the territory when you lead a double life.

"That sounds lonely, too."

"It's safer. Mixing the two can get complicated."

"Complicated how?"

Sweat beads on my forehead. This conversation is like trying to tiptoe in stilettos through bubble wrap without making the bubbles go snap.

"People have expectations about who I should be, what I should want. It's easier to maintain boundaries."

"But doesn't that get exhausting, always being what people expect instead of who you are?"

It's my entire life.

"I suppose," I reply.

"Maybe we have more in common than you'd think," he says softly.

I turn to face him, the outline of his features only just visible in the dim light. "Max, you were born into a life of privilege. I had the rug pulled right out from under my feet before I was even a teenager."

"Your world may have changed suddenly, and mine more gradually, but neither of us got to enjoy the childhood other people get. We both had to grow up too fast."

Thoughts ping like pinballs in my mind. I've always regarded myself as the underdog, the scrappy kid whose life went off the rails, who's had to fight for everything she's got, hiding behind the façade of Fabiana Fontaine. Max has the world laid out for him on a gold platter.

I've always thought we couldn't be more different if we tried.

But now that I'm lying here, next to this person I've always envied for his privilege and family, his position and carefree life, there's truth in his words.

We *are* more alike than I'd ever given credit. It's why I can see him for who he really is under his layers. I recognize myself in him.

We both perform for others.

We both hide our true selves.

Only we do it for very different reasons.

"Fabiana," he says, and there's something in the way he says my fake name that makes my chest tighten. "You don't have to be anything other than yourself with me."

If only you knew how impossible that is.

"That's very kind of you to say."

"I'm not being kind. I'm being selfish. As I said, I want to know you. Really know you."

"Why?" I ask, my voice breathy, not sure I want to hear his reply.

"Because…because I've never met anyone quite like you."

"Rude, sharp, name calling?" I joke in an attempt to break some of the tension between us.

"Intriguing," he replies, the word hitting me like an arrow through the heart.

A change of subject is needed, and fast, before I do or say something I might regret.

"My nona told me the pies from the bakery here are amazing. We used to get them when I was a kid." Suddenly, I can almost taste the strawberry and rhubarb, the apple, the blueberry.

"You're from around here?"

Oops. That backfired.

I give him my standard answer. "I'm from the north."

"We're in the north. Are you telling me you're from around here? You never said."

I can't share the name of my family estate. That could give the game away, if he's even aware of what happened to my family. Instead, I give him the name of the little town a few kilometers from what was once our gate.

"Campoverde?" he repeats in surprise, lifting his head from the pillow. "But that's not far from here. You're a local."

"Not really. I don't remember coming to this town before."

"But you know the pies."

"I do."

He relaxes back onto his pillow. "That's settled then."

"What's settled?"

"Pie for breakfast."

I let out a light laugh. "A man after my own heart."

There's silence for a beat before he replies quietly, "I am."

Instantly, my belly butterflies take flight, and I clear my throat in a vain attempt to halt their progress. But here's the thing about lying in a bed with a man, talking about things that matter to you, opening up more than you have with anyone before. It brings you closer to him, it makes you want things you can't have. It makes you want to open up to him, to tell him who you really are.

I want to be the real me with him, Valentina Romano.

But it would mean risking everything if I was.

Chapter 22

Max

I'M COCOONED in warmth and comfort, my heart telling me this is exactly where I'm meant to be, right here, in this moment. The cool of the night air has given way, and as I open my eyes, blurry in the soft morning light, I can hear the gentle patter of rain against the window, and the sound of soft, rhythmic breathing.

I let out a contented sigh, increasingly aware of a weight on my chest. I blink a few times as I look down to see a trail of golden hair across my shoulder like silk, an arm slung high across my belly, a hand placed loosely on my arm. Fabiana is breathing in and out, in and out, a soft, steady rhythm that somehow manages to be both comforting and utterly exhilarating.

The wall of pillows is discarded on the floor, and somehow, in the night we gravitated to one another, becoming entwined in a way that makes me want to stay like this forever.

This is both the best and worst way I could start the morning.

Best because having her this close, having her breath against my skin, watching her face completely relaxed in sleep, is everything I didn't know I was desperate for.

Worst because I'm acutely aware that this is undoubtedly an accident of sleep rather than a conscious choice, and any moment now she's going to wake up, realize our current configuration, and probably leap out of bed in horror.

So, I'm memorizing every second of this. How she feels against me, the softness of her skin, her warm breath on my chest.

Despite my instinct to drop a kiss on the top of her head, to wrap my arms around her and hold her close, I don't dare move. I don't want this moment to end. I want to lie like this with her in my arms, together, our breathing synced, our hearts as one.

She shifts slightly, and I freeze like a guilty man caught stealing the crown jewels. I'm stealing moments of intimacy with her that don't technically belong to me.

Yet.

I'm determined to change that.

Yesterday was…well, it was like no other day I've had with a woman. We talked, we opened up, we shared parts of ourselves that I, for one, had never shared with a living soul before. And she understood. She got me.

She saw the real me—the private me, the parts of me I keep hidden—and she didn't run away. She stayed, even opening up to share parts of herself with me. She held back. There are parts of her story she's keeping locked away. But I'm hopeful that in time, she'll trust me enough to tell me what she holds close.

Now, here in our bed, in this rain-drenched town in the middle of nowhere, I'm closer to this woman in my arms than I've ever felt to anyone in my life.

She stirs and lets out a soft sound that reaches inside and tugs at my heart. She lifts her hand from my arm to rub her eyes and then raises her head to look up at me.

"Good morning," I murmur softly.

Blinking, realization dawns, and her whole body stiffens.

The moment's gone.

She pulls away, sitting bolt upright. "I'm sorry. I...I don't know what came over me."

"It's fine. Really."

She looks at me as though I had just told her the sky is green.

"You drooled on me," I say with a smile.

Her mouth forms an O, which she instantly brushes with the back of her hand. "Oh, my gosh. How humiliating."

"I think it's cute."

"Drool isn't cute, Max."

"Don't tell Toffee that," I reply, and my dog's head lifts, her ears pricked as her tail begins to thump against the cushion.

Just as I feared, Fabiana leaps out of bed, pulling the blankets up to meet her pillow. "I'm going to use the bathroom. Good with you? Good." She's like a blur, buzzing around the room, collecting her clothes and darting into the bathroom.

Toffee and I share a look.

"Well, that happened," I say, and she rushes over to me, her tail wagging. I pull the covers back. "Come on then, girl. I'll take you outside."

I throw on some clothes and take Toffee out. When we get back to the room, wet from the rain, Fabiana is dressed and packing her bag, her hair tied up in her usual ponytail, glasses back on. All signs of the woman who lay sleeping on my chest are now gone.

"We might not be leaving today," I tell her as I remove my wet cap. "It's still raining."

"So, I shouldn't pack?"

"Let's get some breakfast and talk to the locals. They'll have a handle on what's happening."

"Were you serious about pie for breakfast?"

"One thing you should know about me: I'm always serious about pie."

She smiles, and it's the first I've seen today. She slips on a jacket, and I pass her my spare cap.

Toffee trots along beside us as we make our way up the rain-soaked street to the bakery, which Fabiana located on her phone. Luckily, it's open, and we shake off the rain as we head inside, the smell of fresh-baked goods making my belly rumble.

"This smells just like those pies did all those years ago," she says, pulling her phone from her pocket and filming the scene.

The cabinet is filled with pies and pastries and colorful cakes, the wooden shelves above stacked with a variety of breads.

Fabiana removes her spectacles to wipe the rain away. "The problem with glasses."

I snatch them from her and slide them onto my face. "How do I look?" I ask, grinning at her.

"Like a man wearing my glasses. Give them back." She reaches for them.

I lift them up and down, looking out to the street. "These make zero difference. Did you know that?"

She claims them, slotting them back onto her own face. "That's because you obviously need glasses."

"Is that so?" I ask with a laugh. "That's not what the Air Force says."

She lifts her chin. "Do you mind if I film you choosing your breakfast?"

"I wouldn't expect anything less."

She clicks on her camera as I make my way to the counter.

"Good morning, Your Royal Highness," a woman about my mother's age says from behind the counter as she dips into a curtsy. She's got a round, smiling face and light brown hair, speckled with gray, tied up in a net.

"Good morning. I hope it's okay that I've brought my dog in here. It seems cruel to leave her out in the rain."

"Your dog is welcome," she replies, and I note her name badge says *Marlene*.

"Did you hear that, Toffee? Marlene says you can be in here, but you need to behave yourself, or you'll get all of us kicked out."

Toffee looks up at me with eager eyes, her tail swishing from side to side across the wooden floor.

"Have you heard anything about the road today?" Fabiana asks.

"The fallen trees are being cleared this morning, and the forecast says the rain will let up later today, so we're hoping the river will recede before too long," Marlene replies.

"Does that mean we can get to Villadorata?" Fabiana asks.

Marlene gives a mournful head shake. "Not unless your car can transform into a boat."

"Well, actually," I begin only for both Fabiana and Marlene's eyes to widen to the size of soccer balls. "Kidding. My car is just a car."

"I thought you were going to tell us the palace issues James Bond cars to members of the royal family," Fabiana says.

"That would be fire," I reply with a laugh. "Now, Marlene, I've heard you have the best pies in the county."

Marlene squares her shoulders with pride. "We've won plenty of awards." She gestures at a shelf littered with cups and trophies.

"So, you have. Well done!"

Her face colors. "Thank you, sir. Whatever you want is on the house."

"You're very kind, but I insist on paying. Name your best pies."

Our food ordered—a slice of apple pie for me and a slice of strawberry and rhubarb for Fabiana, and two cups of coffee—we take a seat at one of the wooden tables, Toffee at our feet.

"I've never had a slice of pie for breakfast before," Fabiana says.

"You sure are living on the wild side."

"More than you know," she replies, and I wonder if there's truth to her words.

"If they've cleared the trees to the north, we can head back to the summer palace today."

"If it's okay with you, I'd still like to go see my nona,

even if she has messaged me again today to tell me she's in good hands with Rudolf." She rolls her eyes.

"They're in love, I tell you."

She shakes her head. "She never liked the man."

"People can change their minds," I say, and she slides her eyes briefly to mine before she looks away.

"Your breakfast!" Marlene announces, placing the food and coffee on the table between us. "I hope you enjoy!"

"Thank you so much," Fabiana says.

"It looks amazing," I add.

"Tell us, Marlene, what is there to do in this town on a rainy day?" Fabiana asks.

"Eat pastries, drink coffee, and then when the time is right, switch to wine and pasta." She throws us a wink.

"What if we wanted to do something in between all the eating and drinking?" I ask.

"If you had children, I would suggest you go to The Giggle Garden down the hill, but as you don't, perhaps you would like to go to the library and read a book, sir," she replies.

"Reading a book sounds fantastic to me," Fabiana says before she eats some of her pie. "Oh, this is just as good as I remember it."

"You've been here before, miss?" Marlene asks.

Something passes across Fabiana's face, but it's gone before I can work out what it is. "No, but I've had your pies. They're famous around here."

Marlene beams with pride. "Thank you."

"What's The Giggle Garden?" I ask.

"An indoor children's play area. It has things like a ball pit and a huge slide. The children love it. Me?" She shudders. "Not so much. It's too loud."

"A ball pit? With a huge slide?" I repeat, turning to Fabiana.

She shakes her head. "No, Max."

"Why not?" I ask.

She looks up at Marlene as though looking for a comrade. "Because it's for kids, right?"

"So?" I lean closer to Fabiana and add for her ears only, "We had fun in our fort last night, didn't we?"

Her cheeks bloom pink, and she picks up her coffee cup and takes a sip.

"You go on the big slide and in the ball pit if that's what you want to do, Prince Max," Marlene says.

"See?" I say to Fabiana. "Marlene said I could, so…"

She laughs, shaking her head. "Sure. Why not? We can pretend we're both four foot nothing and play in a ball pit. But you have to let me do some filming."

I reach across the table and shake her hand. "Deal."

Chapter 23

Valentina

I CANNOT BELIEVE I'm doing this.

I'm wearing a pair of socks with rubber pads on the bottom of my feet as I dash between soft-padded obstacles, brightly colored enough to induce a migraine. What's more, I'm clutching a foam gun in my hands while firing large yellow foam bullets at Max.

All the local kids are at school, so we have the place to ourselves, and we're taking full advantage of it.

It's immature. It's childish. And it's so much freaking fun. More fun than I've had in years.

We've bounced on the trampoline, slid down the slide into the ball pit, and then declared fully fledged war on one another with the aid of our bright yellow and red foam guns.

Being with Max brings out this side of me. Fun-loving, free-spirited, joyful.

If Judith Giovanni could see me now, she'd fire me before you could say *unresolved childhood issues.*

I find a foam barrier on the upper level and crouch behind it, my heart hammering against my ribs like it's trying to escape. Through a gap in the padding, I spot Max moving stealthily along the lower walkway, and I have to hold my hand over my mouth to keep from laughing out loud.

I'm being stalked by a member of the royal family brandishing a foam gun and a grin the size of Ledonia, intent on making sure I have fun.

I take a mental note to write the following video caption: *Prince Surprisingly Athletic in Foam Combat.*

He catches my eye, and I retreat, my back against the barrier.

He's seen me. *Dang it!*

"I know you're up there, Fontaine," he calls out, confirming my worst fears. "Your royal correspondent instincts won't save you now."

"We'll see about that, Your Royal Highness!" I call back as a foam bullet whizzes past my ear, close enough that I can feel it.

I let out a shriek before I take flight, dashing along the high bridge. With him hot on my heels, I'm aiming for the slide so I can whoosh down to the ground floor and take cover.

Through the mesh netting, I catch a glimpse of Max vaulting over a low barrier with the kind of athletic grace that makes me want to drop my gun and fall right into his arms.

But this is war. No time for that sort of carrying on.

"You think you're so clever, Fontaine, but I'm onto you!"

I hide behind a soft pillar. I lean around the pillar, line him up, and fire three quick shots. "Oh, yeah? Take that, Canossa!"

To my astonishment, one actually hits his chest. He comes to a sudden stop, glancing down before looking back at me. His look of mock betrayal sends me into a fit of giggles that the Valentina of just last week would have been deeply mortified by.

But this is the new Valentina, the Valentina who's shared more of herself with this man currently stalking her than she has with anyone before. The Valentina who understands the prince, who empathizes with him.

The Valentina who can finally admit she's falling for him.

The feeling is both exhilarating and utterly terrifying.

This should never have happened. And I fought it. *Really*, I did. Tooth and nail. That initial attraction, mixed with distrust and dislike of the man I thought Max was, has transformed into something so much more. So much deeper.

And I want it. I want *him*.

He's made his intentions toward me perfectly clear. He's allowed himself to be vulnerable with me, to trust me wholeheartedly with who he is.

For my part, I've held myself back, frightened that I can't be who I truly am with him.

But perhaps it's time to put that to rest. Perhaps it's

time to give him my full story. Perhaps it's time for me to allow myself to be totally real with this man, totally vulnerable, in a way I haven't been with anyone in all these years.

He makes me want to stop hiding.

My heart is hammering in my chest, and it's no longer just because of the game. I've been Fabiana Fontaine to the world for years, pretending to be this tough journalist so I can keep the lights on for Nona and me. In some ways, I've become her.

But I'm more than the journalist with the inside track.

I'm Valentina Romano, and I think it's about time I let her shine.

"You can run but you can't hide. Fontaine. I'm coming for you!"

I let out an excited giggle as I push myself up from my hideout and run like the wind along the bridge. I turn a corner and, to my surprise, there he is, the man I dare to want something more with.

We both stop and stare at one another, panting from the exertion. His lips curve upwards, his eyes sparkling with mischief. There's only one thing to do.

I dive onto the big slide, headfirst, sailing downwards at a rate of knots, letting out a maniacal scream as I do. I hit the ball pit, balls jettisoned into the air in the soft cage, my belly beginning to hurt from laughter.

The next thing I know, Max is roaring down the slide behind me. He lands, balls flying about, and as he catches my eye, a grin stretching from ear to ear, we break into fits of laughter, the heady concoction of being chased around this padded play area by the man I'm falling for rolling out of me, my whole body shaking.

Running and laughing with him like this brings back flashes of being children together in the palace gardens, before I had to become someone else. An innocent time, before my world imploded, before I had to become someone else.

And then, something shifts between us, and our laughter evaporates, replaced by something stronger. Something no longer childish. A muscular arm snakes around me, pulling me against him. My heart thuds as my body responds, melding to his, and I finally allow myself to give in to my overwhelming feelings for this man who's captured my heart and mind.

His eyes darken with intensity, and as I drop my gaze to his mouth, he tangles his fingers in my hair, pulling my lips against his. They're soft and perfect and just how I'd imagined they'd be, and I breathe in his delicious scent as I kiss him back with the urgency I feel for him, an urgency that can only be satisfied with one thing.

He lets out a soft moan as he deepens our kiss, his big hands holding me possessively against him. Our kiss is nothing short of magical, and I sink into it, full of passion and want, my heart thudding with everything I hold for this incredible man.

I'm lost in the moment, and as everything around us fades to nothing, it's just him and me and the way we feel about one another, finally taking form in the most wonderful, wonderful way.

Eventually, after we've kissed for longer than any self-respecting adults should in a ball pit, we pull back, resting our foreheads against one another's, our breath mingling.

"Max, that was… you are…" My voice is shaking and I'm unable to find the words to tell him how I feel.

"You are," he replies, smiling at me, his eyes dark. He leans in and places another long, lingering kiss on my lips. "I never expected this," he says, echoing my very thoughts. "But now that I've found you, I don't want to let you go."

"I... I feel the same way," I murmur, and when I look into his eyes, it's like the whole world disappears.

He brushes another soft, tantalizing kiss against my lips, and makes my whole body quiver.

"If I'd known you felt this way about foam warfare, I would have suggested we do this long ago."

"Just so you could kiss me?" I tease.

"Absolutely."

I need to tell him. I need to come clean. It's not fair to him to think that he has feelings for someone I'm not.

My heart is thudding so hard it could burst out of my chest with all the emotion I have for this beautiful, wonderful man who's holding me possessively against him. He trails delectable kisses along my jawline, sending shivers down my spine as he reaches my neck, and I want to lose myself once more in this perfect moment with this perfect man.

But everything is screaming at me to finally open myself up to him fully, to tell him who I really am.

Fear is holding me back.

What if he rejects me?

What if he tells me everything between us was based on a lie?

What if he tells me he never wants to see me again?

Telling him the full story, allowing him to see all of me, scares me to death.

As much as I want to, I can't tell him. Not now. Not during this perfect moment. It has the potential to destroy it—to destroy us—and that's the last thing I want.

I must, and I'm determined to find the right time. Then he can know the real me, and I can hold my breath and hope that he accepts me—*loves me*—for who I really am.

Chapter 24

Max

Of all the places I'd hoped Fabiana and I might share our first kiss, a ball pit in a child's indoor play area in a small town in the mountains didn't even make the list.

But you know what? I wouldn't change it for all the horrible tea in Malveaux.

Finally kissing her, feeling her soft, womanly curves pressed against me, understanding what it's like to hold her in my arms and claim her mouth with mine, is even more mind-blowing than I'd anticipated.

And let me tell you, I'd anticipated nothing short of fireworks.

The feel of her, the scent of her, the way she responds to my touch. It makes everything worthwhile. If it hadn't been for the proprietor telling us that the road south is now open, I bet we'd still be in that ball pit together.

Although that moment was absolute physical perfection, what strikes me most is how *right* it felt. How naturally she fit against me, how her laughter had dissolved into something deeper. For over a week, I've been watching her sharp wit and professional armor loosen, and in that ridiculous ball pit, surrounded by plastic spheres in primary colors, I finally saw past all of that to the woman underneath.

Fabiana has quickly become so important to me, morphing from the woman I thought I loathed into someone who has filled my heart and my mind. The transformation hasn't just been in how I see her, it's been in how I see myself. Around her, I'm not performing. I'm not the prince who has to charm his way through every interaction or the disappointment who needs to prove his worth. I'm just me.

It's nothing short of intoxicating.

The woman who once wrote scathing articles about my every misstep now knows the real me, and she kissed me back with a passion that told me none of my imperfections matter to her.

I grip the steering wheel as I turn to look at her in the passenger seat. She fell asleep a handful of kilometers ago, her face serene, beautiful. My heart expands in my chest. This woman has captivated me, mind, body, and soul. For the first time in my life, I'm not just attracted to someone. I'm not just infatuated or temporarily enchanted. This thing between us runs so much deeper than that.

I'm falling in love, completely and irrevocably, in love with a woman who sees me exactly as I am, and somehow finds that worthy of her affection.

The irony isn't lost on me that my greatest critic has become my greatest champion. But perhaps that's exactly why this is so real, so solid. She didn't fall for the prince in the tabloids or the charming facade I present at state dinners. She didn't fall for the life and soul party prince and all his antics.

She fell for the real me.

The roads opened about a couple of hours ago, and eager to see her grandmother, we collected our things from the inn, bid the townsfolk goodbye, and headed south.

We're now driving along the plains, past fields and small towns, their church spires visible from the road. The gray of the skies has given way to bright sun, and it's hard not to let it feel like it's a metaphor for our new, exciting togetherness.

She stirs, her eyes opening before she stretches her arms above her head, her hands reaching toward the ceiling of my car.

"Hello, sleepyhead," I say, and as she smiles at me, her whole face lights up and my heart expands.

"Where are we?" she asks.

"We're about an hour from the city. You've been asleep for a while."

"Have I?"

"I think I wore you out in the ball pit."

She presses her lips together, her iridescent green eyes sparkling. "I'd do it again in a heartbeat."

I reach for her hand and give it a squeeze. "It's a date, but maybe we could choose a more romantic spot than a child's play area next time."

I've already made some plans while she's been sleeping.

A candlelit dinner on the balcony, overlooking the palace grounds. A horse ride to the lake, where we can picnic and swim together in the warm summer sun.

"Not a ball pit?" she teases.

I laugh. "Not a ball pit."

We spend the rest of the journey chatting about inconsequential things until we reach the busy streets of Villadorata.

"Where do you and your grandmother live?" I ask as we come to a stop at a set of lights.

"Why don't you drive to the palace? I can make my way from there."

"I won't hear of it."

"Max. I need to collect my car. It's only practical."

"I can have someone drop it off for you."

She shakes her head, her stubborn independence shining through. "It's better this way. Then I can drive back to see you tomorrow morning."

Realization dawns. "You don't want me to meet your grandmother." I try to keep the hurt out of my voice.

"I need to talk to her about a couple of things first," she says carefully.

I pull my brows together as I study her face. "What do you mean?"

"Please don't ask me. I promise to tell you everything, Max, just…not yet." Her features are taut with tension.

As much as I want to know what she's hiding, as much as I want there to be nothing between us, I need to give her the space she needs.

"Whatever you need," I say softly.

She holds my gaze, and something moves between us. "Thank you. I will tell you."

A horn sounds, and we both jump.

"The light's green," she says, and I press the accelerator, moving the car along the street.

We reach the palace entrance, and the guard waves us through. I drive around to the staff carpark where I climb out to collect Fabiana's suitcase for her, placing it in her car.

"Thanks, Max, for everything, but especially for driving me to the station when I found out about my nona."

I pull her against me and brush a kiss across her lips. "Anything," I say in a murmur against her mouth, wishing we were somewhere private, and I could kiss her how I want to.

She smiles up at me, her eyes soft. "I don't deserve you."

I stop her words with my lips. "Don't say that."

"It's the truth. You're an amazing human being."

I grin. "Well, now that you mention it…"

She laughs as she bats me playfully on the arm.

"When will I see you tomorrow?" I ask.

"I can come here first thing," she replies without hesitation. "I'm still the journalist reporting on the real Max. I've got a job to do."

"I'd hope there are some things you'll keep to yourself, such as what a good kisser I am," I tease.

She grins. "Oh, I think the world needs to know that. Plus, how good you are at making forts."

She's only teasing.

"I'll miss you."

"I'll miss you," she replies. "As much as I don't want to, I really must go." She turns to leave, pulling her keys from her bag. Looking back at me, she says, "I'll see you tomorrow."

"I'll clear my schedule. Give my best to your grandmother," I say as I close her door over.

She winds down the window and her car shudders as she turns the ignition. "I will."

Looking up at me, stunning in the late afternoon light, her eyes soft, I can't resist kissing her one more time. Leaning down, I press my lips against hers, and immediately her hand slides around my neck as she kisses me back.

"Fabiana," I murmur, overwhelmed by the feelings I have for this woman.

"Until tomorrow."

I straighten up, my heart full of her. I watch as she pulls her car from the parking space. She throws me one final smile with a wave before she drives off, and I watch her leave.

I never expected to feel this way about any woman, let alone Fabiana Fontaine. But now that I do, whatever the thing she's keeping from me is, I'm determined to make her mine.

Chapter 25

Valentina

"Nona, it's so good to see you!" I rush across the living room floor and pull my grandmother into a hug, breathing in her familiar lavender and vanilla perfume. The late afternoon sunlight streams through the lace curtains, illuminating the dust motes dancing in the familiar surroundings.

It's so strange to think that when I left this house, I thought Max was nothing more than an over-privileged, immature man-child, and now I'm falling for the person he really is, the most wonderful man I've met.

What a difference a week can make.

"Valentina, my darling girl," she says as she gives me a squeeze. "Why are you home? Is everything all right?"

"I came to see you, Nona. How's your ankle?" I sink into the familiar worn cushions of our old sofa, the springs protesting. The contrast between this humble living room, with its faded family photos and Nona's knitting basket, and the palace's gilded opulence, is starker now, more than ever.

"It was only a sprain. I'm doing very well. Hobbling a bit, of course, and that old cane of your grandfather's has come in very handy." She gestures at a cane with a brass handle shaped like a pheasant, leaning up against the sofa.

"A cane?" I don't like the thought of my grandmother having to use a cane to get around. But she's a lot like me. She's tough. Strong.

"Should you elevate it? Ice it? Is it swollen?" I ask as I peer down at her feet.

"Stop fussing, Valentina."

"I'm allowed to fuss. You're my grandmother," I protest.

"Fiddlesticks."

"Nona," I warn. "It's my job to care about you."

"I told you not to come home just for me. I'm in very good hands. Rudolf has been taking good care of me. Not that I need taking care of, of course, but a little extra help is always welcome."

"It's nice that Mr. Beckman has been looking in on you," I say, and her face lights up at the mention of his name.

"He's just splendid. Very kind."

"And a good dancer, apparently."

"You might think I'm an old woman, my dear, but there's still life in me yet. I want to enjoy my autumn years."

A dull ache blooms in my chest at the thought of a world without her in it. "Don't talk like that."

"Like what? I'm old. It happens. But that doesn't mean I want to stop living."

I smile. "You sound like Max."

"Oh? How are things with the prince?"

"He's good." My cheeks begin to heat, completely giving me away.

Nona raises her brows at me. "I knew it! There was romance in San Fiorenzo!"

"Maybe," I concede, and she claps her hands together like she's an excited seal. "But it's very early days," I add quickly.

"I'm so pleased you took my advice. You've spent so long closed off from the world in this house, working, working, always working. You need to *live*."

"Well, if kissing a prince is living, I suppose you could say I'm doing that," I lead.

Her eyes widen. "Oh, Val. You kissed him?" I nod, happiness threatening to burst out of me. "I told you to put yourself out there. I told you not to blame him for his father's misdeeds, and you did it. You kissed him."

I shrug, the memory of being in Max's arms filling my chest with a warm glow.

"Tell me everything."

So, I do. I tell her about how getting to know Max changed my opinion of him, how the staff like him, how he behaved with the teens, how he gradually opened up to me more and more, showing me that he's a good, decent man who feels constricted by his role. A man who loves life with a zest that's infectious.

"That rainstorm certainly did the trick."

"It wasn't as though it was planned, Nona."

"Sometimes the universe has to push us off our intended path to get us where we truly belong."

I shake my head at her, grinning. "Since when did my grandmother talk about 'the universe'?"

"I've been on TikTok."

I blink at her in disbelief. "You have?"

"I started out watching your videos. I did so enjoy the archery one. That prince of yours is very athletic."

I'm about to protest as I did before that Max isn't my prince when I stop myself.

Perhaps he is my prince now?

The thought sends a warm glow of sunshine through my chest.

"How did you go from watching Max shoot an arrow to learning about the ways of the universe?"

"Oh, it's all on there, plus a lot of drivel."

I shake my head, laughing. "You will never cease to surprise me, Nona."

"We should always try to be surprising. Now, does Prince Max know you're Valentina Romano?"

My chest tightens, and I find myself unconsciously touching the spot where Max's hands had rested during our last kiss. "Not yet. It's been such a close-held secret for so long. But I want to tell him. I almost did."

She gives my hand a squeeze. "Oh, sweetheart. The complicated webs we weave. Do you love him?"

The directness of her question is like a jolt.

"I...I think I do."

Her hand flies to her mouth.

Tears prick my eyes. "I didn't mean to fall for him. It just...happened."

She pulls me roughly against her, patting my back. "It's

okay, darling girl. We can't help who we fall in love with. You just so happened to fall in love with the country's most eligible bachelor."

I pull back from her to see her eyes dancing, and I can't help but let out a watery laugh. "I suppose I did."

"Does he love you back?"

I think of the way he looks at me, the softness in his eyes. The way he kissed me, full of passion and something more. Something deep. Although he hasn't said it in so many words, it feels as though he does.

"I think he might, or at least he's on his way to."

"Well then, it's obvious what you have to do."

I pull my lips into a line. "I have to tell him."

"You must. The longer you wait, the more it will look like a deliberate deception on your part."

Her words hit me with the force of a blow, and I suck in a breath. "But what if telling him ruins everything, Nona? What if he can never trust me again? He thinks I'm Fabiana Fontaine, an uncomplicated journalist doing a job, not the daughter of a traitor his father sent away."

"You can't build love on a foundation of lies, sweetheart."

"But what if he looks at me the way everyone else did when Papa was accused? What if I see disappointment in his eyes instead of love?" My voice cracks. "I'm not sure I can take that."

"What if he doesn't?" she asks simply.

I wring my hands, spikes of anxiety prickling my body. "Right now, when he looks at me, he sees someone worthy of his attention. Someone he can trust. What if I tell him the truth and all of that disappears? What if he realizes that every conversation we've had, every moment of closeness, was built on my lie?" I sink back against the sofa, my heart heavy. "I've never felt this way about anyone. The thought of losing him, of seeing disgust in his eyes? It terrifies me."

She lifts her chin, levelling me with her gaze. "You forget who you are. You are Valentina Romano, daughter of Arabella and Vittorio Romano, a once great lord of this country with a lineage that reaches back to the Middle Ages."

"Exactly! A man who destroyed everything when he embezzled money from royal charities," I spit, the old bitterness rising like bile in my throat. "Do you know what it was like, Nona? Watching the neighbors whisper when I walked by? Having friends' parents suddenly decide I wasn't welcome in their homes anymore? I was twelve years old, just a kid, and suddenly I was the daughter of a traitor."

My throat burns as I stand up abruptly, pacing across the room. "And now I'm supposed to tell Max, the son of the man who banished my father, that I've been lying to him this entire time? That every moment we've shared has been built on a deception."

"Your father has always maintained his innocence," Nona says quietly. "And I believed him then, just as I believe him now."

Nona's beliefs come more from familial loyalty than anything based on cold, hard facts.

"He maintained his innocence and then ran away," I say, not capable of keeping the bitterness down. "He's never tried to come back to clear his name, Nona. What kind of innocent man just gives up?"

"He didn't give up, sweetheart. He was protecting you—"

"By abandoning me?"

The words come out sharper than I intended.

"He did what he had to do," she says quietly.

"Nona, I was twelve. He left me to deal with the whispers, the shame. If he was really innocent, he should have stayed and fought."

Nona's face softens with understanding. "You're angry with him."

My shoulders slump. "I love him because he's my father, but I also resent him."

"Regardless of what happened back then with your dad, you're not responsible for his choices. As you said, you were a child." She rises to her feet, reaching for grandfather's cane.

My hands shake as I reach to steady her, but she gently pushes me away.

"This family has spent all these years in shame," she says, her voice steady. "Isn't it time to stop hiding?"

"You make it sound so simple."

"Simple? No, darling. Of course, it's not simple. But it's necessary if you want any kind of future, for yourself and for this man." She gestures around our once grand living room with its peeling wallpaper and furniture that's progressively falling apart. "Look at what fear has given us. Look at what hiding has cost us."

I look around the room at the sunken sofa, the tattered chairs, the frayed rugs. Every cent I've earned has gone into maintaining this house and it still looks like it's one step away from becoming Miss Havisham's house, old and decrepit, a house where hope once lived. A house where I've hidden away for years.

"Valentina, whatever has come before, if you want a future with him, you need to tell him the truth. The longer you wait, the harder it becomes to explain why you waited."

Of course she's right, and we both know it.

"I know," I whisper. "I have to tell him. Tomorrow, I'll

ask him to go somewhere private. I'll tell him everything. I'll tell who I am, why I hid it, all of it. And I'll tell him how I feel about him as well." I press my lips together, the thought of losing Max like a physical pain in my ribs.

Nona reaches over to tuck a strand of hair behind my ear. "Your grandfather used to say that love worth having is love that survives the truth. If this prince of yours truly cares for you, he'll find a way to forgive you."

"What if he doesn't?" I ask, my voice cracking.

She presses a kiss on my forehead. "Then he was never worthy of my beautiful, clever granddaughter's heart."

Chapter 26

Max

I'M in my office the following morning, catching up on communications. I checked in with Rocco first thing and was glad to hear that the kids had moved inside and camped on the living room floor before they headed home yesterday afternoon.

Now that the trains are running again, a recovered Pippa Chen is the sole occupier of the royal train, whizzing back south.

There's a knock at my door, and I look up, calling out, "Come in."

And then in walks the woman of my dreams, and my heart leaps at the sight of her. Fabiana Fontaine. My Fabiana.

Unlike her usual look, she's got her hair loose around her shoulders, her glasses nowhere to be seen, and she's wearing a white button-up shirt and a pair of jeans that hug her curves in a way that sends me wild.

I pick her up and spin her around, ecstatic to have her back in my arms. I press an urgent kiss to her soft lips, breathing in her scent. "I missed you. It's been less than a day, and I missed you."

"I like hearing that," she says, her lips pulled into a smile.

"How's your grandmother?"

"She's doing great."

"You must be relieved."

"It's certainly a weight off my mind."

"Good." I kiss her once more. "I get to kiss you whenever I like, don't I?"

She giggles, and it's the most wonderful sound. "Do it again."

So, I do just that, kissing her lipstick right off her face. "I have something to ask you."

"What is it?"

"Fabiana Fontaine, will you do me the honor of attending the Autumn Ball with me as my guest?"

"The Autumn Ball?" she asks, her eyes as big as two full moons on a clear night. "But then everyone will know about us."

"Is that so terrible?"

She gazes at me, and I can't imagine a more perfect

moment with this beautiful woman in my arms. "It's not terrible at all. It's just—"

"I get it. It's your job. I've thought about that. The ball isn't for a couple of weeks, during which time you will have finished your series on me."

"That's true."

"Then we can come out as a couple and people can't say anything terrible about us."

"They still will."

"Let them."

She bites her lip, and something passes over her features.

"What is it?"

"Max, there's something I need to tell you," she begins, her features tight, and I want to reach out and touch her, to soften the hard edges of her face, smooth the worry from her forehead.

Could this be what she's withheld from me?

"You can tell me anything."

She begins to pace the room, her hands clutched together. I wait, my heart hurting for her. Whatever this thing is she's been so hesitant to tell me, it certainly weighs heavily on her.

"This isn't easy for me," she says, coming to a stop beside me.

I reach for her hand, lift it to my lips, and brush a kiss across her knuckles. "I find the best thing to do is to just come out and say it."

She nods her head a few times, the look in her eyes intense. "You're right," she says as she grips my hand so tight she's in fear of cutting off the blood supply. "You're right." She takes a deep breath and begins. "Here goes. I'm not—" she begins, just as the door flies open with a bang and Amelia rushes in.

She's got her phone in hand, her face pale.

When her eyes land on us, she comes to a sudden stop. "There you are, Max!" Her gaze fixes on Fabiana, and her eyes widen. For a moment, she just stares at her, her mouth opening as if to say something, before snapping shut again. Something flashes across her features, then her expression hardens as she looks back at me.

"Amelia?" I question, not sure what to make of this odd entrance.

"Oh, please tell me you already know about this!" she exclaims.

"About what?" I ask, frustrated that Fabiana didn't have the chance to finish what she'd begun to tell me. "Ami, we're in the middle of something important here."

"Is it true?" she asks Fabiana.

Fabiana looks equally confused. "Is what true?"

"This!" Amelia brandishes her phone in the air.

"Have you had too much caffeine today, Ami, because you're seriously wired," I say with a snicker.

Amelia marches over to me and grabs me by the arm, pulling me away from Fabiana.

"What the heck, Ami?" I protest.

"You need to read this *now*, Max," she hisses as she thrusts her phone in front of me.

"What's going on?" Fabiana asks, and I'm surprised to hear a tremor in her voice.

I shrug. "No clue, but Ami's being a total drama queen. As usual."

"Read it," my sister insists, thrusting her phone at me once more, so close it almost hits my nose.

"Since you asked so nicely." I take it from her and immediately my belly tightens with apprehension as I read the headline.

*Royal RomCom or Rom*Con*?*

I look back at my sister. "What is this?"

"Keep reading," she instructs again, sounding more like bossy Sofia than my fun-loving sister.

I scroll down to see that the article is accompanied by a grainy photo of Fabiana and me kissing in the palace carpark. My heart leaps into my mouth. "Oh, no." I turn to Fabiana. "They know."

"Know what?" she asks, her voice low and steady.

"About us. Have you seen this?" As I hold the phone up for her, I feel a hand on my arm. I look back at Ami.

"Read the full article," Amelia instructs.

"Why? What does it say?" Fabiana asks. She's clasping her hands together so tightly her knuckles have turned white.

I understand. She's a journalist, here to do a job. The last thing she needs is for the country to learn we're romantically involved.

I scroll past the photo and begin to read.

Fabiana Fontaine's exposé on Prince Max is starting to look more like an exposé of passion than anything professional, the couple being caught in a clinch in the palace grounds yesterday. Is this part of your ploy, Ms. Fontaine? Or just a perk of the job?

"How the heck did they photograph us?" I ask, indignant. "We were in the staff carpark." I glance at Fabiana. Her face is blanched white, her eyebrows knitted together so tightly they could crush walnuts. I reach for her hand, but she wraps her arms around herself.

"Keep reading," my sister instructs.

But things get even more delicious when you delve a little deeper, which is exactly what we at The Post *have done.*

A very reliable source has assured us that Fabiana Fontaine, the woman currently enjoying Prince Max's smiles, among other things, is not who she purports to be.

She is, in fact, someone else entirely.

The words jump out at me, and something twists in my gut.

Masquerading as Fabiana…been doing it for years…Valentina Romano… daughter of the disgraced lord, Vittorio Romano… Does the prince know?

Does the prince know.

"This is ludicrous. Made up rubbish," I say as I shove the phone back at Amelia. I turn to Fabiana. "They're saying you're not who you are. That you're in fact Valentina Romano, daughter of Lord Vittorio Romano. That's preposterous, right? Who writes these things?"

But the look on Fabiana's face tells me it might not be quite as preposterous after all.

My heart stutters. "Fabiana?" I question.

Fabiana's hand flies to her mouth, her eyes wild. "Max, please let me explain."

Wait. What?

One half of me is amused, and the other half has begun to wonder whether I should in fact be freaking out.

"What do you mean 'explain'?" I ask tentatively, watching her carefully.

"I was just about to tell you, I swear. That's what I was trying to do when your sister turned up just now," she says.

"How convenient, Fabiana," Amelia remarks, her arms crossed as she glares at her. "Or should that be Valentina Romano, the girl who used to come here with her father all those years ago?"

Carefully, with my limbs like jelly, I look back up at Fabiana. "You're Valentina Romano?"

Slowly, with her eyes trained on me, Fabiana's hand drops from her mouth. "I am," she says simply.

She's not who she said she is.

She's someone else instead.

"Oh, my!" Amelia exclaims, her eyes wide. "It's true. Father will have kittens!"

"What?" I ask, not believing my ears. "You're making a joke, right? Something I don't get." My brain begins to feel like someone just scrambled the TV channels.

Fabiana shakes her head slowly. "It's not a joke, Max. I am Valentina Romano. That's what I was trying to tell you. That's what I've been holding back from you." Tears prick her eyes, and her lip begins to tremble. "We used to play together. At garden parties, at royal events. I was Valentina then, and you... you were just Max, before everything became so complicated."

We used to play together. I remember her. I remember Valentina, the little girl with dark hair and those bright green eyes, who would always try to one-up me in our games.

Panic tastes like metal in my mouth, and I swallow, the tightness in my throat amplifying with each thud of my heart. "You're not Fabiana Fontaine?"

"She's a made-up person. Someone I've hidden behind for years." She places her hand over her heart, sucking in a ragged breath. "I wanted to tell you, Max, but it was so hard for me." Her voice is catching.

I clench my jaw, my chest buzzing. "It was too hard for you to be honest with me? To tell me the truth after what we've grown to mean to one another?"

"You don't understand. I had to change my identity. My father's disgrace had clung to me throughout my teenage years. I was forced to leave my school, to move to Villadorata to live with my grandmother, but everyone knew who I was. Everyone knew what he'd done. Becoming Fabiana made me free of that, free to carve out a new life, to forget that my father destroyed my family legacy."

Her words rumble over me, my mind reeling. This woman I thought I knew, this woman I thought I was falling in love with, isn't who she said she is.

It's all been a lie.

A horrible joke.

And I'm the punchline.

"Your necklace. That's what the V is for. Valentina."

She looks down, giving a brief nod of her head.

"Romano. Your father was the one who—" Amelia's voice trails off as the full magnitude hits her. "He ran away after embezzling Crown funds."

"I remember that," I say, my eyes riveted to Fabiana.

Fabiana—*Valentina*—has the good sense to look ashamed. "It might have been a story to you, but to me it was my life, and it changed in a day." She holds her hands out, palms up. "Max, please see it from my point of view. I was going to come here and do the project and leave, and no one would be the wiser. I never intended to fall in love with you, and when I realized I was falling for you, I was terrified that you would see me the way everyone else did, as if I was tainted by my father's crimes."

My breath comes short and fast, but there's one word that I cling to, even though it's hopeless.

Love.

"You love me?" I ask, my voice shaking.

She looks up at me, her eyes filled with tears. "Yes," she whispers, her breath caught in her throat.

"How do I know you're not lying now?"

"Because I've got everything to lose if I do."

"You can destroy me with what you've learned about me. Was that your plan all along? Is this all just revenge for what happened to your father?"

Aghast, she exclaims, "No! I came here in good faith to do a job. I might not be the royal family's biggest fan because of what happened, but I agreed to represent you as I saw you, and that's what I've been doing."

"It's all falling into place," Amelia says. "The way you always seem to know what's going on in our lives. You had the inside track. You've spent time here. You probably have a cast of spies everywhere."

"Is that true?" I ask.

"I did come here before it all happened."

I blink at her in total astonishment. "So, when I showed you around the palace that time, you could have been my tour guide?" I spit.

"I couldn't let on that I'd been here before. What would a journalist have been doing here as a child?" she replies.

I throw my hands in the air. "More lies."

"I didn't want you to find out like this." Fabiana reaches for me, touching her hand to my forearm.

Instantly, I tense. "Why did you do it?" I ask, forcing steadiness in my voice, my gaze boring into hers, searching for the answers I need so desperately to hear.

"I told you. I had to do it. I had no other choice. Max, my life was destroyed back then by what happened. I needed to become someone else."

My heart is thrashing in my ears, my throat tight as I struggle to breathe.

I feel utterly betrayed. Betrayed, humiliated, angry. Hurt.

"I told you things that I've never told anyone before."

She hangs her head. "Yes."

"I trusted you, and now I find out from some journalist that you've been lying this whole time? Every conversation we had, every moment you saw me vulnerable. Was any of it real? Or were you just gathering material for your story?"

"No! It was never like that, Max. I promise you." Her throat works. "I'm so sorry."

I stare at her in utter disbelief.

With my jaw set, I grind out, "I think it's time you left." My voice surprises me with how calm it sounds.

"Max, please."

I pull my lips into a line and shake my head from side to side. "There is nothing you can say that will change the way I feel."

Her chest rises and falls with each breath she takes as a tear makes a track down her cheek. "I understand," she says softly, and then she collects her things, and heads to the door. When she reaches the hallway, she looks back at me one last time.

I turn away, a sharp ache tearing through my chest. The woman I thought I was falling for just broke my heart —and the worst part is, she never even existed.

Chapter 27

Valentina

I stumble home, my heart heavier than a sky that's lost its sun. I drive through the busy Villadorata streets, unshed tears blurring my vision, replaying the scene over and over in my mind, blindly hoping for a different outcome. An outcome in which I still have Max in my life. An outcome in which he looks in my eyes and tells me he understands, that he forgives me for what he knew I had to do.

That he loves me.

But no matter how many times I roll through the scene,

it always ends with the look of shock and betrayal on his face.

His sending me away.

It being over between us.

Part of me knew this day would come, the day in which my Fabiana Fontaine mask was forced to drop, and I became me again. I thought I would be the one to control it. I would be the one to win. But now that it's happened, I never imagined it would hurt this much.

I may have been pretending to be someone else, but my love for Max is real. I fell for the man he is, the man who has qualities the length of the longest river. I may not have shared all the details of my life, but what I did share was the truth. He saw the real me, even if he thinks it was all lies.

What started out as a need for protection, at first a sanctuary from what had become of my life, ended up as a prison, and in the end, I was too busy protecting myself that I destroyed the one thing worth protecting.

The cruel irony is that I was finally ready to tell him the truth when it was ripped away from me. How would he have reacted if I'd had the chance to tell him myself? Would he have been this hurt, this angry, this betrayed?

I'll never know.

When I park outside our dilapidated house, my instinct is to run upstairs and hide, bury my face in my pillow, and sob until my tears are all dried up. Instead, I pull the article up on my phone and read the whole thing from start to finish. It was written by Miranda Thorne, the journalist I'd met at the state dinner, who got my back right up. She'd dropped hints that she knew more about me than I'd want her to know, and it turns out she was right on the money.

But where did she get her information? No one knows who I really am. I've been Fabiana Fontaine for years.

I open a social media app and do a quick search for Fabiana Fontaine. A bunch of people are already talking about Miranda Thorne's revelations, some questioning if it's true, some deciding it has to be, and I should be thrown in jail.

Jail!

I click my phone off. I can't take it right now, not when my whole world has imploded around my ears.

I need a hug from the one person who knows everything there is to know about me.

I find her in the conservatory, watering the orchids she's always loved. She takes one look at me and drops her watering can, opening her arms and wrapping them around me.

"My darling girl, what's happened?" she asks, and the concern in her voice brings out the tears I'd been holding in. I bury my head in her shoulder as she soothes me with her words, my shoulders heaving as I let it all out.

My public exposure as a fraud.

Max's reaction to learning the truth.

That I was trapped in an impossible position.

The finality of his words when he told me to leave.

"Shall we have a nice cup of tea?" Nona suggests when finally, my tears stop.

"Okay," I reply, my voice hoarse.

A few minutes later, we're at the kitchen table, and Nona's pouring us both a cup from her favorite teapot.

She pushes a cup and saucer across the table. "Take a sip," she instructs, and I do as she says, the hot liquid sliding down and warming my throat. "Now, tell me all about it."

"A journalist called Miranda Thorne discovered my real identity and published it in *The Post*, along with a photo of Max and me kissing."

"Oh, how dreadful! Did she name you?"

I nod.

"And did she connect you to your father and what happened to him?"

I nod again.

"How did she know? We've been so careful."

"I'm not sure, but it's all over social media now. Fabiana Fontaine is officially dead."

She gives my hand a squeeze. "Oh, sweetheart. Does the palace know?"

A stab of pain shoots through me as I picture Max's face. "I was there when Princess Amelia came in to tell Max about it. He…he didn't take it well."

And there we have it, the understatement of the year.

"Did you explain to him why you did what you did?"

"Of course I did, but he didn't want to know." I toy with my teacup. "He sent me away."

"He's shocked, that's all. He'll come around. You two were building something special together."

I press my lips together, my heart tight in my chest. "I don't think he will, Nona. He was pretty hurt."

The way he looked at me was like a lightning strike, straight to my heart. I hurt him. He put his trust in me. I might have wanted to tell him who I really was, but the truth of the matter is I hadn't. Even when we shared the bed at the inn, when we kissed that first time in the ball pit, when he drove me back to the city. I put it off. I let my fear get the better of me.

And look at how that worked out.

His words ring in my ear. *There is nothing you can say that will change the way I feel.*

"I don't think I'll be hearing from the prince any time soon, Nona. Not unless he's going to take legal action or something."

"Legal action," she repeats, appalled. "Why on earth would he do that?"

"They would say I got the job on false pretenses," I reply with a defeated shrug. And more than that, he told me things he hadn't told anyone. Now, seeing me as a liar, he'll be worried that I'll do something with those secrets. Sell them. Profit from them.

I would never do that. I'll take them to the grave.

I'd give him my word on that if I thought it meant anything to him.

"If he truly loves you, the you that you've shown him, then a name won't change that."

I let out a heavy sigh. "It already has."

"Then he's not a man who's worthy of you."

I manage a small smile through my malaise. "Thanks, Nona. You're always in my corner."

"As far as I'm concerned, there are no other corners to be in."

My phone buzzes, and I pull it from my purse to see my boss's name on the screen.

"I'm not sure I can face her right now," I say, wrestling with whether I should answer or not.

"Well, then don't. She'll keep. You're allowed to feel sad about this, and in your own time."

I turn the phone over on the table, but no sooner has the ringing stopped than it starts up again.

I shoot Nana a look.

"Switch it off," she instructs. She pours some fresh tea into my cup, and I take another sip. "Your father never stole a single penny. I would stake my life on it."

"Nona," I warn. "Do you mind if we don't? I'm not in the mood for conspiracy theories."

"There are things about that time. Inconsistencies."

I close my eyes. Nona has never accepted what

happened, and when she gets on a roll, there's no stopping her.

"Things that were never looked into properly. That Lord Blackwood always resented your father's influence with the King."

This gets my attention. "Lord Blackwood? As in Cyril Blackwood?"

"Yes, the snake. He always had it in for your father, right from their time in boarding school."

"I met him at a dinner at the palace just over a week ago."

Was that only last week?

"Dreadful man. He bought our family land, and at a bargain basement price, as well."

"Did he?"

"Your father was innocent. Someday the truth will come out. Mark my words."

"I'm not even sure it matters anymore. The damage is done. Max will never trust me again."

There's a loud rat-a-tat-tat on the door, and Nona and I both look at one another in surprise.

I push myself to my feet. "I'll get it." I make my way down the hallway and pull open the front door, only to be faced with not only my boss, looking as frazzled as someone with their finger in an electric socket, but a horde of other people, flashes going, people calling my name—both Valentina and Fabiana.

"Come on, let me in," Judith says, her voice high with panic as she pushes past me into the hallway, leaving a waft of perfume in her wake.

Immediately, I slam the door shut behind her. "What the heck?"

"You, my dear, have caused quite the ruckus," she says, her bright red pantsuit crumpled and her thick-rimmed hot pink glasses askew.

"How do they even know where I live?"

She finds a hallway mirror and straightens herself out. "Because everyone knows who you really are now, my dear girl," Judith responds before she turns to me and says, "It would have been nice to have been clued in."

"About that." I begin when Nona's voice calls from the kitchen.

"Val? Who is it?"

"It's Judith Giovanni, my boss," I call back.

She nods in the direction of the kitchen. "Come on then. Let's meet your grandmother, shall we, *Valentina Romano?*"

She marches down the hallway, one hand held in the air. "Come! You can tell me all about it."

Judith Giovanni is not someone to argue with, and even though I'm certain she's here to fire me—or worse—I do as she says, reaching the kitchen, where I introduce her to Nona.

"I can see where your granddaughter gets her fine features," Judith says, making Nona smile. "Now, do you have anything stronger than tea? That mob out there was intense."

A handful of minutes later, we're in the living room, a decanter of whiskey on the coffee table, from which Judith has already had her first glass and is onto her second. I stand at the window and pull back the lace curtains to see a mess of people outside, with television vans and journalists and photographers as well as members of the public, all hoping to catch a glimpse of me, the woman who duped a prince.

"You look like a Valentina," Judith says as she eyes me from across the room. "You're not a natural blonde, are you?"

"No, I'm not," I take a seat opposite her. "It's part of my disguise. I don't actually need glasses either."

"As far as disguises go, it's not exactly high-tech, is it?" she replies before she takes another sip of her drink. "Jolly good whiskey."

"It's about a hundred years old," I reply. "And as for my disguise, the last time anyone knew I was Vittorio Romano's daughter, I was twelve."

"And you've changed a lot since then," Judith finishes for me.

"She was a cute twelve-year-old who blossomed into a beauty," Nona says with pride in her voice.

"Well, you're certainly in a pickle now. Lying to us all about who you really are, and getting caught kissing a prince no less."

I cast my eyes down, my heart throbbing. "You're here to fire me."

"Fire you? Are you quite mad? You're the hottest thing in the country right now. You've seen it yourself outside. Everyone wants a piece of you."

I look back up at her in surprise. "But I lied to you about who I am."

With a flick of her wrist, her gold bangles jangle. "Semantics, my dear girl. Yes, I would have preferred to have been given a heads-up, particularly when it all blew up. But you did what you had to do to survive. I admire that. It shows tenacity and determination."

"See, Val? Not everyone is against you," Nona says.

Just the royal family and about thirty reporters currently taking up residence outside.

Never one to mince her words, Judith replies, "There are a lot who are against you, however, but that's what makes this the story of the year. Not since Princess Amelia and Ethan Roberts were duped into a reality television program has the nation been so enraptured. And we learned about it all only today! Imagine what the next weeks will bring."

I groan. *Imagine.*

"I'm not sure I want to be a story, let alone the biggest story since the Princess Amelia reality TV palaver," I say.

"You don't have a choice in the matter." Judith places her glass back on the coffee table and leans her elbows on her knees. "First things first. What happened between you and the prince? Was it just a kiss? Or was it something more?"

I flick my gaze to Nona. She gives a brief head nod. "Not just a kiss," I say.

Judith's face lights up. "Marvellous! Would you be willing to write about it for the paper?"

I shake my head vehemently. I've already hurt Max enough. The last thing I want to do is go public about what happened between us. "I won't do that."

"We'll pay you well. You name the price."

"That story is not for sale."

"What will you do then?" she asks.

"I don't know," I reply truthfully. "I've hardly even caught my breath after Miranda Thorne's revelation today."

Judith harrumphs. "I can't stand the woman. She's made a deal with the devil, if you ask me. She'll get her comeuppance."

"One can only hope," Nona admonishes.

"While you work out what you're going to say about you and the prince, we will pay you handsomely for Valentina Romano's full exclusive story."

"Do you mean about what happened with her father?" Nona asks.

"About all of it. The country now knows that my top

journalist not only had a rather thrilling love affair with Ledonia's most eligible bachelor, but she's also the daughter of a disgraced lord and has been in hiding for years. It's gold!"

"It's not gold. It's my granddaughter's life," Nona grinds out.

"Of course it is." Judith drains her glass and rises to her feet. "Have something on my desk by the end of the week, Valentina." She pauses. "Valentina. I'll need to get used to that."

I stand. "The story won't be about what happened between the prince and me."

"Make it about the real you and your father, and we'll see about that later. Now, it was a pleasure to meet you, Lady V, and you, as it happens, *Valentina*." She marches out of the living room only to reappear. "Is there a back door? I'd rather not have to fight through the rabble again."

I take her to the back door where she reminds me to send my story to her, and then rushes away, leaving only a cloud of her perfume in her wake.

Chapter 28

Valentina

I sit at my desk in our dusty old library, staring at an empty screen. I can still hear the journalists outside several days on, and I do my best to block out their constant, intrusive noise.

I let out a breath as I run my fingers through my hair, now the natural brunette I've not seen since I was a teenager. It's a small way in which I can shrug off my past, show the world the real me.

I've looked like my Fabiana persona for so many years,

when now I look in the mirror, I'm someone I don't recognize. It's an odd sensation, but one I find I like.

I'm not pretending anymore. I'm Valentina Romano. If I'm not your cup of tea, don't drink me.

I type a sentence and then delete it. Then another and delete that. Where do I start with this article? There's so much that's happened in the past weeks. I've gone from being Fabiana Fontaine, a royal journalist who hid my identity behind my entertaining, sometimes frivolous reports and TikToks, to a woman who fell in love with the prince. Now, *I'm* the story, hunted by the press, hiding out in my nona's house, a prisoner of a different sort.

What's more, once I was a woman who wasn't looking for love. I didn't think I even needed it in my life. Now, I've fallen for a man who won't see me. A man I've not heard from since that fateful day at the palace.

A man I can never forget.

My heart literally aches when I think of what I've done to him. What I did to myself. He opened up to me, allowed himself to be vulnerable with me, and in return I broke his trust by not telling him my truth.

If I could go back…But I can't. What's done is done. There's no point in even thinking about it.

All I can do now is move forward with my life as Valentina Romano and try to right some of my wrongs.

I type a few words and then stop to read them.

My apology will never be enough, *by Fabiana Fontaine*

Yes. That's it.

As I type, the words begin to flow, and I know exactly what to write, what I *need* to write. It's what's in my heart, the part of my story that needs to be told before anything else.

This will be my last column as Fabiana Fontaine, because as most of you now know, she doesn't actually exist.

I am Lady Valentina Romano.

Yes, *that* Romano. The daughter of the disgraced lord who fled this country fifteen years ago, leaving behind scandal, shame, and a twelve-year-old girl who thought changing her name would change her fate.

Part of me is angry my father left me to face the consequences of his actions alone. Part of me is angry that he's never admitted his guilt, making it impossible for me to fully move on. And the twelve-year-old part of me that still remembers his care packages and piggyback rides just misses my papa and wishes things could be different.

For years, I've hidden behind Fabiana's sharp wit, using her as my armor against a world that knew my family's disgrace. And it worked. I had a career, a life. I became so comfortable living as someone else that I forgot the weight of lies until I met someone who deserved the truth.

I was too much of a coward to give it to him.

And now I've hurt someone who meant so much to me. I cannot change what I've done, no matter how much I want to. So, this is an open letter to him.

I hope he'll read it, but I don't expect he will.

This man trusted me with his genuine self,

giving to me unreservedly. He showed me kindness I didn't deserve.

In return, I kept my secret from him. I chose the comfortable lie over the difficult truth, and in doing so, I betrayed the trust of the one person I should have protected, the one person who grew to mean so much to me in such a short time.

I was a coward, pure and simple.

There's no justification that doesn't sound like excuse-making. I lied. I built our relationship on deception, then had the audacity to fall in love while maintaining that deception.

Because yes, I fell in love with him. Completely. Totally.

Hopelessly.

I've forfeited any right to forgiveness. Loving someone requires honesty, and I failed in that respect quite spectacularly.

What I need to tell you all is that every cruel thing I've written about him was wrong. He isn't the man-child I once described. He's the best man I've ever known. Strong, kind, with the kind of humility I was blind to, the kind of humility that shows up in him every single day. The humility I missed when I labelled him as less than he is.

So, this is where Fabiana Fontaine signs off. What remains is simply Valentina, the flawed, regretful, and finally truthful daughter of a once proud lord.

This man deserved better than my lies, and he certainly deserves better than my flawed love.

But he has both.

Valentina Romano xx

I don't add any hashtags as I read over what I wrote. I don't change a word. It's raw, it's real, and it's exactly how I feel. I share it with Judith. It's not what she's looking for. It's not a tell-all about my relationship with Max. It doesn't shed any light on what happened to my father all those years ago.

What it is, is my simple truth, an apology that needs to be made.

The article is published within three hours, and if I thought the media circus outside my front door was intolerable before, now it's the Olympics of overexposure, complete with commentators narrating how I take out the rubbish.

"They'll move on to the next story soon enough, Val," Nona says as I once again stand at the window, wishing the mob away.

I turn to look at her and Mr. Beckman, sitting side by side on the sofa. They've been grinning at each other like a couple of teenagers since he snuck in through the back door about half an hour ago.

"I think I just added a drum full of fuel to the fire with my article," I say.

"You said what needed to be said. Now, you can leave Fabiana Fontaine behind. You can reinvent yourself as Valentina."

"It's always best to be your authentic self," Mr. Beckman agrees as he gives Nona's hand a squeeze.

"Unless, of course, you're a horrible person like that Miranda Thorne," Nona replies.

"Oh, she's public enemy number one as far as I'm concerned," he agrees.

I flop down on the sofa opposite them. It gives a creak in protest, and one of the springs digs uncomfortably into my butt cheek.

It's a metaphor for my life right now.

I shift along until I find a sunken spot without metal armor. "I don't exactly have any choice but to be my authentic self."

"Do you *want* a choice?" Nona asks.

I worry my lip. If I had the chance to do it all again, would I remain as Fabiana Fontaine? Would I protect myself from falling in love with the prince?

Although it hurts like heck, I wouldn't give up those precious moments spent with him. Not for the world.

"I don't want the choice," I reply.

"That's my girl. Be proud of who you are. You are my granddaughter, after all."

"And what a grandmother you have," Mr. Beckman says, gazing at my nona with love in his eyes.

Seriously, it's like his eyes have morphed into little heart emojis.

"What would I do without you, Nona?" I ask, my throat heating up.

"You'd have a conservatory full of dead orchids for starters."

I smile. "I'll be sure to ask St. Nick for a green thumb this year."

My phone buzzes, and I pick it up to see which journalist is calling me now only to see Ronan Clementine's name appear on my screen. Instantly, my heart rate kicks up.

My first thought is that it's actually Max, and for some

reason he's using Mr. Clementine's phone. Totally illogical, but when is hope logical?

"I think it's the palace PR guy," I say.

Nona leans forward with interest. "I suggest you answer that one, Val."

Apprehension builds in me, but I answer anyway. Part of being the new Valentina Romano is being brave.

"Hello?"

"This is Ronan Clementine, Ms. Fontaine…or rather, should I say, Lady Romano."

"Hello, Mr. Clementine," I reply, my heart drumming.

"I understand you've been, err, swamped, shall we say, and I wanted to ensure you receive a package that's being sent to you today."

My heart sinks. It's probably legal documents. They're going to sue me. "A package?" I ask.

"Expect it in about an hour."

"All right." When he doesn't reply, I say, "Mr. Clementine?"

He clears his throat. "Ah, Ms. Chen says to say hello." I can hear a voice in the background. "Hello, Fab, to be precise."

I smile despite myself. "Say hi back."

"I certainly will. And Lady Romano? For what it's worth, I think it's a shame what happened. You had been producing some good work for the prince. He owes you a debt."

I swallow down a rising lump. "He doesn't owe me anything."

Within the hour, a package arrives, just as Mr. Clementine said it would, and I collect it from the delivery man, who looks just as frazzled as Judith had on my doorstep. I carry it into the living room and place it on the coffee table.

"It's a lot bigger than I thought it would be," I say as I stare at the package. It's at least ten times the size of the usual document packages I receive.

"Are you going to open it?" Mr. Beckman asks.

I twist my mouth. "I'm not sure."

"Shall I do the honors?" Mr. Beckman asks. "I've never seen a package from the palace. It's all rather exciting."

"No, I'll do it." I slide a knife along the taped edges and push the cardboard to each side. There's a layer of tissue paper, sealed with a black and gold sticker. "What the heck is this?" I pull back the tissue paper and suddenly, I can't breathe and my hand flies to my mouth.

"What is it, Val?" Nona asks with concern in her voice.

She and Mr. Beckman crowd around me, peering inside the package.

"Looks like a dress to me," Mr. Beckman says.

"Valentina, my darling, it matches your eyes perfectly," Nona croons.

I reach out and touch the emerald green silk, deep and rich. With trembling hands, I pull the dress from the box, and it spills out. Gold embroidery shimmers on the bodice and edges of the strapless dress, cut in a sweetheart shape. As I shake it out, the skirt billows out like a princess dress. A fairy-tale dress.

A note drops to the floor, and I lean down to pick it up and read it. All it says is the date of the ball and the location, at the grand ballroom at the palace.

In shock, I look up at Nona. She's smiling at me, her eyes soft.

"He wants you at the ball, my darling," she says.

"But…why?" I ask.

"Love is a very powerful thing," Mr. Beckman says, nodding his head sagely. "You've captured that man's heart. Mark my words."

Clutching the dress in my hands, I sit back down, suddenly overwhelmed.

"So?" Nona asks. "Will you go?"

I stare at the dress for a long moment, my mind racing through all the possibilities. The best case, the worst case, and everything in between.

"I honestly don't know," I admit. "Part of me wants to believe this means something wonderful. But the other part —?" I trail off, unable to finish the thought.

"The other part?" Mr. Beckman asks kindly.

"I guess the other part is terrified that hoping for too much will break whatever's left of my heart."

Nona and Mr. Beckman exchange concerned looks.

"Why don't you sleep on it, dear," Nona suggests. "There's no rush to decide. The ball isn't for a few days."

I slide the dress back into the box and close it over. I head toward the stairs. "I need to sleep on it. Tomorrow I'll decide."

"You'll know the right thing to do," Nona says.

The dress is the most beautiful thing I've ever seen, but I'm not sure I'm brave enough to wear it.

I'm not sure I'm brave enough to hope.

Chapter 29

"Max, your sash is crooked." My mother tweaks my blue satin sash as a muscle jumps in my jaw, nerves popping like corn in my belly. "What's with you tonight, darling? You're so on edge."

"I'm fine," I lie, forcing a smile. I'm anything but.

She places her palm against my chest, smiling up at me. In her Ledonian red ball gown, she looks really quite beautiful, her hair swept up off her elegant neck with a tiara nestled in her curls. "You've been through a lot lately. You can sit this one out if you want. Your father will understand."

Sitting this one out is the last thing on my mind. "I'm good. Don't worry about me."

"Darling, even though you're a grown man, I'll always worry about you," she says with a soft smile. "It's a mother's job." She pats my chest.

"All set?" Father asks as he steps into the room, looking resplendent in his red jacket, the same as mine, only his with significantly more gold detailing, appropriate for his status.

"My baby brother is having his mummy fix his outfit," Amelia teases from her position on the sofa beside Ethan.

"Less of the baby, thanks," I sniff.

She rises to her feet, puffing out her full skirt. "You'll always be the baby of the family, Max. That's life."

Ethan quirks a brow. "A six-foot two baby? Isn't he almost twenty-eight?"

Amelia and her husband share a smile, and it does something to my heart.

I want what they have.

Alex, who arrived in Villadorata with his wife and children this afternoon, comes to stand next to me. "Still taller," he declares as he slaps me on the back. "Hello, Max."

"No, you're not. I'm at least a centimeter taller than you," I reply.

"You could both be a couple of linebackers," Maddie says as she kisses me on the cheek.

"Is that a good thing?" Amelia asks.

"Oh, yeah," Maddie replies, her eyes dancing. "Are you okay, Max? You've had a rough few weeks, right?"

"I'm doing okay," I lie.

"Max, I thought you were bringing a date," Sofia asks, adjusting her tiara in the mirror.

Marco places a kiss on her bare shoulder. "You look beautiful, my love."

"I might be," I reply, my nerves cranking up.

Sofia turns to me. "So? Where is she?"

"I don't know," I reply honestly.

Father knits his brows. "Who is this woman who's keeping the entire family waiting? The ball is about to begin."

"Yes, Max, who is she?" Sofia asks, and every eye in the room turns to me.

"I've invited Valentina Romano," I say simply.

Mother's expression immediately fills with compassion. "I remember that little girl. She had the sweetest smile." She pauses. "Do you think she'll come after everything that's happened?"

"I'm not sure," I admit, my chest tight. "But I had to try."

Father studies me for a long moment. "You care for her."

"I do."

"Then I hope she comes," he says quietly, his hand on my shoulder.

I do, too.

"Let's get out there, shall we? The Autumn Ball waits for no man," I say.

"Or woman," Sofia says.

"Max is right. Let's greet our guests," Mummy says, and we begin to file from the room, heading to the ballroom.

I feel a hand on my arm and turn to see Amelia. "What?" I ask, both eager and terrified to get to the ball.

Will she come?

"What's going on with you?" she asks.

We're alone in the room now, so I come clean. "I've invited...well, I'm hoping Fabiana will be here. Valentina, I mean."

"Fabiana? Are you mad?" she guffaws.

"Maybe?"

She narrows her gaze. "You fell in love with her, didn't you?"

Slowly, I nod my head.

"Even though she lied to you about who she was?"

"I've realized she had good reason. She needed to put distance between herself and her family name. I couldn't hear it at first, but I understand now."

"Are you sure, Max? About her, I mean. She's been pretending to be someone else for years, someone who persecuted you."

I shrug. "I guess we'll see."

She studies my face before she pulls me into a hug. "I want the world for you."

"I know you do."

We join the rest of the family, and together we enter the ballroom, announced at the top of the sweeping staircase as is tradition. As it is every year, the room is decorated in an autumnal theme, with garlands of maple and oak leaves wound around marble columns, and delicate bronze pheasant figurines nestled among floral arrangements in reds and yellows and oranges.

I smile and make small talk with everyone I meet, always keeping an eye on the double doors. *Hoping... hoping...*

Mother announces the dancing, and each of my siblings and their spouses step onto the floor, looking elegant and in love, just as they always do. Several women catch my eye, hoping for a dance, but all I do is smile at them and look away.

There's only one woman I want to dance with, and she's not here.

It had felt so romantic to simply invite her tonight by sending her a dress anonymously. Now, with almost half the evening gone, I wish I'd been more direct. I wish I'd simply turned up on her doorstep and told her how I feel about her. Tell her what I've learned.

But I didn't, and right now, with the ballroom double doors firmly shut, what hope I'd held that she would come begins to dwindle like the last echo of a fanfare in the palace courtyard.

An elderly woman in a black velvet dress, her long gray hair captured in a bun, approaches me. She has a pleasant face, and when she smiles her eyes twinkle in the golden glow of the ballroom.

She inclines her head, dipping into a shallow curtsy. "Good evening, Your Royal Highness," she says.

"Good evening," I reply, wracking my brain for which member of the aristocracy this woman is. I come up with nothing. "I don't believe we've met," I say, keeping one eye on the door.

"My name is Lady Violetta Romano," she says, and immediately she captures my full attention

"You're Valentina's grandmother?" I ask, my heart stuttering.

"I am," she replies, her chin lifted with pride. "I hope you'll pardon an old woman's boldness, but I felt I must speak with you."

Hope leaps in my chest. "Is she here?" I scan the room but see no sign.

"I want to ask you a question, and I hope you'll give me the respect to respond truthfully."

"Of course I will."

"My granddaughter has made mistakes, but she's suffered enough. If you've invited her here out of anger or for some kind of public humiliation, please tell me now. I cannot stand by and watch her heart break again."

That she would think I was capable of such a thing... But I understand. Valentina told me the truth, and I sent her away. *Of course,* her grandmother will be dubious about my intentions.

"You have my word, Lady Romano. I have nothing but the very best of intentions where your granddaughter is concerned."

She studies my face for a beat before she says, "I believe you."

"Thank you," I say, meaning it. "Can I see her?"

"I will speak with her. But young man?" Her voice is sharp. "It will be her decision what she does next."

A small smile works its way across my face. "I would expect nothing less of her, Lady Romano."

As I watch her make her way around the dance floor, flashes of recognition appear on guests' faces, and I bet it took a lot for her to come here tonight.

She's here. The woman I love is here.

I can barely contain my excitement, and I have to work hard at stopping myself from tearing after her grandmother and demanding to see her.

But I gave my word, so I need to wait. Wait and hope.

And then, the doors I've watched for so long tonight, open and there, standing alone, breathtaking in the dress I handpicked for her, her hair dark, falling in soft waves around her shoulders, is the woman I love.

Valentina Romano.

She takes a tentative step forward, her hands clasped at her waist, searching the room. When her eyes land on mine, they flash with recognition, her lips parting as she takes a deep breath, and I can no longer contain my need for her that coils in my chest.

I can no longer stand and wait.

I rush toward her, apologizing as I bump into people, stepping on dresses, but not once taking my eyes from hers.

"You came," I say, my heart thrumming in my ears at the sight of her. The dress is everything I imagined it would be on her when I'd chosen it. She looks regal, beautiful, elegant. She's power wrapped in beauty, and I'm utterly transfixed.

"You look—" I begin, but suddenly, I can't find the words. How can I tell her she's more beautiful than I've ever seen her, more beautiful than I've ever seen anyone, a stunning, almost otherworldly vision in emerald.

In the end, I settle on, "You look perfect."

Her full lips—the lips I've thought about kissing again and again, that have tormented me since I sent her away—pull into a hint of a smile, and I no longer want to be here in this crowded room with people watching us, waiting to hear what we have to say.

This is between us. Her and me. No one else.

I take her by the hand. "Will you come with me?"

"Yes," she breathes.

With prying eyes watching our every move, I lead her to the terrace and close the doors firmly behind us. Bathed in the soft moonlight and glow from the ballroom, she looks even more beautiful, and it takes all my strength not to pull her to me and claim her as mine.

That must wait.

"Thank you for coming, Valentina," I say, her lyrical name feeling odd on my lips.

"Did you see my article?"

"I did. It meant everything."

She moves closer to me, and I catch her scent in the air. "Max, I'm so very sorry about lying to you."

"I don't need you to apologize again."

"You don't?"

I can no longer resist my overwhelming need to touch her, to feel her warm body next to mine. I wrap her in my arms and hold her close, my heart thudding against my ribs as though it's trying to escape. "I forgive you wholeheartedly."

"I never dared hope you'd forgive me," she replies softly.

"I only hope *you* can forgive *me*."

She looks up at me, her eyes shining. "For what, Max? You did nothing wrong."

"I sent you away that day," I reply, the memory of the look on her face like a physical pain in my chest.

"How could you not? I lied to you."

"You were only doing what you had to do. I understand that now. You were protecting yourself. I have things to tell you. Important things."

"What?"

I take her by the hand and together we sit on one of the stone benches. "I did some investigating into what happened with your father."

She blinks at me in shock. "Why?"

"After you left the palace that day and I'd calmed down, I read Miranda Thorne's article. It didn't sit right with me. She seemed to know details about your father's case that were oddly specific."

"You sound like an investigative journalist."

"Perhaps that could be a new career for me?" I reply, and we share a smile.

"So, I had Dante do some digging for me."

"Dante? As in your Air Force friend?"

"Former Air Force, now a private investigator. He searched through all the files. He discovered some inconsistencies and followed through on some of them."

"And?" she asks, eagerness in her eyes.

"And it would seem your father was innocent."

Her hand flies to her chest. "What?! Max, how?"

"The man who accused your father of embezzlement and provided most of the evidence against him was Lord Blackwood."

"Lord Blackwood?" she repeats, aghast.

"Here's the key thing Dante discovered. The financial irregularities didn't stop when your father fled the country. Money continued disappearing from the same royal charities for months afterwards, but it was covered up."

"But if Papa had been the one stealing—"

"Exactly. It should have stopped the moment he left the country. But it didn't." I squeeze her hand. "Blackwood had massive gambling debts around that time, debts that were paid off just after your family left Ledonia."

"I don't understand. How could Lord Blackwood frame my father?"

"Dante found forged signatures and backdated papers, but the most damning evidence was a bank account."

"What kind of bank account?"

"One that Blackwood opened under a false name, routing stolen funds through it. He got sloppy. He used his own address for the correspondence. It was all there in the old records, but no one looked closely enough because they already thought they had their man."

She stares at me for a long moment, as if trying to absorb the magnitude of what I've told her. "My papa. All these years he's been living with that shame, and he was innocent all along? The man I believed to be a criminal was telling the truth?" She covers her face with her hands, and my heart aches for her.

"It's a lot to take in."

She lets out a laugh. "You're telling me."

"As the person who exposed Romano, Blackwood was put in charge of financial oversight to prevent future incidents. This gave him perfect cover to continue stealing while appearing to be the solution. He'd positioned himself as the hero who saved the Crown from a traitor."

"People don't suspect their saviors."

"There's more," I say softly.

"More? How could there possibly be? Max, finding this out, you've already done so much for me, for my family."

"He was the one who worked out who you were. He told Miranda Thorne to investigate you."

"Lord Blackwood is the villain," she says, her face a study in shock.

"Dante and I presented all the evidence to my parents yesterday. Lord Blackwood has been arrested, and your father's name will be officially cleared. The palace is issuing a full public exoneration."

"My father is…vindicated?" she asks, her voice thin.

"He is."

She lets out a whimper, her eyes filling with tears, and I pull her against me.

"You're free, my love."

She pulls back to look into my eyes. "I don't know what to say. I am so incredibly grateful to you and what you've done."

"Perhaps you don't need to say anything at all." I smile at her, and she slides her hands around the back of my neck.

"I have one thing to say."

"If it's 'I love you,' then I beat you to it," I say in a murmur.

She lets out a gurgling laugh. "I love you, too."

And then I pull her against me, and I press my lips to hers, showing her exactly what she means to me. This woman I once thought I despised but now cannot imagine my life without. The woman I love.

Epilogue

Valentina

Two Months Later

I FIND Max in the gardens at Belladonna Palace, throwing a ball for Toffee on one of the lawns. Now six months old, she's growing into those huge puppy paws of hers, but is just as full of life as she always has been.

I watch as my handsome boyfriend—aka Ledonia's most eligible bachelor—crouches down to pet his dog, ruffling her fur, and telling her what a good dog she is. His sweater pulls just slightly across his broad shoulders as he moves, his forearms flexing, his face lit up in an affectionate smile that always undoes me whenever I see it.

Really, it shouldn't be possible for a man to look that handsome while covered in dog hair, but somehow, he does.

He looks up at me, and his smile deepens as he rises to his feet. "My love," he says, pulling me into an embrace and brushing a kiss across my lips. "I missed you."

"You've only been here for a day without me," I reply with a light laugh, because the truth is I missed Max, too. Over the last couple of months, since that fateful night at the Autumn Ball, we've rarely been apart, despite his royal duties and my new status as Valentina Romano, serious journalist.

The media attention has been a lot, but thankfully the palace has provided me with a security guard named Davide, whose only facial expression seems to be serious—although his moustache does twitch now and then when I make a joke. He follows me around from the office to my interviews and everything in between. Nona calls him Mr. Muscles, and he towers over me at 6'6", and he's forever parting the Red Sea of reporters for me.

Max gives me a squeeze, and I breathe in his wonderful Max scent, the very scent that caused me to fall right off my seat only a hundred yards from where we are right now. "Can't a man miss his woman?" he asks.

"Oh, he can." My heart squeezes as I look up into the eyes of this beautiful man I get to call my own.

Toffee barks at us, clearly feeling left out, her tail swiping from side to side. I greet her before Max collects the ball and hurls it for her across the lawn, and she tears after it.

"How did Judith like the new article?" he asks.

"She's still pushing for our story, but she liked my take on my life as Fabiana."

"From Lady to Liar to Love," he says, quoting the title.

"You've got to love alliteration. And that's the last time I'm mentioning that life. From now on, it's newsworthy topics for me."

"The state of the economy, global warming, whether Ledonia should change its national shade of red?" he teases.

"The last one in particular."

"Good trip up here?" he asks as he takes my hand in his and together, we follow Toffee. She bounds over to one of the kids and drops her ball at his feet.

"Hey, Cedric!" I call out, giving him a wave.

He throws the ball for Toffee and waves back at me, his face pulled into a genuine smile. "Tent Lady!" He runs over to us.

"Her name is Valentina, Cedric," Max says.

"Nah, she's Tent Lady," Cedric replies, and I give him a fist bump.

"Tent Lady. I'll take it," I reply with a shrug. "How's today gone?"

"We rock climbed, and Max couldn't work out how to get past this one spot, so Rocco had to help him," Cedric says, his eyes bright.

"Oh, I sincerely hope Pippa filmed that," I reply.

"She did," Max replies with a roll of his eyes. "My failings will be all over your social media platforms by the weekend."

I shove him playfully on the arm. "We agreed, remember? Show the country you doing the things the kids on the program do," I say.

"I remember," he replies with a soft smile that does things to my heart.

Royally Off-Limits

Toffee grows impatient once more, and Cedric picks up her ball and runs with it toward the cluster of tents, chased by an excited dog.

"Where's your family?" Max asks. "I thought they came up with you?"

"They're freshening up after the train ride. Thanks for sending the royal train, by the way. There's nothing like traveling in style."

"Nothing but the best for you, my darling."

I smile up at him, my heart filled to the brim with love. "I'm so glad you see it that way."

He pushes a strand of hair from my face, his fingertips sending a shiver down my spine. "For you, anything." He leans down and presses his lips against mine once more, and instantly distant voices begin to hoot and holler.

Embarrassed, I look over at the group of teens, watching us with grins on their faces.

"Give a guy some privacy, will you?" Max calls back, and I give a mortified wave.

"To be fair, we are on the lawn where about twenty kids are staying in tents," I say.

"Perhaps we need to take this elsewhere." He waggles his eyebrows at me. "Come on. Let's go see your family." He takes my hand in his once more and leads me back to the house, where Rocco is talking with Pippa on the patio. His grin is half nerves, half pure adoration, like he can't quite believe she's talking to him.

"Are they…?" I ask Max under my breath.

"He's had a thing for her since our first visit. Told me he's going to ask her out."

"Cute," I reply, watching as Pippa giggles, her pretty face flushed. "My guess is it'll be a 'yes'."

"I hope so. The guy's obsessed."

Pippa greets me with a hug. "Fab!"

"Pip," I reply, genuinely pleased to see her. I greet Rocco with, "How's it going?"

"Good, good," he replies, no doubt wishing we hadn't interrupted. He may well have been at the crucial moment in the conversation.

"I got some amazing footage today," Pippa says.

"I heard! I'd love to see it," I reply.

"Can I show it to you later?" Her eyes dart to Rocco, and she instantly turns shy.

My hunch is right on the money.

"Of course. No rush," I reply with a smile.

"Leave you to it," Max says, throwing Rocco a wink, who instantly shifts his weight, looking about as comfortable as Toffee wearing booties in the snow.

I give Pippa's hand a squeeze. "No drinking the fountain water, remember?"

"I remember."

Max and I make our way into the house, where we find Nona and Mr. Beckman in the living room.

"Good afternoon, Lady Romano, Mr. Beckman," Max says as he greets them both warmly. "It's wonderful to have you here at Belladonna."

"Thank you so much for having us, Your Royal Highness," Nona says, clutching his hands.

"Max, please," he corrects.

"Or Maxie," I tease, and he smiles at me, shaking his head.

"This place is stunning," Mr. Beckman says. "I can see why you love it here so much."

"I'm glad you like it. It's very special to me." His eyes flash to mine. He's not only referring to the fact that he's always loved this house, ever since he was a little boy. This is the place where our love began, where he showed me who he really is, and where I began to fall in love with him.

"Where's Lord Romano?" Max asks.

"If we're going to call you Max, you must call me Vittorio," a voice says from behind us, and we both turn to see my father, standing in the doorway, looking totally at home in his tweed jacket and salt and pepper hair.

My heart skips a beat at the sight of him here, still not used to having him back in Ledonia. And now he's in the home of the family that once ruined him. But the son of the man who convicted him was the one who worked to clear his name.

It's been a lot for him, for all of us, and I'm so grateful to have him back.

Papa returned to Ledonia amid a media storm soon after the Autumn Ball, where Max changed my life forever. He's been working to regain our Tenuta Fioralba, our family land, taken from him all those years ago, and he has a new zest for life that can only come from knowing his name has been cleared and he's back in the country he loves.

"Welcome to Belladonna, Vittorio," Max says as he clasps my father's hand in his.

"I cannot tell you how good it is to be here," Papa replies. "I owe you a great debt, Max. A great debt indeed."

"If the investigation had been done correctly in the first place…" Max begins.

"Let's not rake over old stones, son. What's done is done, and all we can do is move on," Papa replies magnanimously.

There's something magical about seeing the two men I love shaking hands and showing genuine care for one another. The way I feel about my father will always be complicated, thanks to the decision he made all those years ago to leave. But he's still my father, and I love him. Having him here with Nona and Mr. Beckman and Max is beyond special for me.

After everyone has drunk tea, we join the kids around the fire, eating sausages and laughing and telling stories and making s'mores, just like we did that first time I was here. Max provides comfortable chairs for Nona and Mr. Beckman, who eat their food and then retire early, as the elderly often do.

"I have something to show you," Max says softly as he snakes his hand around my waist.

"Now?"

"Now."

"Where are you two off to?" Papa asks from his spot by the fire.

"I have something to show Val," Max replies mysteriously. He leads me from the warmth of the fire around the back of the house, where the goats roam around a field, and I can hear the horses settling in for the night in the stables.

"Where are you taking me?" I ask as we begin to climb the hill.

"Somewhere special."

"A ball pit?" I ask.

He squeezes my hand. "Best kiss ever."

We make our way past a thicket of trees, and as we approach a white wooden pergola, my breath catches in my throat. Strung from the ceiling and down the columns are a host of fairy lights illuminating the space, with a red plaid picnic blanket and oversized cushions arranged on the floor, surrounded by candles.

"This is so romantic," I say as we step up onto the pergola.

"Would you care to take a seat, mademoiselle," Max asks with a glint in his eye, and as I settle onto the surprisingly comfortable picnic blanket, he places another blanket over us to keep us warm against the autumnal night air.

We lean back against the large cushions and look down the hill toward the house, the tents, and the fire in the distance. I snuggle against his chest, and he wraps his arms around me, holding me close.

"This is wonderful," I say, taking in the view.

"I used to play on this pergola as a boy. Sofia would be the queen of the castle—"

"Of course."

"—and Amelia, Alex, and I would be her army, fighting off whatever enemy it was that day."

"I fear for the future of our country," I joke. "Thank you so much for inviting my family here. It means a lot to them, especially my papa."

He places a kiss on the top of my head. "I know it does, but I've done it for purely selfish reasons."

I turn to look up into his eyes, his face lit in the soft glow of the lights. "Why do you say that?"

"Because I had a rather important question to ask your nona and papa."

My brows spring upwards, no clue what that question might be. "You did?"

He shifts his weight, and before I know what's happening, he bends a knee, popping open a small velvet box encasing a stunning Ledonian red ruby, flanked by diamonds.

My heart stutters as I look from the ring into Max's eyes.

Does this mean…?
Is he about to…?
Oh, my.

"My darling Valentina," he begins, his voice low and steady, his eyes dark with intensity. "We may not have had a typical journey to get where we are now, but I wouldn't have changed it for the world. In these past months, you've grown to mean everything to me, and I want you in my life now, and always."

My heart is thrashing in my chest, my belly clenched tight as my breath comes short and sharp.

It's happening.

"Valentina Romano, will you do me the great honour of never really growing up with me, of always making sure to do what's in our hearts, and most importantly, of becoming my wife?"

He barely finishes his sentence before I throw myself at him, peppering his face with kisses, saying, "Yes, yes, yes! Yes, I'll marry you. Max, I love you, I love you!"

He lets out a soft laugh before he captures my lips with his, sweeping me up in the most heartfelt kiss, filled with love.

We remain locked together, holding one another close as tears spring to my eyes, tears of joy and of love and of everything we've been through to get to this point.

To become *us*. Max and Valentina, not Man-Child and Fabiana, but the real us. The people we were always meant to be.

Eventually, as we pull apart, he murmurs, "Would you like to try the ring on?"

"The ring! Of course," I say with a gurgling laugh I can barely contain.

I hold my hand out for him, shaking slightly, and he slides the ring onto my finger. We both look down at it, sparkling in the light, looking absolutely perfect.

"Max, it's beautiful," I whisper.

"Not as beautiful as you," he replies, and as I look up into his eyes, I cannot imagine my life without him in it, this man I once thought was an overgrown child, a pointless member of the royal family, without a serious bone in his body, a man I had nothing good to say about other than comment on his genetic jackpot. A man I love with all my heart, a man who has made everything in my life so much better. A man I get to spend the rest of my life with.

The End

Do you want to know what happens next? For a free **BONUS EPILOGUE** set in Valentina and Max's future, follow this link: https://BookHip.com/FBBVLQS

More in the Royally Kissed series

Don't miss out on what happens with the four royal Ledonian siblings, Alex, Sofia, Amelia, and Max. Plua read where it all began with King Frederic and Queen Astrid's arranged marriage story set in 1992...

Frederic and Astrid's story: About an arranged match meant to protect the monarchy. As they navigate palace expectations and public scrutiny, their marriage of convenience slowly begins to feel anything but convenient. A closed-door romance filled with humor, heart, and a prince who never intended to fall in love.

Alex and Maddie's story: A regular Texas girl becomes heir to the throne of Malveaux, and finds herself trading rodeos for royal soirees, accidentally punching a prince, and torn between an unexpected crown and the fiery love she never saw coming

Sofia and Marco's story: A rule-following princess hosts a Husband-Hunting Ball to check all the right boxes—only to fall head-over-heels for the one man she never planned on: her chosen suitor's charming brother

Amelia and Ethan's story: A runaway princess ditches her tiara and strict palace rules—only to fall for a disguised Hollywood heartthrob who's as eager to escape fame as she is to rewrite her royal destiny

Max and Valentina's story: Prince Max needs a PR makeover and Valentina's there to keep him in check—yet palace rules and one undeniable spark threaten to turn professional help into forbidden desire

Also by Kate O'Keeffe

Royal Romcoms:

Royally Arranged
The Backup Princess
Royally Matched
The Royal Runaway
Royally Off-Limits

Hockey Romcoms:

Mistletoe Face Off
The Rebound Play
Offside and Off-Limits

Small Town Romcoms:

Kissing My Fake Boyfriend
Kissing My Best Friend
Kissing the Enemy Next Door

Romcoms Set in Britain:

Dating Mr. Darcy
Marrying Mr. Darcy
Falling for Another Darcy
Falling for Mr. Bingley (spin-off novella)

Never Fall for Your Back-Up Guy
Never Fall for Your Enemy
Never Fall for Your Fake Fiancé
Never Fall for Your One that Got Away

Romcoms Set in New Zealand:

One Last First Date
Two Last First Dates
Three Last First Dates
Four Last First Dates
No More Bad Dates
No More Terrible Dates
No More Horrible Dates

Co-Authored with Melissa Baldwin:

One Way Ticket

Acknowledgments

Writing this book has been an amazing journey. Giving the peripheral character of Fabiana Fontaine—aka Valentina Romano—the depth and rich backstory she deserved was both deeply satisfying and genuinely fun. Creating her complexities, her struggles, and her strength brought me such joy as an author.

Max has been waiting for his happily ever after for three books now, and watching him grow into the man who could finally embrace it has been incredibly rewarding. He's matured through each story, and seeing him reach this point where he's ready for his HEA—and actually gets it—feels like the perfect culmination of his journey. It's wonderful to finally give him the love and happiness he's earned.

My heartfelt thanks go to Jackie Rutherford, my expert critique partner, whose insights and guidance have been invaluable in shaping this story.

Thank you to Jane Litherland and Wendy Connolly, my alpha readers, who saw this book in its earliest stages and helped me strengthen it with their thoughtful feedback and encouragement. Thanks also to my awesome assistant, Cathy Jeppson, who helps to keep me sane when I release a book, which is no small thing!

Most importantly, I want to thank my readers. You are the most *essential* element in bringing this book to life. Without you, these characters would exist only in my imagination. Your enthusiasm, your messages, and your love for these stories keep me writing.

This book is for you, and I hope Max and Fabiana's story touches your heart as much as writing it has touched mine.

Kate xoxo

About the Author

Kate O'Keeffe is a *USA Today* bestselling author known for her fun, feel-good romantic comedies brimming with humor, heart, and happily ever afters. A native of New Zealand, Kate has crafted numerous popular series, garnering a devoted international readership.

With a flair for witty banter and irresistible heroines navigating the ups and downs of modern dating, Kate's novels showcase strong friendships, comedic entanglements, and the of course sometimes bumpy but always hopeful road to love.

When she's not writing, Kate can often be found reading romcoms, binging her favourite shows, or spending time with her friends and family in the beautiful Hawke's Bay region of New Zealand.

www.ingramcontent.com/pod-product-compliance
Lightning Source LLC
Chambersburg PA
CBHW022058090426
42743CB00008B/642